Data Visualization with D3 4.x Cookbook

Second Edition

Discover over 65 recipes to help you create breathtaking data visualizations using the latest features of D3

Nick Zhu

BIRMINGHAM - MUMBAI

Data Visualization with D3 4.x Cookbook

Second Edition

First published: October 2013

Second edition: February 2017

Production reference: 2270217

Published by Packt Publishing Ltd.
Livery Place
35 Livery Street
Birmingham
B3 2PB, UK.
ISBN 978-1-78646-825-3

www.packtpub.com

Credits

Author

Nick Zhu

Reviewer

Scott Becker

Commissioning Editor

Wilson Dsouza

Acquisition Editor

Shweta Pant

Content Development Editor

Arun Nadar

Technical Editor

Sachit Bedi

Copy Editor

Dhanya Baburaj

Project Coordinator

Ritika Manoj

Proofreader

Safis Editing

Indexer

Mariammal Chettiyar

Graphics

Jason Monteiro

Production Coordinator

Deepika Naik

About the Author

Nick Zhu is a professional programmer and data engineer with more than a decade experience in software development, big data, and machine learning. Currently, he is one of the founders and CTO of Yroo.com - meta search engine for online shopping. He is also the creator of dc.js—a popular multidimensional charting library built on D3.

About the Reviewer

Scott Becker is a partner at Olio Apps, a software consulting company in Portland Oregon. He has built numerous systems including a marketplace for geospatial datasets, HIPAA compliant video services for the medical industry, and visualizations of breaches in data security products. He is currently building a next generation time tracking system at www.shoutbase.com. He has also produced a video course on data visualization with D3.js available at deveo.tv.

www.PacktPub.com

For support files and downloads related to your book, please visit `www.PacktPub.com`.

Did you know that Packt offers eBook versions of every book published, with PDF and ePub files available? You can upgrade to the eBook version at `www.PacktPub.com` and as a print book customer, you are entitled to a discount on the eBook copy. Get in touch with us at `service@packtpub.com` for more details.

At `www.PacktPub.com`, you can also read a collection of free technical articles, sign up for a range of free newsletters and receive exclusive discounts and offers on Packt books and eBooks.

`https://www.packtpub.com/mapt`

Get the most in-demand software skills with Mapt. Mapt gives you full access to all Packt books and video courses, as well as industry-leading tools to help you plan your personal development and advance your career.

Why subscribe?

- Fully searchable across every book published by Packt
- Copy and paste, print, and bookmark content
- On demand and accessible via a web browser

Customer Feedback

Thanks for purchasing this Packt book. At Packt, quality is at the heart of our editorial process. To help us improve, please leave us an honest review on this book's Amazon page at `https://www.amazon.com/dp/1786468255`.

If you'd like to join our team of regular reviewers, you can e-mail us at `customerreviews@packtpub.com`. We award our regular reviewers with free eBooks and videos in exchange for their valuable feedback. Help us be relentless in improving our products!

Table of Contents

Preface

D3.js is a JavaScript library designed to display digital data in dynamic graphical form. It helps you bring data to life using HTML, SVG, and CSS. D3 allows great control over the final visual result, and it is the hottest and most powerful web-based data visualization technology on the market today.

D3 v4 is the latest release of the D3 library. This second edition cookbook has been completely updated to cover and leverage the D3 v4 API, modular data structure, as well as revamped force implemented. It is designed to provide you with all the guidance you need to get to grips with data visualization with D3. With this book, you will create breathtaking data visualization with professional efficiency and precision with the help of practical recipes, illustrations, and code samples.

This cookbook starts off by touching upon data visualization and D3 basics before gradually taking you through a number of practical recipes covering a wide range of topics you need to know about D3.

You will learn the fundamental concepts of data visualization, functional JavaScript, and D3 fundamentals, including element selection, data binding, animation, and SVG generation. You will also learn how to leverage more advanced techniques such as interpolators, custom tweening, timers, queueing, hierarchy, force manipulation, and so on. This book also provides a number of pre-built chart recipes with ready-to-go sample code to help you bootstrap quickly.

What this book covers

Chapter 1, *Getting Started with D3.js*, is designed to get you up and running with D3.js, covering fundamental aspects, such as what D3.js is, and how to set up a typical D3.js data visualization environment.

Chapter 2, *Be Selective*, covers one of the most fundamental tasks you need to perform with any data visualization project using D3: selection. Selection helps you target certain visual elements on the page.

Chapter 3, *Dealing with Data*, explores the most essential question in any data visualization project: how to represent data in both programming constructs and its visual metaphor.

Chapter 4, *Tipping the Scales*, covers the one key task that you need to perform over and over again as a data visualization developer, that is, mapping values in your data domain to visual domain, which is the focus of this chapter.

Chapter 5, *Playing with Axes*, explores the usage of the axes component and some related techniques commonly used in the visualization based on the Cartesian coordinates system.

Chapter 6, *Transition with Style*, deals with a saying that is arguably one of the most important cornerstones of data visualization, "a picture is worth a thousand words." This chapter covers transition and animation support provided by the D3 library.

Chapter 7, *Getting into Shape*, deals with **Scalable Vector Graphic (SVG)**, which is a mature **World Wide Web Consortium (W3C)** standard widely used in visualization projects.

Chapter 8, *Chart Them Up*, explores one of the oldest and trusted companions in data visualization: charts. Charts are a well-defined and well-understood graphical representation of data.

Chapter 9, *Lay Them Out*, focuses on the D3 layout. D3 layouts are algorithms that calculate and generate placement information for a group of elements capable of generating some of the most complex and interesting visualizations.

Chapter 10, *Interacting with Your Visualization*, focuses on D3 human visualization interaction support or, in other words, how to add computational steering capability to your visualization.

Chapter 11, *Using Force*, covers one of the most fascinating aspects of D3: force. Force simulation is one of the most awe-inspiring techniques that you can add to your visualization.

Chapter 12, *Know Your Map*, introduces the basic D3 cartographic visualization techniques and how to implement a fully functional geographic visualization in D3.

Chapter 13, *Test Drive Your Visualization*, guides you to implement your visualization like a pro with **Test-Driven Development (TDD)**.

Appendix A, *Building Interactive Analytics in Minute*, serves as an introduction to Crossfilter.js and DC.js on interactive dimensional charting.

What you need for this book

- A text editor to edit and create HTML, CSS. and JavaScript files
- A modern web browser (Firefox 3, IE 9, Chrome, Safari 3.2, and later)
- A local HTTP server to host data file for some of the more advanced recipes in this book. We will cover how to set up a Node-based or Python-based simple HTTP server in the first chapter.
- Optionally, you will need a Git client if you would like to check out the recipe source code directly from our Git repository

Who this book is for

If you are a developer or an analyst familiar with HTML, CSS, and JavaScript, and you wish to get the most out of D3, then this book is for you. This book can also serve as a desktop quick-reference guide for experienced data visualization developers.

Sections

In this book, you will find several headings that appear frequently (Getting ready, How to do it, How it works, There's more, and See also).

To give clear instructions on how to complete a recipe, we use these sections as follows:

Getting ready

This section tells you what to expect in the recipe, and describes how to set up any software or any preliminary settings required for the recipe.

How to do it...

This section contains the steps required to follow the recipe.

How it works...

This section usually consists of a detailed explanation of what happened in the previous section.

There's more...

This section consists of additional information about the recipe in order to make the reader more knowledgeable about the recipe.

See also

This section provides helpful links to other useful information for the recipe.

Conventions

In this book, you will find a number of text styles that distinguish between different kinds of information. Here are some examples of these styles and an explanation of their meaning.

Code words in text, database table names, folder names, filenames, file extensions, pathnames, dummy URLs, user input, and Twitter handles are shown as follows: "Create a new user for JIRA in the database and grant the user access to the jiradb database we just created using the following command:"

A block of code is set as follows:

```
var timeFormat = d3.time.format.iso;
var data = crossfilter(json); // <-A

var hours = data.dimension(function(d){
  return d3.time.hour(timeFormat.parse(d.date)); // <-B
});
```

New terms and **important words** are shown in bold. Words that you see on the screen, for example, in menus or dialog boxes, appear in the text like this: "Select **System info** from the **Administration** panel."

Warnings or important notes appear in a box like this.

Tips and tricks appear like this.

Reader feedback

Feedback from our readers is always welcome. Let us know what you think about this book-what you liked or disliked. Reader feedback is important for us as it helps us develop titles that you will really get the most out of.

To send us general feedback, simply e-mail feedback@packtpub.com, and mention the book's title in the subject of your message.

If there is a topic that you have expertise in and you are interested in either writing or contributing to a book, see our author guide at www.packtpub.com/authors .

Customer support

Now that you are the proud owner of a Packt book, we have a number of things to help you to get the most from your purchase.

Downloading the example code

You can download the example code files for this book from your account at http://www.packtpub.com. If you purchased this book elsewhere, you can visit http://www.packtpub.com/support and register to have the files e-mailed directly to you.

You can download the code files by following these steps:

1. Log in or register to our website using your e-mail address and password.
2. Hover the mouse pointer on the **SUPPORT** tab at the top.
3. Click on **Code Downloads & Errata**.
4. Enter the name of the book in the **Search** box.
5. Select the book for which you're looking to download the code files.
6. Choose from the drop-down menu where you purchased this book from.
7. Click on **Code Download**.

You can also download the code files by clicking on the **Code Files** button on the book's webpage at the Packt Publishing website. This page can be accessed by entering the book's name in the **Search** box. Please note that you need to be logged in to your Packt account.

Once the file is downloaded, please make sure that you unzip or extract the folder using the latest version of:

- WinRAR / 7-Zip for Windows
- Zipeg / iZip / UnRarX for Mac
- 7-Zip / PeaZip for Linux

The code bundle for the book is also hosted on GitHub at `https://github.com/PacktPublishing/Data-Visualization-with-D3-4.x-Cookbook`. We also have other code bundles from our rich catalog of books and videos available at `https://github.com/PacktPublishing/`. Check them out!

Errata

Although we have taken every care to ensure the accuracy of our content, mistakes do happen. If you find a mistake in one of our books-maybe a mistake in the text or the code-we would be grateful if you could report this to us. By doing so, you can save other readers from frustration and help us improve subsequent versions of this book. If you find any errata, please report them by visiting `http://www.packtpub.com/submit-errata`, selecting your book, clicking on the **Errata Submission Form** link, and entering the details of your errata. Once your errata are verified, your submission will be accepted and the errata will be uploaded to our website or added to any list of existing errata under the Errata section of that title.

To view the previously submitted errata, go to `https://www.packtpub.com/books/content/support` and enter the name of the book in the search field. The required information will appear under the **Errata** section.

Piracy

Piracy of copyrighted material on the Internet is an ongoing problem across all media. At Packt, we take the protection of our copyright and licenses very seriously. If you come across any illegal copies of our works in any form on the Internet, please provide us with the location address or website name immediately so that we can pursue a remedy.

Please contact us at `copyright@packtpub.com` with a link to the suspected pirated material.

We appreciate your help in protecting our authors and our ability to bring you valuable content.

Questions

If you have a problem with any aspect of this book, you can contact us at `questions@packtpub.com`, and we will do our best to address the problem.

1
Getting Started with D3.js

In this chapter, we will cover:

- Setting up a simple D3 development environment
- Setting up an NPM-based D3 development environment
- Understanding D3-style functional JavaScript

Introduction

This chapter is designed to get you up and running with D3.js and covers fundamental aspects, such as what D3.js is and how to set up a typical D3.js data visualization environment. One particular section is also devoted to covering some lesser known areas of JavaScript that D3.js relies heavily on.

What is D3? D3 refers to *Data-Driven Documents*, and according to the official D3 Wiki:

> D3 (**Data-Driven Documents** *or D3.js) is a JavaScript library for visualizing data using web standards. D3 helps you bring data to life using SVG, Canvas and HTML. D3 combines powerful visualization and interaction techniques with a data-driven approach to DOM manipulation, giving you the full capabilities of modern browsers and the freedom to design the right visual interface for your data.*

> *-D3 Github Wiki (2016, August)*

In a sense, D3 is a specialized JavaScript library that allows you to create amazing data visualizations using a simple (data driven) approach by leveraging the existing Web standards. D3.js was created by Mike Bostock (`https://bost.ocks.org/mike/`) and superseded his previous work on a different JavaScript data visualization library called Protovis. For more information on how D3 was created and on the theory that influenced both Protovis and D3.js, please check out the links in the following information box. Here, in this book, we will focus more on how to use D3.js to power your visualization. Initially, some aspects of D3 maybe a bit confusing due to its different approach for data visualization. I hope that over the course of this book, a large number of topics, both basic and advanced, will make you comfortable and effective with D3. Once it is properly understood, D3 can improve your productivity and expressiveness with data visualizations by orders of magnitude.

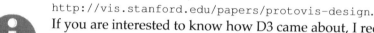

For a more formal introduction to the idea behind D3, refer to the *Declarative Language Design for Interactive Visualization* paper published by *Mike Bostock* on *IEEE InfoVis 2010* at `http://vis.stanford.edu/papers/protovis-design`.

If you are interested to know how D3 came about, I recommend that you check out the *D3: Data-Driven Document* paper published by *Mike Bostock, Vadim Ogievestsky,* and *Jeffery Heer* on *IEEE InfoVis 2011* at `http://vis.stanford.edu/papers/d3`.

Protovis, the predecessor of D3.js, also created by *Mike Bostock* and *Jeff Heer* of the Stanford Visualization Group can be found at `https://mbostock.github.io/protovis/`.

Setting up a simple D3 development environment

The first thing you will need when you start a D3-powered data visualization project is a working development environment. In this recipe, we will show you how a simple D3 development environment can be set up within minutes.

Getting ready

Before we start, make sure that you have your favorite text editor installed and ready on your computer.

How to do it...

We"ll start by downloading D3.js through the following steps:

1. Download the latest stable version of D3.js from `https://d3js.org/`. You can download the archived, older releases from `https://github.com/d3/d3/tags`. Additionally, if you are interested in trying out the bleeding edge D3 build on master branch, then you can fork `https://github.com/d3/d3`.

2. Once it is downloaded and unzipped, you will find two D3 JavaScript files, `d3.js` and `d3.min.js`, and other informational files in the extracted folder. For development purpose, it is recommended that you use the `d3.js` file, the *non-uglified* (minimized) version, since it can help you trace and debug JavaScript inside the D3 library. Once extracted, place the `d3.js` file in the same folder with an `index.html` file containing the following HTML:

```html
<!-- index.html -->
<!DOCTYPE html>
<html>
<head>
    <meta charset=""utf-8"">
    <title>Simple D3 Dev Env</title>
    <script type=""text/javascript"" src=""d3.js""></script>
</head>
<body>

</body>
</html>
```

This is all you need to create, in its simplest form, a D3-powered data visualization development environment. With this setup, you can essentially open the HTML file using your favorite text editor to start your development and also to view your visualization by opening the file in your browser.

The source code for this recipe can be found at `https://github.com/NickQiZhu/d3-cookbook-v2/tree/master/src/chapter1/simple-dev-env`.

How it works...

D3 JavaScript library is very self-sufficient. It has no dependency on any other JavaScript library except what your browser already provides.

If your visualization's target browser environment includes Internet Explorer 9, it is recommended that you use the compatibility library **Aight**, which can be found at `https://github.com/shawnbot/aight`, and **Sizzle selector engine**, which can be found at `http://sizzlejs.com/`.

Having the following character encoding instruction in the header section was critical before D3 v4 release since the older version of D3 used UTF-8 symbols, such as π, in its source; however, with D3 v4.x, it is no longer necessary. It is still considered a good practice however, since other JavaScript libraries you will include might be using UTF-8 symbols, as shown in the following example:

```
<meta charset=""utf-8"">
```

D3 is *completely open source* under a custom license agreement created by its author Michael Bostock. This license is pretty similar to the popular MIT license, with only one exception where it explicitly states that Michael Bostock's name cannot be used to endorse or promote products derived from this software without his permission.

There's more...

Throughout this cookbook, numerous recipe code examples will be provided. All example source code is provided and hosted on GitHub (`https://github.com/`), a popular open source social coding repository platform.

How to get source code

The easiest way to get all the recipe source code that you will need is to clone the Git repository (`https://github.com/NickQiZhu/d3-cookbook-v2`) for this book. If you are not planning to set up a development environment for the recipes, then you can safely skip this section.

In case you are not familiar with Git, its clone concept is similar to the checkout concept in other version control software. However, cloning does a lot more than simply checking out the files. It also copies all branches and histories to your local machine, effectively cloning the entire repository to your local machine so you can work even when you are completely offline with this cloned repository in your own environment.

First, install a Git client on your computer. You can find a list of Git client software at `https://git-scm.com/downloads`, and a detailed guide on how to install it on different operating systems at `https://git-scm.com/book/en/Getting-Started-Installing-Git`.

 Another popular way to get Git and GitHub working is to install the GitHub client, which gives you a richer set of features than simply Git. However, at the time of writing this book, GitHub only offered client software for Windows and Mac OS; refer to `https://desktop.github.com/`.

Once the Git client is installed, simply issuing the following command will download all recipe source code to your computer:

```
> git clone git@github.com:NickQiZhu/d3-cookbook-v2.git
```

Setting up an NPM-based development environment

The simple setup demonstrated in the previous recipe is enough for implementing most recipes in this book. However, when you work on a more complex data visualization project that requires the use of a number of JavaScript libraries, the simple solution we discussed before might become a bit clumsy and unwieldy. In this section, we will demonstrate an improved setup using **Node Packaged Modules** (**NPM**), a de facto JavaScript library repository management system. If you are as impatient as me and want to get to the meaty part of the book, the recipes, you can safely skip this section and come back when you need to set up a more production-ready environment for your project.

Getting ready

Before we start, please make sure that you have NPM properly installed. NPM comes as part of the Node.js installation. You can download Node.js from `https://nodejs.org/`. Select the correct Node.js binary build for your OS. Once installed, the following `npm` command will become available in your terminal console:

```
> npm -v
2.15.8
```

The preceding command prints out the version number of your NPM client to indicate that the installation is successful.

How to do it...

With the NPM installed, we can now create a package descriptor file to automate some of the manual setup steps:

1. First, under your project folder, create a file named `package.json` that contains the following code:

```
{
  ""name": "d3-project-template",
  ""version": "0.1.0",
  "description": "Ready to go d3 data visualization project template",
  "keywords": [
    "data visualization",
    "d3"
  ],
  "homepage": "<project home page>",
  "author": {
    "name": "<your name>",
    "url": "<your url>"
  },
  "repository": {
    "type": "git",
    "url": "<source repo url>"
  },
  "dependencies": {
      "d3":"4.x"
  },
  "devDependencies": {
      "uglify-js": "2.x"
  }
}
```

2. Once the `package.json` file is defined, you can simply run the following:

```
> npm install
```

How it works...

Most of the fields in the `package.json` file are for informational purpose only, such as its name, description, home page, author, and the repository. The name and the version fields will be used if you decide to publish your library into an NPM repository in the future. What we really care about, at this point, are the `dependencies` and `devDependencies` fields:

- The `dependencies` field describes the runtime library dependencies that your project has, that is, the libraries your project will need to run properly in a browser.
- In this simple example, we only have one dependency on D3. `d3` is the name of the D3 library that is published in the NPM repository. The version number `4.x` signifies that this project is compatible with any of the version 4 releases, and NPM should retrieve the latest stable version 4 build to satisfy this dependency.

D3 is a self-sufficient library with zero external runtime dependency. However, this does not mean that it cannot work with other popular JavaScript libraries. I regularly use D3 with other libraries to make my job easier, for example, JQuery, Zepto.js, Underscore.js, and ReactJs to name a few.

- The `devDependencies` field describes development time (compile time) of library dependencies. What this means is that libraries specified under this category are only required in order to build this project, and not required to run your JavaScript project.

Detailed NPM package JSON file documentation can be found at `https://docs.npmjs.com/files/package.json`.

Executing the `npm install` command will automatically trigger NPM to download all dependencies that your project requires, including your dependencies' dependencies recursively. All dependency libraries will be downloaded into the `node_modules` folder under your project's root folder. When this is done, you can just simply create your HTML file as shown in the previous recipe, and load your D3 JavaScript library directly from `node_modules/d3/build/d3.js`.

The source code for this recipe with an automated build script can be found at `https://github.com/NickQiZhu/d3-cookbook-v2/tree/master/src/chapter1/npm-dev-env`.

Relying on NPM is a simple and yet more effective way to save yourself from all the trouble of downloading JavaScript libraries manually and the constant need for keeping them up to date. However, an astute reader may have already noticed that with this power we can easily push our environment setup to the next level. What if you are building a large visualization project where thousands of lines of JavaScript code will be created? Then obviously, our simple setup described here will no longer be sufficient. However, modular JavaScript development by itself can fill an entire book; therefore, we will not try to cover this topic since our focus is on data visualization and D3. In later chapters, when unit test-related recipes is discussed, we will expand the coverage on this topic to show how our setup can be enhanced to run automated build and unit tests.

> D3 v4.x is very modular; so if you only need a part of the D3 library for your project, you can also selectively include D3 submodule as your dependency. For example, if you only need `d3-selection` module in your project, then you can use the following dependency declaration in your `package.json` file:
> ```
> "dependencies": {
>         "d3-selection":"1.x"
> }
> ```

There's more...

Although in previous sections it was mentioned that you can just open the HTML page that you have created using your browser to view your visualization result directly, this approach does have its limitations. This simple approach stops working once we need to load data from a separate data file (this is what we will do in later chapters, and it is also the most likely case in your daily working environment) due to the browser's built-in security policy. To get around this security constraint, it is highly recommended that you set up a local HTTP server so your HTML page and the data file can be accessed from this server instead of being loaded from a local file system directly.

Setting up a local HTTP server

There are probably more than a dozen different ways to set up an HTTP server on your computer based on the operating system you use and the software package you decide to use to act as an HTTP server. Here, I will attempt to cover some of the most popular setups.

Python Simple HTTP server

This is my favorite for development and fast prototyping. If you have Python installed on your OS, which is usually the case with any Unix/Linux/Mac OS distribution, then you can simply type the following command in your terminal with Python 2:

```
> python -m SimpleHTTPServer 8888
```

Alternatively, type the following command with Python 3 distribution:

```
> python -m http.server 8888
```

This little python program will launch an HTTP server and start serving any file right from the folder where this program is launched. This is by far the easiest way to get an HTTP server running on any OS.

 If you don't have python installed on your computer yet, you can get it from https://www.python.org/getit/. It works on all modern OS, including Windows, Linux, and Mac.

Node.js HTTP server

If you have Node.js installed, perhaps as part of the development environment setup exercise we did in the previous section, then you can simply install the http-server module. Similar to the Python Simple HTTP Server, this module will allow you to launch a lightweight HTTP server from any folder and start serving pages right away.

First, you need to install the http-server module using the following command:

```
> npm install http-server -g
```

The -g option in this command will install http-server module globally, so it will become available in your command-line terminal automatically. Once this is done, you can launch the server from any folder you are in by simply issuing the following command:

```
> http-server -p 8888
```

This command will launch a Node.js-powered HTTP server on the default port 8080, or if you want, you can use the -p option to provide a custom port number for it.

If you are running the `npm install` command on Linux, Unix, or Mac OS, you may need to run the command in the `sudo` mode or as root in order to use the `-g` global installation option.

Understanding D3-style JavaScript

D3 is designed and built using functional style JavaScript, which might come as a bit unfamiliar or even alien to someone who is more comfortable with the procedural or object-oriented JavaScript styles. This recipe is designed to cover some of the most fundamental concepts in functional JavaScript required to make sense of D3, and furthermore enable you to write your visualization code in the D3 style.

Getting ready

Open your local copy of the following file in your web browser:
`https://github.com/NickQiZhu/d3-cookbook-v2/blob/master/src/chapter1/functional -js.html`.

How to do it...

Let's dig a little deeper into the good part of JavaScript, the more functional side. Take a look at the following code snippet:

```
function SimpleWidget(spec) {
  var instance = {}; // <-- A

  var headline, description; // <-- B

  instance.render = function () {
    var div = d3.select('body').append("div");

    div.append("h3").text(headline); // <-- C

    div.attr("class", "box")
    .attr("style", "color:" + spec.color) // <-- D
      .append("p")
      .text(description); // <-- E

    return instance; // <-- F
  };
```

```
instance.headline = function (h) {
  if (!arguments.length) return headline; // <-- G
  headline = h;
  return instance; // <-- H
};

instance.description = function (d) {
  if (!arguments.length) return description;
  description = d;
  return instance;
};

return instance; // <-- I
}

var widget = SimpleWidget({color: "#6495ed"})
  .headline("Simple Widget")
  .description("This is a simple widget demonstrating
    functional      javascript.");
widget.render();
```

The preceding code snippet generates the following simple widget on your web page:

How it works...

Despite its simplicity, the interface of this widget has this undeniable similarity to the D3 style of JavaScript. This is not by coincidence but rather by leveraging a JavaScript programming paradigm called functional objects. Like many interesting topics, this is another topic that can fill an entire book by itself; nevertheless, I will try to cover the most important and useful aspects of this particular paradigm in this section, so you can not only understand D3's syntax but you'll also be able to create your code in this fashion. As stated on D3's project Wiki, this functional programming style gives D3 much of its flexibility:

> *D3's functional style allows code reuse through a diverse collection of components and plugins.*

> -D3 Wiki (2016, August)

Functions are objects

Functions in JavaScript are objects. Like any other object in JavaScript, function object is just a collection of name and value pair. The only difference between a function object and a regular object is that function can be invoked and additionally associated with the following two hidden properties: function context and function code. This might come as a surprise and seem unnatural, especially if you come from a more procedural programming background. Nevertheless, this is the critical insight most of us need in order to make sense of some of the *strange* ways that D3 uses functions.

 JavaScript in its pre-ES6 form is generally not considered very object oriented; however, function object is probably one aspect where it outshines some of its other more object-oriented cousins.

Now, with this insight in mind, let's take a look at the following code snippet again:

```
var instance = {}; // <-- A

var headline, description; // <-- B

instance.render = function () {
  var div = d3.select('body').append("div");

  div.append("h3").text(headline); // <-- C

  div.attr("class", "box")
    .attr("style", "color:" + spec.color) // <-- D
```

```
        .append("p")
        .text(description); // <-- E

    return instance; // <-- F
  };
```

At the lines marked as A, B, and C, we can clearly see that `instance`, `headline`, and `description` are all internal private variables belonging to the `SimpleWidget` function object. While the `render` function is a function associated with the `instance` object which itself is defined as an object literal. Since functions are just objects, they can also be stored in an object/function, referred to by variables, contained in an array, and being passed as function arguments. The result of the execution of the `SimpleWidget` function is the returning of object instance at line I as follows:

```
function SimpleWidget(spec) {
...
    return instance; // <-- I
}
```

 The `render` function uses some of the D3 functions that we have not covered yet, but let's not pay too much attention to them for now since we will cover each of them in depth in the next couple of chapters. Also, they basically just render the visual representation of this widget and do not have much to do with our topic on hand.

Static variable scoping

Curious readers will probably be asking by now how the variable scoping is resolved in this example since the render function has seemingly strange access to not only the `instance`, `headline`, and `description` variables but also the `spec` variable that is passed into the base `SimpleWidget` function. This seemingly strange variable scoping is actually determined by a simple static scoping rule. This rule can be thought as the following: whenever the runtime searches for a variable reference, the search will be first performed locally. When a variable declaration is not found (as in the case of `headline` on line C), the search continues toward the parent object (in this case, the `SimpleWidget` function is its static parent and the `headline` variable declaration is found at line B). If still not found, then this process will continue recursively to the next static parent, so on and so forth, till it reaches a global variable definition; if it is still not found, then a reference error will be generated for this variable. This scoping behavior is very different from variable resolution rules in some of the most popular languages, such as Java and C#.

It might take some time to get used to; however, don't worry too much about it if you still find it confusing. With more practice and by keeping the static scoping, rule in mind, you will be comfortable with this kind of scoping in no time.

One word of caution here, again for folks from Java and C# backgrounds, is that JavaScript does not implement block scoping. The static scoping rule we described only applies to function/object but not at the block level, as shown in the following code:

```
for(var i = 0; i < 10; i++){
  for(var i = 0; i < 2; i++){
    console.log(i);
  }
}
```

You might be inclined to think this code should produce 20 numbers. However, in JavaScript, this code creates an infinite loop. This is because JavaScript does not implement block scoping, so the variable `i` in the inner loop is the same variable `i` used by the outer loop. Therefore, it gets reset by the inner loop and can never end the outer loop.

This pattern is usually referred as functional when compared with the more popular prototype-based **Pseudo-classical pattern**. The advantage of the functional pattern is that it provides a much better mechanism for information hiding and encapsulation since the private variables, in our case, the `headline` and `description` variables, are only accessible by nested functions through the static scoping rule; therefore, the object returned by the `SimpleWidget` function is flexible yet more tamper-proof and durable.

If we create an object in the functional style, and if all of the methods of the object make no use of this, then the object is durable. A durable object is simply a collection of functions that act as capabilities.

-Crockfort D. 2008

Getter-setter function

Let's take a look at the following code; something strange has happened on line G:

```
instance.headline = function (h) {
  if (!arguments.length) return headline; // <-- G
  headline = h;
  return instance; // <-- H
};
```

You might be asking where this `arguments` variable on line G came from. It was never defined anywhere in this example. The `arguments` variable is a built-in hidden parameter that is available to functions when they are invoked. The `arguments` variable contains all arguments for a function invocation in an array.

 In fact, `arguments` is not really a JavaScript array object. It has *length* and can be accessed using an index; however, it does not have many of the methods associated with a typical JavaScript array object, such as `slice` or `concat`. When you need to use a standard JavaScript array method on `arguments`, you will need to use the following apply invocation pattern:
`var newArgs = Array.prototype.slice.apply(arguments);`

This hidden parameter when combined with the ability to omit function argument in JavaScript allows you to write a function such as `instance.headline` with unspecified number of parameters. In this case, we can either have one argument h or none. Because `arguments.length` returns 0 when no parameter is passed, the `headline` function returns `headline` if no parameter is passed, otherwise it turns into a setter if parameter h is provided. To clarify this explanation, let's take a look at the following code snippet:

```
var widget = SimpleWidget({color: "#6495ed"})
    .headline("Simple Widget"); // set headline
console.log(widget.headline()); // prints "Simple Widget"
```

Here, you can see how the headline function can be used as both setter and getter with different parameters.

Function chaining

The next interesting aspect of this particular example is the capability of chaining functions to each other. This is also the predominant function invocation pattern that the D3 library deploys since most of the D3 functions are designed to be chainable to provide a more concise and contextual programming interface. This is actually quite simple once you understand the variable, parameter function concept. Since a variable-parameter function, such as the `headline` function, can serve as setter and getter at the same time, returning the `instance` object when it's acting as a setter allows you to immediately invoke another function on the invocation result, hence the chaining.

Let's take a look at the following code:

```
var widget = SimpleWidget({color: "#6495ed"})
    .headline("Simple Widget")
    .description("This is ...")
    .render();
```

In this example, the `SimpleWidget` function returns the `instance` object (as on line I).

```
function SimpleWidget(spec) {
...
    instance.headline = function (h) {
        if (!arguments.length) return headline; // <-- G
        headline = h;
        return instance; // <-- H
    };
...
    return instance; // <-- I
}
```

Then, the `headline` function is invoked as a setter, which also returns the `instance` object (as on line H). The `description` function can then be invoked directly on its return, which again returns the `instance` object. Finally, the `render` function can be called.

Now, with the knowledge of functional JavaScript and a working ready-to-go D3 data visualization development environment, we are ready to dive into the rich concepts and techniques that D3 has to offer. However, before we take off, I would like to cover a few more important areas, how to find and share code and how to get help when you are stuck.

There's more...

Let's take a look at some additional helpful resources.

Finding and sharing code

One of the great things about D3 when compared with other visualization options is that it offers a wealth of examples and tutorials that you can draw your inspiration from. During the course of creating my own open source visualization charting library and the creation of this book, I had relied heavily on these resources. I will list some of the most popular options available in this aspect. This list is by no means a comprehensive directory, but rather a starting place for you to explore:

- The D3 gallery (`https://github.com/d3/d3/wiki/Gallery`) contains some of the most interesting examples that you can find online regarding D3 usage. It contains examples on different visualization charts, specific techniques, and some interesting visualization implementations in the wild, among others.

- Christophe Viau's D3 Gallery (`http://christopheviau.com/d3list/gallery.html`) is another D3 gallery with categorization that helps you find your desired visualization example online quickly.
- The D3 tutorials page (`https://github.com/d3/d3/wiki/Tutorials`) contains a collection of tutorials, talks, and slides created by various contributors over time that demonstrates in detail how to use different D3 concepts and techniques.
- D3 plugins can be found at `https://github.com/d3/d3-plugins`. Maybe some features are missing in D3 for your visualization needs? Before you decide to implement your own, make sure that you check out the D3 plugin repository. It contains a wide variety of plugins that provide some of the common and, sometimes, uncommon features in the visualization world.
- The D3 API (`https://github.com/d3/d3/blob/master/API.md`) is very well documented. This is where you can find detailed explanations for every function and property that the D3 library has to offer.
- Mike Bostok's Blocks (`http://bl.ocks.org/mbostock`) is a D3 example site, where some of the more intriguing visualization examples can be found and is maintained by its author Mike Bostock.
- JS Bin (`http://jsbin.com/ugacud/1/edit`) is a prebuilt D3 test and experiment environment completely hosted online. You can easily prototype a simple script using this tool or share your creation with other members in the community.
- JS Fiddle (`http://jsfiddle.net/qAHC2/`) is similar to JS Bin; it also is a hosted-online JavaScript code prototyping and sharing platform.

How to get help

Even with all the examples, tutorial, and cookbook such as this, you might still run into challenges when you create your own visualization. The good news here is that D3 has a broad and active support community. Simply *googling* your question can most often yield a satisfying answer. Even if it doesn't, don't worry; D3 has a robust community-based support as the following:

- D3.js on Stack Overflow (`http://stackoverflow.com/questions/tagged/d3.js`): Stack Overflow is the most popular community-based free Q&A site for technologists. D3 is a specific category on the Stack Overflow site to help you reach the experts and get an answer to your question quickly.
- The D3 Google group (`https://groups.google.com/forum/?fromgroups#!forum/d3-js`): This is the official user group for not just D3 but also other related libraries in its ecosystem.

2

Be Selective

In this chapter we will cover:

- Selecting a single element
- Selecting multiple elements
- Iterating through a selection
- Performing subselection
- Function chaining
- Manipulating raw selection

Introduction

One of the most fundamental tasks that you will need to perform with any data visualization project using D3 is selection. Selection helps you target certain visual elements on the page. If you are already familiar with the W3C-standardized CSS selector or other similar selector APIs provided by popular JavaScript libraries, such as jQuery and Zepto.js, then you will find yourself right at home with D3's selection API. Don't worry if you haven't used the selector API before; this chapter is designed to cover this topic in steps with the help of some very visual recipes. It will cover pretty much all common use cases for your data visualization needs.

Introducing selection

Selector support is standardized by W3C, so all modern web browsers have built-in support for the selector API. However, the basic W3C selector API has limitations when it comes to Web development, especially in the data visualization realm. The standard W3C selector API provides only the selector, but not the selection. What this means is that the selector API helps you to select element(s) in your document; however, to manipulate the selected element(s), you still need to loop through each element. Consider the following code snippet using the standard selector API:

```
var selector = document.querySelectorAll("p");
selector.forEach(function(p){
    // do something with each element selected
    console.log(p);
});
```

The preceding code essentially selects all <p> elements in the document and then iterates through each element to perform some task. This can obviously get tedious quickly, especially when you have to manipulate many different elements on the page constantly, which is what we usually do in data visualization projects. This is why D3 introduced its own selection API, making development less of a chore. In the rest of this chapter, we will cover how D3's selection API works and some of its powerful features.

CSS3 selector basics

Before we dive into D3's selection API, some basic introduction on the W3C level-3 selector API is required. If you are already comfortable with CSS3 selectors, feel free to skip this section. D3's selection API is built based on the level-3 selector or is more commonly known as CSS3 selector support. In this section, we plan to go through some of the most common CSS3 selector syntaxes that are required to understand the D3 selection API. The following list contains some of the most common CSS3 selector conventions you will typically encounter in a data visualization project:

- #foo: Selects elements with foo as the value of id

  <div id="foo">

- foo: Selects element foo

- `.foo`: Selects elements with `foo` as the value of `class`

  ```
  <div class="foo">
  ```

- `[foo=goo]`: Selects elements with the `foo` attribute value and sets it to `goo`

  ```
  <div foo="goo">
  ```

- `foo goo`: Selects the `goo` element inside the `foo` element

  ```
  <foo><goo></foo>
  ```

- `foo#goo`: Selects the `foo` element with `goo` as the value of `id`

  ```
  <foo id="goo">
  ```

- `foo.goo`: Selects the `foo` element with `goo` as the value of `class`

  ```
  <foo class="goo">
  ```

- `foo:first-child`: Selects the first child of the `foo` elements

  ```
  <foo> // <-- this one
  <foo>
  <foo>
  ```

- `foo:nth-child(n)`: Selects the nth child of the `foo` elements (n is one-based, starting at 1 for the first child)

  ```
  <foo>
  <foo> // <-- foo:nth-child(2)
  <foo> // <-- foo:nth-child(3)
  ```

CSS3 selector is a pretty complex topic. Here, we have only listed some of the most common selectors that you will need to understand and that you need to be effective when working with D3. For more information on this topic, please visit the W3C level-3 selector API document at `http://www.w3.org/TR/css3-selectors/`.

If you are targeting an older browser that does not support selector natively, you can include Sizzle before D3 for backward compatibility. You can find Sizzle at `http://sizzlejs.com/`.

Currently, the next-generation selector API level-4 is in the draft stage with W3C. You can have a peek at what it has to offer and its current draft at `https://drafts.csswg.org/selectors-4/`.

Major browser vendors have already started implementing some of the level-4 selectors; if you are interested to find out the level of support in your browser, try out this handy website: `http://css4-selectors.com/browser-selector-test/`.

Selecting a single element

It is very common that at times you will need to select a single element on a page to perform some visual manipulation. This recipe will show you how to perform a targeted single element selection in D3 using a CSS selector.

Getting ready

Open your local copy of the following file in your web browser:

`https://github.com/NickQiZhu/d3-cookbook-v2/blob/master/src/chapter2/single-selection.html`

How to do it...

Let's select something (a `paragraph` element perhaps) and produce the classic *hello world* on screen.

```
<p id="target"></p> <!-- A -->

<script type="text/javascript">
    d3.select("p#target") // <-- B
    .text("Hello world!"); // <-- C
</script>
```

This recipe simply produces text **Hello world!** on your screen.

How it works...

The d3.select command is used to perform a single-element selection in D3. This method accepts a string that represents a valid CSS3 selector or an element object if you already have a reference to the element you want to select. The d3.select command returns a D3 selection object on which you can chain modifier functions to manipulate the attribute, content, or inner HTML of this element.

> More than one element can be selected using the selector, provided only the first element is returned in the selection.

In this example, we simply select the paragraph element with target as the value of id at line B, and then set its textual content to Hello world! on line C. All D3 selections support a set of standard modifier functions. The text function we have shown in this particular example is one of them. The following are some of the most common modifier functions you will encounter throughout this book:

- selection.attr: This function allows you to retrieve or modify a given attribute on the selected element(s):

```
// set foo attribute to goo on p element
d3.select("p").attr("foo", "goo");
// get foo attribute on p element
d3.select("p").attr("foo");
```

- selection.classed: This function allows you to add or remove CSS classes on the selected element(s):

```
// test to see if p element has CSS class goo
d3.select("p").classed("goo");
// add CSS class goo to p element
d3.select("p").classed("goo", true);
// remove CSS class goo from p element. classed function
// also accepts a function as the value so the decision
// of adding and removing can be made dynamically
d3.select("p").classed("goo", function(){return false;});
```

- selection.style: This function lets you set the CSS style with a specific name to the specific value on the selected element(s):

```
// get p element's style for font-size
d3.select("p").style("font-size");
// set font-size style for p to 10px
```

```
d3.select("p").style("font-size", "10px");
// set font-size style for p to the result of some
// calculation. style function also accepts a function as
// the value can be produced dynamically
d3.select("p").style("font-size", function(){
    return parseFloat(d3.select(this).style('font-size')) +
        10 + 'px';
});
```

- Variable `this` in the preceding anonymous function is the DOM element object for the selected element <p>; therefore, it needs to be wrapped in `d3.select` again in order to access its `style` attribute.

- `selection.text`: This function allows you to access and set the text content of the selected element(s) as follows:

```
// get p element's text content
d3.select("p").text();
// set p element's text content to "Hello"
d3.select("p").text("Hello");
// text function also accepts a function as the value,
// thus allowing setting text content to some dynamically
// produced content
d3.select("p").text(function(){
  return Date();
});
```

- `selection.html`: This function lets you modify the element's inner HTML content as shown in the following:

```
// get p element's inner html content
d3.select("p").html();
// set p element's inner html content to "<b>Hello</b>"
d3.select("p").html("<b>Hello</b>");
// html function also accepts a function as the value,
// thus allowing setting html content to some dynamically
// produced message
d3.select("p").html(function(){
  return d3.select(this).text() +
    " <span style='color: blue;'>D3.js</span>";
});
```

These modifier functions work on both single-element and multi-element selection results. When applied to multi-element selections, these modifications will be applied to each and every selected element. We will see them in action in other, more complex recipes that will be covered later in this chapter.

When a function is used as a value in these modifier functions, there are actually some built-in parameters passed to these functions to enable data-driven calculation. This data-driven approach is what gives D3 its power and its name (**Data-Driven Document**) and will be discussed in detail in the next chapter.

Selecting multiple elements

Often selecting a single element is not good enough, but rather you want to apply a certain change to a set of elements on the page simultaneously. In this recipe, we will play with the D3 multi-element selector and its selection API.

Getting ready

Open your local copy of the following file in your web browser:

`https://github.com/NickQiZhu/d3-cookbook-v2/blob/master/src/chapter2/multiple-selection.html`.

How to do it...

This is what the `d3.selectAll` function is designed for. In the following code snippet, we will select three different `div` elements and enhance them with some CSS classes:

```
<div></div>
<div></div>
<div></div>

<script type="text/javascript">
    d3.selectAll("div") // <-- A
    .attr("class", "red box"); // <-- B
</script>
```

This code snippet produces the following visual:

Multi-element selection

How it works...

First thing you probably will notice in this example is how similar the usage of D3 selection API is when compared to the single-element version. This is one of the powerful design choices of the D3 selection API. No matter how many elements you target and manipulate, whether one or many, the modifier functions are exactly the same. All the modifier functions we mentioned in the previous section can be applied directly to multi-element selection; in other words, D3 selection is set-based.

Now, with that being said, let's take a closer look at the code example shown in this section, though it is generally pretty simple and self-descriptive. At line A, the `d3.selectAll` function is used to select all the `div` elements on the page. The return of this function call is a D3 selection object that contains all the three `div` elements. Immediately after that, on line B, the `attr` function was called on this selection to set the `class` attribute to `red box` for all three `div` elements. As shown in this example, the selection and manipulation code are very generic, and will not change even if now we have more than three `div` elements on the page. This seems to be an insignificant convenience for now, but in later chapters, we will show how this convenience can make your visualization code simpler and easier to maintain.

Iterating through a selection

Sometimes it is handy to be able to iterate through each element within a selection and modify each element differently according to their position. In this recipe, we will show you how this can be achieved using D3 selection iteration API.

Getting ready

Open your local copy of the following file in your web browser:

```
https://github.com/NickQiZhu/d3-cookbook-v2/blob/master/src/chapter2/selection-
iteration.html.
```

How to do it…

D3 selection object provides a simple iterator interface to perform iteration in a similar fashion to how you will iterate through a JavaScript array. In this example, we will iterate through the three selected div elements we worked with in the previous recipe and annotate them with an index number as follows:

```
<div></div>
<div></div>
<div></div>

<script type="text/javascript">
d3.selectAll("div") // <-- A
            .attr("class", "red box") // <-- B
            .each(function (d, i) { // <-- C
                d3.select(this).append("h1").text(i); // <-- D
            });
</script>
```

The preceding code snippet produces the following visual:

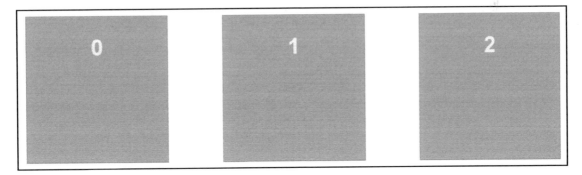

Selection iteration

How it works...

This example is built on top of what we have already seen in the previous section. In addition to selecting all the `div` elements on the page at line A and setting their class attributes at line B, in this example, we will call the `each` function on the selection to demonstrate how we can iterate through a multi-element selection and process each element, respectively:

 This form of calling a function on another function's return is called **Function Chaining**. If you are unfamiliar with this kind of invocation pattern, please refer to `Chapter 1`, *Getting Started with D3.js*, where the topic was explained.

The following list explains the `selecteach` and `append` functions:

- `selection.each(function)`: The `each` function takes an iterator function as its parameter. The given iterator function can receive two optional parameters `d` and `i` with one more hidden parameter passed in as the `this` reference, which points to the current DOM element object. The first parameter `d` represents the datum bound to this particular element (if this sounds confusing to you, don't worry, we will cover data binding in depth in the next chapter). The second parameter `i` is the index number for the current element object being iterated through. This index is zero-based, meaning it starts from zero and increments each time a new element is encountered.

- `selection.append(tagName)`: Another new function introduced in this example is the `append` function. This function creates a new element with the given element name and appends it as the last child of each element in the current selection. It returns a new selection containing the newly appended element. Now, with this knowledge, let's take a closer look at the code example in this recipe:

```
d3.selectAll("div") // <-- A
    .attr("class", "red box") // <-- B
    .each(function (d, i) { // <-- C
        d3.select(this).append("h1").text(i); // <-- D
    });
```

The iterator function is defined on line C with both d and i parameters. Line D is a little bit more interesting. At the beginning of line D, the this reference is wrapped by the d3.select function. This wrapping essentially produces a single-element selection containing the current DOM element, which the this variable represents. Once wrapped, the standard D3 selection manipulation API becomes available on d3.select(this). After that, the append("h1") function is called on the current element selection appending a newly created h1 element to the current element. Afterward, it simply sets the textual content of this newly created h1 element to the index number of the current element. This produces the visual of numbered boxes as shown in this recipe as illustrated in the screen capture. Again, you should notice that the index starts from 0 and increments 1 for each element.

> The DOM element object itself has a very rich interface. If you are
> interested to know more about what it can do in an iterator function,
> please refer to the DOM element API at
> https://developer.mozilla.org/en-US/docs/Web/API/element.

Performing subselection

It is quite common that you will need to perform scoped selection when working on visualization. For example, selecting all div elements within a particular section element is one such use case of scoped selection. In this recipe, we will demonstrate how this can be achieved with different approaches and their advantages and disadvantages.

Getting ready

Open your local copy of the following file in your web browser:

https://github.com/NickQiZhu/d3-cookbook-v2/blob/master/src/chapter2/sub-select ion.html.

How to do it...

The following code example selects two different div elements using two different styles of subselection supported by D3:

```
<section id="section1">
    <div>
        <p>blue box</p>
```

```
        </div>
    </section>
    <section id="section2">
        <div>
            <p>red box</p>
        </div>
    </section>

    <script type="text/javascript">
        d3.select("#section1 > div") // <-- A
                .attr("class", "blue box");

        d3.select("#section2") // <-- B
                .select("div") // <-- C
                .attr("class", "red box");
    </script>
```

This code generates the following visual output:

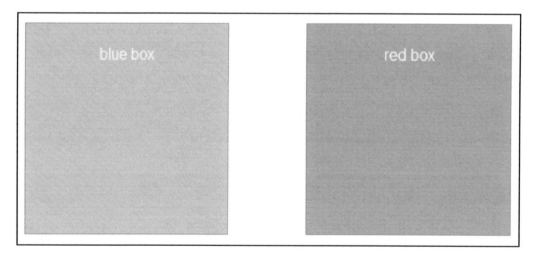

Subselection

How it works...

Though it produces the same visual effect, this example demonstrates two very different subselection techniques. We will discuss them separately here so you can understand their pros and cons as well as when to use one versus the other:

- **Selector level-3 combinators:** On line A, d3.select is used with a special-looking string, which consists of one tag name connected with another one using a greater-than sign (U+003E, >). This syntax is called *combinators* (the greater-than sign here indicates it is a child combinator). Level-3 selector supports a few different kinds of structural combinators. Here, we will give a quick introduction to the most common ones.

- **The descendant combinator:** This combinator has the syntax just like selector selector. The descendant combinator, as suggested by its name, is used to describe a loose parent-child relationship between two selections. The reason why it is called a loose parent-child relationship is that the descendant combinatory does not care if the second selection is a child or a grandchild or a great-grandchild of the parent selection. Let's take a look at some examples to illustrate this loose relationship concept:

```
<div>
<span>
The quick <em>red</em> fox jumps over the lazy brown dog
    </span>
</div>
```

If we use the following selector:

```
div em
```

It will select the em element since div is the ancestor of the em element and em is a descendent of the div element.

- **Child combinator:** This combinator has the syntax such as selector > selector. The child combinator offers a more restrictive way to describe a parent-child relationship between two elements. A child combinator is defined using a greater-than sign (U+003E, >) character separating the two selectors, as follows:

```
span > em
```

It will select the em element since em is a direct child of the span element in our example. The selector div > em will not produce any valid selection since em is not a direct child of the div element.

The level-3 selector also supports sibling combinators; however, since it is less common, we will not cover it here; interested readers can refer to W3C level-3 selector documentation at `http://www.w3.org/TR/css3-selectors/#sibling-combinators`. The W3C level-4 selector offers some interesting additional combinators, that is, following-sibling and reference combinators that can yield some very powerful target selection capability; refer to `https://drafts.csswg.org/selectors-4/#combinators` for more details.

- **The D3 nested subselection**: On lines B and C, a different kind of subselection technique was used. In this case, a simple D3 selection was made first on line B by selecting the `section #section2` element. Immediately afterward, another `select` was chained to select a `div` element on line C. This kind of nested selection defines a scoped selection. In plain English, this basically means to select a `div` element that is nested under `#section2`. In semantics, this is essentially the same as using a descendant combinator `#section2 div`. However, the advantage of this form of subselection is that since the parent element is separately selected, it allows you to handle the parent element before selecting the child element. To demonstrate this, let's take a look at the following code snippet:

```
d3.select("#section2") // <-- B
    .style("font-size", "2em") // <-- B-1
    .select("div") // <-- C
    .attr("class", "red box");
```

As shown in the preceding code snippet, you can see that before we select the `div` element, we can apply a modifier function to `#section2` on line B-1. This flexibility will be further explored in the next section.

Function chaining

As we have seen so far, the D3 API is completely designed around the idea of function chaining. Therefore, it forms a DSL for building HTML/SVG elements dynamically. In this code example, we will take a look at how the entire body structure of the previous example can be constructed using D3 alone.

If DSL is a new concept for you, I highly recommend checking out this excellent explanation on DSL by *Martin Fowler* in the form of an excerpt from his book *Domain-Specific Languages*. The excerpt can be found at `http://www.informit.com/articles/article.aspx?p=1592379`.

Getting ready

Open your local copy of the following file in your web browser:

`https://github.com/NickQiZhu/d3-cookbook-v2/blob/master/src/chapter2/function-chain.html`.

How to do it...

Let's take a look at how a function chain can be used to produce concise and readable code that produces dynamic visual content:

```html
<script type="text/javascript">
  var body = d3.select("body"); // <-- A

  body.append("section") // <-- B
      .attr("id", "section1") // <-- C
    .append("div") // <-- D
      .attr("class", "blue box") // <-- E
    .append("p") // <-- F
      .text("dynamic blue box"); // <-- G

  body.append("section")
      .attr("id", "section2")
    .append("div")
      .attr("class", "red box")
    .append("p")
      .text("dynamic red box");
</script>
```

This code generates the following visual output (similar to what we saw in the previous chapter):

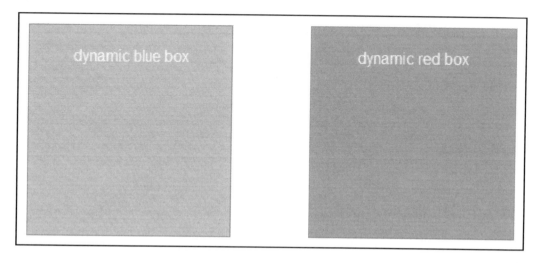

Function chain

How it works...

Despite the visual similarity to the previous example, the construction process of the DOM elements is significantly different in this example. As demonstrated by the code example, there is no static HTML element on the page contrary to the previous recipe where both the section and div elements existed.

Let's examine closely how these elements were dynamically created. On line A, a general selection was made to the top-level body element. The body selection result was cached using a local variable called body. Then, at line B, a new element section was appended to the body. Remember that the append function returns a new selection that contains the newly appended element; therefore, on line C, the id attribute can then be set on a newly created section element to section1. Afterward, on line D, a new div element was created and appended to #section1 with its CSS class set to blue box on line E. For the next step, similar to the previous line, on line F, a paragraph element was appended to the div element with its textual content set to dynamic blue box on line G.

As illustrated by this example, this chaining process can continue to create any structure of arbitrary complexity. In fact this is how a typical D3-based data visualization structure is created. Many visualization projects simply contain only a HTML skeleton and rely on D3 to create the rest. Getting comfortable with this way of function chaining is critical if you want to become efficient with the D3 library.

 Some of D3's modifier functions return a new selection, such as the `select`, `append`, and `insert` functions. It is a good practice to use different levels of indentation to differentiate the selection your function chain is being applied on.

Manipulating the raw selection

Sometimes, having access to the D3 raw selection array might be beneficial in development whether it's for debugging purposes or for integrating with other JavaScript libraries, which require access to raw DOM elements; in this recipe, we will show you ways to do that. We will also see some, internal structure of a D3 selection object.

Getting ready

Open your local copy of the following file in your web browser:

`https://github.com/NickQiZhu/d3-cookbook-v2/blob/master/src/chapter2/raw-selection.html`.

How to do it...

Of course, you can achieve this using the `nth-child` selector or the selection iterator function `each`, but there are cases where these options are just too cumbersome and inconvenient. This is when you might find dealing with the raw selection array a more convenient approach. In this example, we will see how the raw selection array can be accessed and leveraged:

```
<table class="table">
    <thead>
    <tr>
        <th>Time</th>
        <th>Type</th>
        <th>Amount</th>
    </tr>
```

```
        </thead>
        <tbody>
        <tr>
            <td>10:22</td>
            <td>Purchase</td>
            <td>$10.00</td>
        </tr>
        <tr>
            <td>12:12</td>
            <td>Purchase</td>
            <td>$12.50</td>
        </tr>
        <tr>
            <td>14:11</td>
            <td>Expense</td>
            <td>$9.70</td>
        </tr>
        </tbody>
</table>

<script type="text/javascript">
    var trSelection = d3.selectAll("tr"); // <-- A
    var headerElement = trSelection.nodes()[0]; // <-- B
    d3.select(headerElement).attr("class", "table-header"); // <-
    - C
    var rows = trSelection.nodes();
    d3.select(rows[1]).attr("class", "table-row-odd"); // <-- D
    d3.select(rows[2]).attr("class", "table-row-even"); // <-- E
    d3.select(rows[3]).attr("class", "table-row-odd"); // <-- F
</script>
```

This recipe generates the following visual output:

Time	Type	Amount
10:22	Purchase	$10.00
12:12	Purchase	$12.50
14:11	Expense	$9.70

Raw selection manipulation

How it works...

In this example, we went through an existing HTML table to color the table. This is not intended to be a good example of how you would color odd versus even rows in a table using D3. Instead, this example is designed to show how raw selection array can be accessed.

A much better way to color odd and even rows in a table would be using the `each` function and then relying on the index parameter `i` to do the job.

On line A, we select all rows and store the selection in the `trSelection` variable. D3 selection has a convenient `node()` function that returns an array containing the selected element nodes. Thus, in order to access the first selected element, you will need to use `d3.selectAll("tr").nodes()[0]`, the second element can be accessed with `d3.selectAll("tr").nodes()[1]`, and so on. As we can see on line B, the table header element can be accessed using `trSelection.nodes()[0]` and this will return a DOM element object. Again, as we have demonstrated in previous sections, any DOM element can then be selected directly using `d3.select` as shown on line C. Line D, E, and F demonstrate how each element in selection can be directly indexed and accessed.

Raw selection access could be handy in some cases especially when you need to use D3 in partnership with other JavaScript libraries since other libraries won't be able to work with D3 selection but only with raw DOM elements.

Additionally, this approach is typically very useful in a testing environment where knowing the absolute index for each element quickly and gaining a reference to them could be convenient. We will cover unit tests in a later chapter in more detail.

In this chapter we covered many different ways of how HTML elements can be selected and manipulated using D3's selection API. In the next chapter, we will explore how data can be bound to such selection to dynamically drive the visual appearance of selected elements which is the fundamental step of data visualization.

3
Dealing with Data

In this chapter, we will cover:

- Binding an array as data
- Binding object literals as data
- Binding functions as data
- Working with arrays
- Filtering with data
- Sorting with data
- Loading data from a server
- Asynchronous data loading using queue

Introduction

In this chapter, we will explore the most essential question in any data visualization project: how data can be represented in both programming constructs, and its visual metaphor. Before we start on this topic, some discussion on data visualization is necessary. In order to understand what data visualization is, first we will need to understand the difference between data and information.

> *Data consists of raw facts. The word raw indicates that the facts have not yet been processed to reveal their meaning...Information is the result of processing raw data to reveal its meaning.*

> *-Rob P., S. Morris, and Coronel C. 2009*

This is how data and information are traditionally defined in the digital information world. However, data visualization provides a much richer interpretation of this definition since information is no longer the mere result of processed raw facts but rather a visual metaphor of the facts. As stated by *Manuel Lima*, in his *Information Visualization Manifesto*, design in the material world, where form is regarded to follow function.

The same dataset can generate any number of visualizations, which may lay equal claim in terms of validity. In a sense, visualization is more about communicating the creator's insight into data than anything else. On a more provocative note, Card, McKinlay, and Shneiderman suggested that the practice of information visualization can be described as follows:

> *The use of computer-supported, interactive, visual representations of abstract data to amplify cognition.*

> *-"Card S. and Mackinly J.", and Shneiderman B. 1999*

In the following sections, we will explore various techniques D3 provides to bridge the data with the visual domain. It is the very first step we need to take before we can create a *cognition amplifier* with our data.

The enter-update-exit pattern

The task of matching each datum with its visual representation, for example, drawing a single bar for every data point you have in your dataset, updating the bars when the data points change, and then eventually removing the bars when certain data points no longer exist, seems to be a complicated and tedious task. This is precisely why D3 was designed, to provide an ingenious way of simplifying the implementation of this task. This way of defining the connection between data and its visual representation is usually referred to as the *enter-update-exit* pattern in D3. This pattern is profoundly different from the typical *imperative method* most developers are familiar with. However, the understanding of this pattern is crucial to your effectiveness with the D3 library; and therefore, in this section, we will focus on explaining the concept behind this pattern. First, let's take a look at the following conceptual illustration of the two domains:

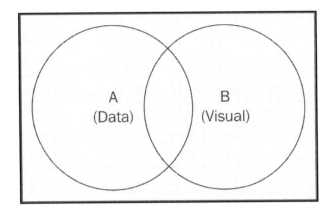

Data and visual set

In the preceding illustration, the two circles represent two joined sets. Set **A** depicts your dataset, whereas set **B** represents the visual elements. This is essentially how D3 sees the connection between your data and visual elements. You might be asking how set theory will help your data visualization effort here. Let me explain.

First, let us consider the question *how can I find all visual elements that currently represent their corresponding data point?* The answer is *A∩B*; this denotes the intersection of sets **A** and **B**, the elements that exist in both Data and Visual domains.

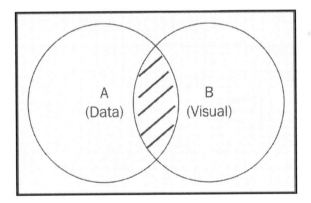

Update mode

In the preceding diagram, the shaded area represents the intersection between the two sets, **A** and **B**. In D3, the `selection.data` function can be used to select this intersection, *A∩B*.

The `selection.data(data)` function, upon selection, sets up the connection between the data domain and visual domain, as we discussed in the previous paragraph. The initial selection forms the visual set **B**, whereas the data provided in the `data` function form dataset **A**. The return result of this function is a new selection (a data-bound selection) of all elements existing in this intersection. Now, you can invoke the modifier function on this new selection to update all the existing elements. This mode of selection is usually referred to as the **Update mode**.

The second question we will need to answer here is *how can I target data points that have not yet been visualized?* The answer is the set difference of **A** and **B**, denoted as $A \setminus B$, which can be seen visually through the following illustration:

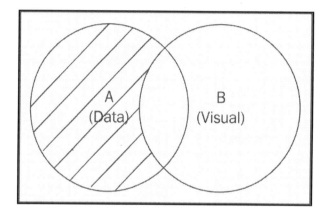

Enter mode

The shaded area in set **A** represents the data points that have not yet been visualized. In order to gain access to this $A \setminus B$ subset, the following functions need to be performed on a data-bound D3 selection (a selection returned by the `data` function).

The `selection.data(data).enter()` function returns a new selection representing the $A \setminus B$ subset, which contains all the pieces of data that has not yet been represented in the visual domain. The regular modifier function can then be chained to this new selection method to create new visual elements that represent the given data elements. This mode of selection is simply referred to as the **Enter mode**.

The third case in our discussion covers the visual elements that exist in our dataset but no longer have any corresponding data element associated with them. You might ask how this kind of visual element can exist in the first place. This is usually caused by removing the elements from the dataset; that is, if you initially visualized all data points within your dataset, and removed some data points after that. Now, you have certain visual elements that are no longer representing any valid data point in your dataset. This subset can be discovered using an inverse of the Update difference, denoted as $B \setminus A$.

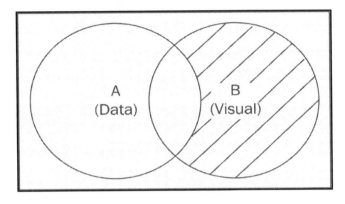

Exit mode

The shaded area in the preceding illustration represents the difference we just discussed. The subset can be selected using the `selection.exit` function on a data-bound selection.

The `selection.data(data).exit` function, when invoked on a data-bound D3 `selection` computes a new selection which contains all visual elements that are no longer associated with any valid data element. As a valid D3 selection object, the modifier function can then be chained to this selection to update and remove these visual elements that are no longer required as part of our visualization. This mode of selection is called the **Exit mode**.

Together, the three different selection modes cover all possible cases of interaction between the data and its visual domain.

Additionally, D3 also offers a fourth selection mode that is very handy when you need to avoid duplicating visualization code or the so-called *DRY* up your code. This fourth mode is called merge mode. It can be invoked using the `selection.merge` function. This function merges the given selection passed to the `merge` function with the selection where the function is invoked and returns a new selection that is a union of both. In the *enter-update-exit* pattern, the `merge` function is commonly used to construct a selection that covers both the Enter and Update modes since that's where most code duplication would otherwise live.

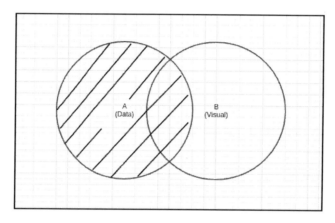

Merge mode

The shaded area in this illustration shows the data points targeted by merge mode that combines both Enter and Update modes, which is essentially the entire set A. This is very convenient since now a single chain of modifiers can be utilized to style both modes and thus lead to less code duplication. We will demonstrate how to leverage merge mode in each recipe of this chapter.

 In software engineering, **Don't Repeat Yourself (DRY)** is a principle of software development, aimed at reducing repetition of information of all kinds (Wikipedia, August 2016). You can also read Mike Bostock's post on *What Makes Software Good?* for more insight on reasons behind this design change at
`https://medium.com/@mbostock/what-makes-software-good-943557f8a4`
`88#.1640c13rp`.

The *enter-update-exit* pattern is the cornerstone of any D3-driven visualization. In the following recipes of this chapter, we will cover the topics on how these selection methods can be utilized to generate data-driven visual elements efficiently and easily.

Binding an array as data

One of the most common and popular ways to define data in D3 visualization is through the use of JavaScript arrays; for example, say you have multiple data elements stored in an array, and you want to generate corresponding visual elements to represent each and every one of them. Additionally, when the data array gets updated, you would want your visualization to reflect such changes immediately. In this recipe, we will accomplish this common approach.

Getting ready

Open your local copy of the following file in your web browser:

```
https://github.com/NickQiZhu/d3-cookbook-v2/blob/master/src/chapter3/array-as-d
ata.html.
```

How to do it...

The first and most natural solution that might come to mind is iterating through the data array elements and generating their corresponding visual elements on the page. This is definitely a valid solution, and it will work with D3; however, the enter-update-exit pattern we discussed in the introduction provides a much easier and more efficient way to generate visual elements. Let's take a look at how we can do that:

```
var data = [10, 15, 30, 50, 80, 65, 55, 30, 20, 10, 8]; // <- A
    function render(data) { // <- B
        var bars = d3.select("body").selectAll("div.h-bar") // <- C
                .data(data); // Update <- D
    // Enter
    bars.enter() // <- E
            .append("div") // <- F
                .attr("class", "h-bar") // <- G
        .merge(bars) // Enter + Update <- H
            .style("width", function (d) {
                return (d * 3) + "px"; // <- I
            })
            .text(function (d) {
```

```
            return d; // <- J
        });
    // Exit
    bars.exit() // <- K
            .remove();
}
setInterval(function () { // <- L
    data.shift();
    data.push(Math.round(Math.random() * 100));
    render(data);
}, 1500);
render(data);
```

This recipe generates the following visual output:

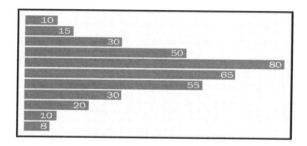

Data as array

How it works...

In this example, data (a list of integers in this case) is stored in a simple JavaScript array as shown on the line A in the preceding code. The render function is defined on the line marked as B so that it can be repeatedly invoked to update our visualization. The selection starts on the line marked as C, which selects all div elements on the web page with the h-bar CSS class. You are probably wondering why we are selecting these div elements since they don't even exist on the web page yet. This is in fact true; however, the selection at this point is used to define the visual set we discussed in the introduction. By issuing this selection, that we made in the previous line, we essentially declare that there should be a set of the div.h-bar elements on the web page to form our visual set. On the line marked as D, we invoke the data function on this initial selection to bind the array as our dataset to the to-be-created visual elements. Once the two sets are defined, the enter() function on line E can be used to select all pieces of data elements that are not yet visualized. When the render function is invoked for the very first time, it returns all elements in the data array, as shown in the following code snippet:

```
var bars = d3.select("body")
                .selectAll("div.h-bar") // <- C
                .data(data); // Update <- D
// Enter
bars.enter() // <- E
    .append("div") // <- F
    .attr("class", "h-bar") // <- G
```

On line F, a new `div` element is created and appended to the `body` element of each data element selected in the `enter` function; this essentially creates one `div` element for each datum. Finally, on line G, we set its CSS class to `h-bar`. At this point, we basically created the skeleton of our visualization, including the empty `div` elements. Next step is to change the visual attributes of our elements based on the given data.

D3 injects a property to the DOM element named __data__ to make data sticky with visual elements so when selections are made using a modified dataset, D3 can compute the difference and intersection correctly. You can see this property easily if you inspect the DOM element either visually using a debugger or programmatically.

```
▼ Properties
 ▼ div.h-bar
     __data__: 30
     accessKey: " "
```

As illustrated by the preceding screenshot, this is very useful to know when debugging.

In the following code snippet, on line H, the merge function is invoked with the selection as its parameter. This function call essentially merges the enter selection with the update selection and returns the union of both selections, thus allowing us to chain modifiers for both enter and update scenarios. Without the merge function, we would need to repeat the code here for both enter and update scenarios. Then, on line I, we applied a dynamic style attribute `width` to be three times the integer value associated with each visual element, as shown in the following code snippet:

```
bars.enter() // <- E
    .append("div") // <- F
        .attr("class", "h-bar") // <- G
    .merge(bars) // Enter + Update <- H
        .style("width", function (d) {
            return (d * 3) + "px"; // <- I
        })
        .text(function (d) {
            return d; // <- J
        });
```

All D3 modifier functions accept this type of dynamic function to compute its value on the fly. This is precisely what it means to *data drive* your visualization. Hence, it is crucial to understand what this function is designed to achieve in our example. This function receives a parameter d, which is the datum associated with the current element. In our example, the first div bar has the value 10 associated as its datum, the second bar has 15, and so on. Therefore, this function essentially computes a numeric value that is three times the datum for each bar and returns it as the element's width in pixels. While, on line J, we used a similar approach to change the text content of the div element to the datum value associated with each element.

The dynamic modifier function actually accepts two parameters, d and i. The first parameter d is the associated datum we just discussed, and i is a zero-based index number for the current element. Some recipes in the previous chapter relied on this index, and in the rest of this chapter, we will take look at other recipes that utilize this index in different ways.

The following is the raw HTML code that resulted from this update process:

```
<div class="h-bar" style="width: 30px;">
    10
</div>
<div class="h-bar" style="width: 45px;">
    15
</div>
....
<div class="h-bar" style="width: 24px;">
    8
</div>
```

The following last section, Exit section, is fairly simple:

```
bars.exit() // <- K
    .remove();
```

The selection returned by the exit() function is just like any other selection. Therefore, although remove is the most common action used against the exit selection, you can also apply other modifiers or transitions to this selection. We will explore some of these options in later chapters

On line K in the preceding code snippet, the `exit()` function is called to compute the set difference of all visual elements that are no longer associated with any data. Finally, the `remove()` function is called on this selection to remove all the elements selected by the `exit()` function. This way, as long as you call the `render()` function after you change our data, you can always ensure that our visual representation and data are kept synchronized.

Now, let's implement the following last block of code as follows:

```
setInterval(function () { // <- L
        data.shift();
        data.push(Math.round(Math.random() * 100));
        render(data);
    }, 1500);
```

On line L, a simple anonymous function was created to remove the top element in the data array using the `shift` function while appending a random integer to the data array using the `push()` function every 1.5 seconds. Once the data array is updated, the `render()` function is called again to update our visualization to keep it synchronized with the new dataset. This is what gives our example its animated bar chart look.

Binding object literals as data

With a more complex visualization, each element we have in a data array might not be a primitive integer value or a string, but a JavaScript object itself. In this recipe, we will discuss how this more complex data structure can be leveraged to drive your visualization using D3.

Getting ready

Open your local copy of the following file in your web browser:

```
https://github.com/NickQiZhu/d3-cookbook-v2/blob/master/src/chapter3/object-as-data.html
```

How to do it...

JavaScript object literal is probably the most common data structure you will encounter when you load data sources on the Web. In this recipe, we will take a look at how these JavaScript objects can be leveraged to generate rich visualization. The following code illustrates how to do it:

```
var data = [ // <- A
        {width: 10, color: 23},{width: 15, color: 33},
        {width: 30, color: 40},{width: 50, color: 60},
        {width: 80, color: 22},{width: 65, color: 10},
        {width: 55, color: 5},{width: 30, color: 30},
        {width: 20, color: 60},{width: 10, color: 90},
        {width: 8, color: 10}
    ];
    var colorScale = d3.scaleLinear()
        .domain([0, 100])
        .range(["#add8e6", "blue"]); // <- B
    function render(data) {
        var bars = d3.select("body").selectAll("div.h-bar")
                .data(data); // Update
        // Enter
        bars.enter()
                .append("div")
                .attr("class", "h-bar")
                .merge(bars) // Enter + Update
                .style("width", function (d) { // <- C
                    return (d.width * 5) + "px"; // <- D
                })
                .style("background-color", function(d){
                    return colorScale(d.color); // <- E
                })
                .text(function (d) {
                    return d.width; // <- F
                });
        // Exit
        bars.exit().remove();
    }
    function randomValue() {
        return Math.round(Math.random() * 100);
    }
    setInterval(function () {
        data.shift();
        data.push({width: randomValue(), color: randomValue()});
        render(data);
    }, 1500);
    render(data);
```

This recipe generates the following visualization:

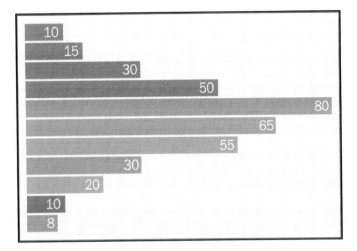

Data as object

 This recipe is built on top of the previous recipe, so if you are not familiar with the fundamental enter-update-exit selection pattern, please take a look at the previous recipe first.

How it works...

In this recipe, instead of simple integers as shown in the previous recipe, now our data array is filled with objects (refer to the line marked as A with an arrow left to it). Each data object contains two attributes: width and color, that are both integers in this case:

```
        {width: 10, color: 23},
        {width: 15, color: 33},
...
        {width: 8, color: 10}
    ];
```

On line B, we have a complicated-looking `color` scale defined:

```
...
.range(["#add8e6", "blue"]); // <- B
...
```

Scales, including color scale, will be discussed in depth in the next chapter, so for now let us just assume this is a scale function we can use to produce CSS-compatible color code, given some integer input value. This is sufficient for the purpose of this recipe.

The major difference between this recipe and the previous one is the way the data is handled as shown on line C in the following code snippet:

```
function (d) { // <- C
    return (d.width * 5) + "px"; // <- D
}
```

As we can see in the preceding code snippet, in this recipe, the datum associated with each visual element is actually an object, not an integer. Therefore, we can access the `d.width` attribute on line D.

If your object has functions of its own, you can also access them here in a dynamic modifier function. This is a convenient way to add some data-specific helper functions in your data source. However, beware that since dynamic functions are usually invoked numerous times during visualization, the function you rely on should be implemented as efficiently as possible. If this is not possible, then it is best to preprocess your data before binding it to your visualization process.

Similarly, on line E in the following code snippet, the `background-color` style can be computed using the `d.color` attribute with the color scale we defined earlier:

```
.style("background-color", function(d){
    return colorScale(d.color); // <- E
})
.text(function (d) {
    return d.width; // <- F
});
```

Again, on line F, we set the text of each bar to display its width.

This recipe demonstrates how JavaScript objects can easily be bound to visual elements using exactly the same method discussed in the previous recipe. This is one of the most powerful capabilities of the D3 library; it allows you to reuse the same pattern and method to handle different types of data, whether simple or complex. We will see more examples on this topic in the next recipe.

Binding functions as data

One of the benefits of D3's excellent support for functional-style JavaScript programming is that it allows functions to be treated as data as well. This particular feature can offer some very powerful capabilities under certain circumstances. This is a more advanced recipe. Don't worry about it if you are new to D3 and have some difficulty understanding it at first. Over time, this functional programming usage will become natural to you.

Getting ready

Open your local copy of the following file in your web browser:

```
https://github.com/NickQiZhu/d3-cookbook-v2/blob/master/src/chapter3/function-a
s-data.html.
```

How to do it…

In this recipe, we will explore the possibility of binding functions as data to your visual elements. This capability is extremely powerful and flexible, if used correctly:

```
<div id="container"></div>

<script type="text/javascript">
    var data = []; // <- A
    var datum = function (x) { // <- B
        return 15 + x * x;
    };
    var newData = function () { // <- C
        data.push(datum);
        return data;
    };
    function render(){
        var divs = d3.select("#container")
                    .selectAll("div")
                    .data(newData); // <- D
```

```
        divs.enter().append("div").append("span");
        divs.attr("class", "v-bar")
            .style("height", function (d, i) {
                return d(i) + "px"; // <- E
            })
            .select("span") // <- F
                .text(function(d, i){
                    return d(i); // <- G
                });
        divs.exit().remove();
    }
    setInterval(function () {
        render();
    }, 1000);
    render();
</script>
```

This preceding code produces the following bar chart:

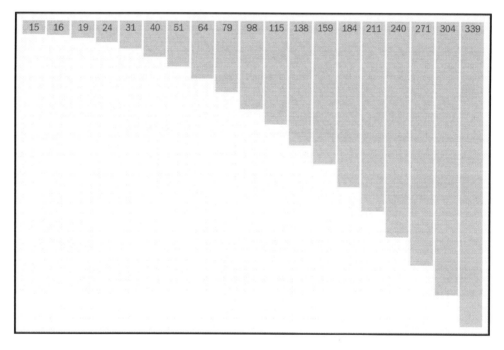

Data as function

How it works...

In this recipe, we chose to visualize the output of formula `15 + x * x` using a series of vertical bars, each of them annotated with its representing integral value. This visualization adds a new bar to the right of the previous one every one and a half seconds. We can of course implement this visualization using the techniques we discussed in the previous two recipes, where we generated an array of integers using the formula, and then just appended a new integer from *n* to *n+1* every 1.5 seconds before re-rendering the visualization. However, in this recipe, we decided to take a more functional approach.

This time we started with an empty data array on line A. On line B, a simple `datum` function was defined to calculate the result of this formula $15+x^2$. Then, on line C, another function `newData` was created to generate the current dataset, which contains *n+1* references to the `next` function. The following is the code for a functional data definition:

```
var data = []; // <- A
var datum = function (x) { // <- B
    return 15 + x * x;
};
var newData = function () { // <- C
    data.push(datum);
    return data;
};
```

This seems to be a strange setup to achieve our goal. Let's take a look at how we can leverage all these functions in our visualization code. On line D, we bound our data to a selection of `div` elements, just as we did in the previous recipes. However, this time, the data is not an array, but rather the `newData` function:

```
var divs = d3.select("#container")
             .selectAll("div")
             .data(newData); // <- D
```

D3 is pretty flexible when it comes to data. If you provide a function to the `data` function, D3 will simply invoke the given function and use the returned value of this function as a parameter of the `data` function. In this case, the data being returned by the `newData` function is an array of function references. As the result of this, now in our dynamic modifier function, on lines E and G, the datum d that is being passed into these functions is actually a reference to the `next` function, as shown in the following code:

```
divs.attr("class", "v-bar")
    .style("height", function (d, i) {
        return d(i) + "px"; // <- E
    })
    .select("span") // <- F
```

```
.text(function(d, i){
    return d(i); // <- G
});
```

As a reference to a function, d can now be invoked with index i as the parameter, which in turn will generate the output of the formula needed for our visualization.

 In JavaScript, functions are special objects, so semantically this is exactly the same as binding objects as data. Additionally data can also be considered as functions. Constant values such as integers can be thought of as an identity function that simply returns what it receives with no modification made.

This technique might not be the most commonly used technique in visualization; but when used properly, it is extremely flexible and powerful, especially when you have a fluid dataset.

 Datum function typically needs to be *idempotent* to make sense. Idempotence is the property of being able to apply the same function with the same inputs multiple times without changing the result beyond the initial application. For more detail on idempotence, visit `http://en.wikipedia.org/wiki/Idempotence`.

Working with arrays

Most of our data is stored in arrays, and we spend a lot of our effort working with arrays to format and restructure data. This is why D3 provides a rich set of array-oriented utilities functions, making this task a lot easier. In this recipe, we will explore some of the most common and helpful utilities in this aspect.

Getting ready

Open your local copy of the following file in your web browser:

`https://github.com/NickQiZhu/d3-cookbook-v2/blob/master/src/chapter3/working-with-array.html`.

How to do it...

The following code example shows some of the most common and helpful array utility
functions offered by the D3 library and their effects:

```
<script type="text/javascript">
    // Static html code were omitted due to space constraint

    var array = [3, 2, 11, 7, 6, 4, 10, 8, 15];
    d3.select("#min").text(d3.min(array));
    d3.select("#max").text(d3.max(array));
    d3.select("#extent").text(d3.extent(array));
    d3.select("#sum").text(d3.sum(array));
    d3.select("#median").text(d3.median(array));
    d3.select("#mean").text(d3.mean(array));
    d3.select("#quantile").text(
            d3.quantile(array.sort(d3.ascending), 0.25)
    );
    d3.select("#deviation").text(d3.deviation(array));
    d3.select("#asc").text(array.sort(d3.ascending));
    d3.select("#desc").text(array.sort(d3.descending));
    d3.select("#bisect").text(
        d3.bisect(array.sort(d3.ascending), 6)
    );
    var records = [
        {quantity: 2, total: 190, tip: 100, type: "tab"},
        {quantity: 2, total: 190, tip: 100, type: "tab"},
        {quantity: 1, total: 300, tip: 200, type: "visa"},
        {quantity: 2, total: 90, tip: 0, type: "tab"},
        {quantity: 2, total: 90, tip: 0, type: "tab"},
        {quantity: 2, total: 90, tip: 0, type: "tab"},
        {quantity: 1, total: 100, tip: 0, type: "cash"},
        {quantity: 2, total: 90, tip: 0, type: "tab"},
        {quantity: 2, total: 90, tip: 0, type: "tab"},
        {quantity: 2, total: 90, tip: 0, type: "tab"},
        {quantity: 2, total: 200, tip: 0, type: "cash"},
        {quantity: 1, total: 200, tip: 100, type: "visa"}
    ];
    var nest = d3.nest()
            .key(function (d) { // <- A
                return d.type;
            })
            .key(function (d) { // <- B
                return d.tip;
            })
            .entries(records); // <- C
    d3.select("#nest").html(printNest(nest, ""));
    // Utility function to generate HTML
```

```
    // representation of nested tip data
    function printNest (nest, out, i) {
        " " " " " " " "


    } " " " " " " " "
</script>
```

The preceding code produces the following output:

```
d3.min => 2
d3.max => 15
d3.extent => 2,15
d3.sum => 66
d3.median => 7
d3.mean => 7.333333333333333
array.sort(d3.ascending) => 2,3,4,6,7,8,10,11,15
array.sort(d3.descending) => 15,11,10,8,7,6,4,3,2
d3.quantile(array.sort(d3.ascending), 0.25) => 4
d3.deviation(array) => 4.18
d3.bisect(array.sort(d3.ascending), 6) => 4


tab
 100
   {quantity: 2, total: 190, tip: 100, type: tab, }
   {quantity: 2, total: 190, tip: 100, type: tab, }
 0
   {quantity: 2, total: 90, tip: 0, type: tab, }
   {quantity: 2, total: 90, tip: 0, type: tab, }
   {quantity: 2, total: 90, tip: 0, type: tab, }
   {quantity: 2, total: 90, tip: 0, type: tab, }
   {quantity: 2, total: 90, tip: 0, type: tab, }
   {quantity: 2, total: 90, tip: 0, type: tab, }
visa
  200
   {quantity: 1, total: 300, tip: 200, type: visa, }
  100
    {quantity: 1, total: 200, tip: 100, type: visa, }
cash, }
   0
   {quantity: 1, total: 100, tip: 0, type: cash, }
   {quantity: 2, total: 200, tip: 0, type: cash, }
```

How it works...

D3 provides a variety of utility functions to help perform operations on JavaScript arrays. Most of them are pretty intuitive and straightforward; however, there are a few intrinsic ones. We will discuss them briefly in this section.

Given our array as [3, 2, 11, 7, 6, 4, 10, 8, 15], the following will be its utility function:

- d3.min: This function retrieves the smallest element, that is, 2.
- d3.max: This function retrieves the largest element, that is, 15.
- d3.extent: This function retrieves both the smallest and the largest elements, that is, [2, 15].
- d3.sum: This function retrieves the addition of all elements in the array, that is, 66.
- d3.medium: This function finds the medium, that is, 7.
- d3.mean: This function calculates the mean value, that is, 7.33.
- d3.ascending/d3.descending: The d3 object comes with a built-in comparator function that you can use to sort the JavaScript array:

```
d3.ascending = function(a, b) {  return a < b ? -1 : a >
   b ? 1 : 0; }
d3.descending = function(a, b) {  return b < a ? -1 : b
   > a ? 1 : 0; }
```

- d3.quantile: This function calculates the quantile on an array that is already sorted in an ascending order, for example, the quantile of 0.25 will be 4.
- d3.deviation: This function calculates the standard deviation of the array, in our case that will be 4.18.
- d3.bisect: This function finds an insertion point that comes after (to the right of) any existing element of an already-sorted array, that is, bisect (array, 6) will produce 4.
- d3.nest: D3's nest function can be used to build an algorithm that transforms a flat array-based data structure into a hierarchical nested structure that is particularly suitable for some types of visualization. D3's nest function can be configured using the key function chained to nest, as seen on lines A and B:

```
var nest = d3.nest()
       .key(function (d) { // <- A
            return d.type;
       })
```

```
        .key(function (d) { // <- B
            return d.tip;
        })
        .entries(records); // <- C
```

- Multiple `key` functions can be provided to generate multiple levels of nesting. In our case, the nesting consists of two levels, first by the `type` amount and then by the `tip` amount, as demonstrated in the following output:

```
tab
  100
    {quantity: 2, total: 190, tip: 100, type: tab, }
    {quantity: 2, total: 190, tip: 100, type: tab, }
```

- Finally, the `entries()` function is used to supply the flat array-based dataset as shown on line C.

Filtering with data

Imagine you need to filter D3 selection based on the associated data elements so that you can hide or show different subdatasets based on the user's input. D3 selection provides a filter function to perform this kind of data-driven filtering. In this recipe, we will show you how this can be leveraged to filter visual elements in a data-driven fashion.

Getting ready

Open your local copy of the following file in your web browser:

```
https://github.com/NickQiZhu/d3-cookbook-v2/blob/master/src/chapter3/data-filte
r.html.
```

How to do it...

The following example code shows how data-based filtering can be leveraged to highlight different visual elements based on its categorization:

```
<script type="text/javascript">
    var data = [ // <-A
        {expense: 10, category: "Retail"},
        {expense: 15, category: "Gas"},
        {expense: 30, category: "Retail"},
```

```
                    {expense: 50, category: "Dining"},
                    {expense: 80, category: "Gas"},
                    {expense: 65, category: "Retail"},
                    {expense: 55, category: "Gas"},
                    {expense: 30, category: "Dining"},
                    {expense: 20, category: "Retail"},
                    {expense: 10, category: "Dining"},
                    {expense: 8, category: "Gas"}
            ];
        function render(data, category) {
            var bars = d3.select("body").selectAll("div.h-bar") // <-B
                    .data(data);
            // Enter
            bars.enter()
                .append("div") // <-C
                    .attr("class", "h-bar")
                    .style("width", function (d) {
                        return (d.expense * 5) + "px";}
                    )
                    .append("span") // <-D
                    .text(function (d) {
                        return d.category;
                    });
            // Update
            d3.selectAll("div.h-bar").attr("class", "h-bar");
            // Filter
            bars.filter(function (d, i) { // <-E
                    return d.category == category;
                })
                .classed("selected", true);
        }
        render(data);
        function select(category) {
            render(data, category);
        }
    </script>

    <div class="control-group">
        <button onclick="select('Retail')">
            Retail
        </button>
        <button onclick="select('Gas')">
            Gas
        </button>
        <button onclick="select('Dining')">
            Dining
        </button>
        <button onclick="select()">
```

```
        Clear
    </button>
</div>
```

The preceding code generates the following visual output once you click on the **Dining** button:

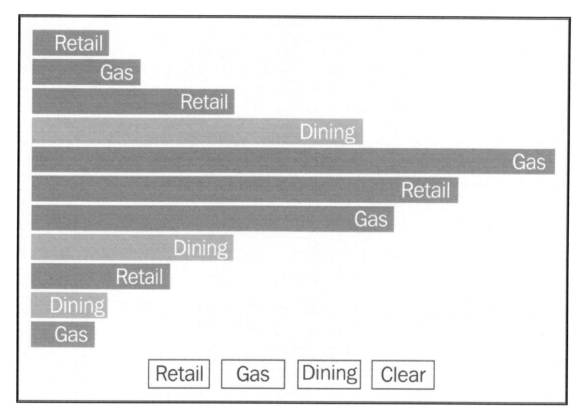

Data-based Filtering

How it works...

In this recipe, we have a dataset that consists of a list of personal expense records with `expense` and `category` as attributes, which is shown on the block of code marked as A. On lines B, C, and D, a set of horizontal bars (HTML `div`) was created using the standard enter-update-exit pattern to represent the expense records. So far, this recipe is similar to the *Binding object literals as data* recipe. Now let's take a look at line E:

```
bars.filter(function (d, i) { // <-E
    return d.category == category;
}).classed("selected", true);
```

D3's `selection.filter` function takes a function as its parameter. It applies the function against every element in the existing selection. The given function for `filter` takes two parameters with a hidden `this` reference:

- `d`: It is the datum associated with the current element
- `i`: It is a zero-based index for the current element
- `this`: This has the hidden reference points to the current DOM element

D3's `selection.filter` function expects the given function to return a Boolean value. If the returned value is `true`, the corresponding element will be included into the new selection that is returned by the `filter` function. In our example, the `filter` function essentially selects all bars that match the user-selected category and applies a CSS class `selected` to each one of them. This method provides you a powerful way to filter and generate data-driven sub-selection, which you can further manipulate or dissect to generate focused visualization.

 D3's `selection.filter` function treats the returned value using JavaScript as *truthy* and *falsy tests*, thus not exactly expecting a strict Boolean value. What this means is that `false`, `null`, `0`, `""`, `undefined`, and **NaN (not a number)** are all treated as `false`, while other things are considered `true`.

Sorting with data

In many cases, it is desirable to sort your visual elements according to the data they represent so that you can highlight the significance of different elements visually. In this recipe, we will explore how this can be achieved in D3.

Getting ready

Open your local copy of the following file in your web browser:

```
https://github.com/NickQiZhu/d3-cookbook-v2/blob/master/src/chapter3/data-sort.html.
```

How to do it...

Let's take a look at how data-driven sorting and further manipulation can be performed using D3. In this example, we will sort the bar chart we created in the previous recipe based on either expense (width) or category, using a user's input:

```
<script type="text/javascript">
    var data = [ // <-A
        {expense: 10, category: "Retail"},
        {expense: 15, category: "Gas"},
        {expense: 30, category: "Retail"},
        {expense: 50, category: "Dining"},
        {expense: 80, category: "Gas"},
        {expense: 65, category: "Retail"},
        {expense: 55, category: "Gas"},
        {expense: 30, category: "Dining"},
        {expense: 20, category: "Retail"},
        {expense: 10, category: "Dining"},
        {expense: 8, category: "Gas"}
    ];
    function render(data, comparator) {
        var bars = d3.select("body").selectAll("div.h-bar") // <-B
                .data(data);
        // Enter
        bars.enter().append("div") // <-C
                .attr("class", "h-bar")
                .append("span");
        // Update
        d3.selectAll("div.h-bar") // <-D
                .style("width", function (d) {
                    return (d.expense * 5) + "px";
                })
                .select("span")
                .text(function (d) {
                    return d.category;
                });
        // Sort
        if(comparator)
            bars.sort(comparator); // <-E
    }
    var compareByExpense = function (a, b) {  // <-F
        return a.expense < b.expense?-1:1;
    };
    var compareByCategory = function (a, b) {  // <-G
        return a.category < b.category?-1:1;
    };
};
```

```
        render(data);
        function sort(comparator) {
            render(data, comparator);
        }
</script>

<div class="control-group">
    <button onclick="sort(compareByExpense)">
        Sort by Expense
    </button>
    <button onclick="sort(compareByCategory)">
        Sort by Category
    </button>
    <button onclick="sort()">
        Reset
    </button>
</div>
```

This preceding code generates sorted horizontal bars as shown in the following screenshot:

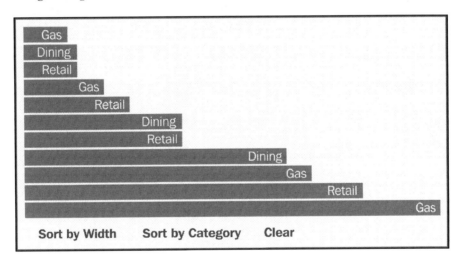

Data-based Sorting

How it works...

In this recipe, we set up a simple row-based visualization (in lines B, C, and D) of some simulated personal expense records containing two attributes, `expense` and `category`, that are defined on line A. This is almost exactly the same as the previous recipe and quite similar to what we have done in the *Binding object literals as data* recipe. Once the basics are done, we then select all existing bars on line E and perform sorting using D3's `selection.sort` function:

```
// Sort
if(comparator)
    bars.sort(comparator); // <-E
```

The `selection.sort` function accepts a comparator function:

```
var compareByExpense = function (a, b) {   // <-F
    return a.expense < b.expense?-1:1;
};
var compareByCategory = function (a, b) {   // <-G
    return a.category < b.category?-1:1;
};
```

The `comparator` function receives two data elements: a and b, to compare, returning either a negative, positive, or zero value. If the value is negative, a will be placed before b; if positive, a will be placed after b; otherwise, a and b are considered equal and the order is *arbitrary*. The `sort()` function returns a new selection with all elements sorted in an order that is determined by the specified comparator function. The newly returned selection can then be manipulated further to generate the desired visualization.

As a and b are placed arbitrarily when they are equal, D3 `selection.sort` is not guaranteed to be stable; however, it is guaranteed to be consistent with your browser's built-in `sort` method on arrays.

Loading data from a server

It is probably very rare that you will only be visualizing static local data. The power of data visualization usually lays on the ability to visualize dynamic data typically generated by a server-side program. Since this is a common use case, D3 comes with some handy helper functions to make this task as easy as possible. In this recipe, we will see how a remote dataset can be loaded dynamically and will update an existing visualization once it is loaded.

Getting ready

Open your local copy of the following file in your web browser:

https://github.com/NickQiZhu/d3-cookbook-v2/blob/master/src/chapter3/asyn-data-load.html.

How to do it...

In the code example of the `asyn-data-load.html` file, we will load data dynamically from the server on the user's request, and once the data is loaded, we will also update our visualization to reflect the new expanded dataset. The following is the code for its implementation:

```
<div id="chart"></div>

<script type="text/javascript">
    function render(data) {
        var bars = d3.select("#chart").selectAll("div.h-bar") // <-A
            .data(data);
        bars.enter().append("div") // <-B
            .attr("class", "h-bar")
                .style("width", function (d) {
                    return (d.expense * 5) + "px";
                })
                .append("span")
                    .text(function (d) {
                        return d.category;
                    });
    }
    function load(){ // <-C
        d3.json("data.json", function(error, json){ // <-D
            render(json);
        });
    }
</script>

<div class="control-group">
    <button onclick="load()">Load Data from JSON feed</button>
</div>
```

Here is what our `data.json` file looks like:

```
[
  {"expense": 15,  "category": "Retail"},
  {"expense": 18,  "category": "Gas"},
```

```
...
{"expense": 15, "category": "Gas"}
]
```

This recipe generates the following visual output after you click on the **Load Data from JSON feed** button once:

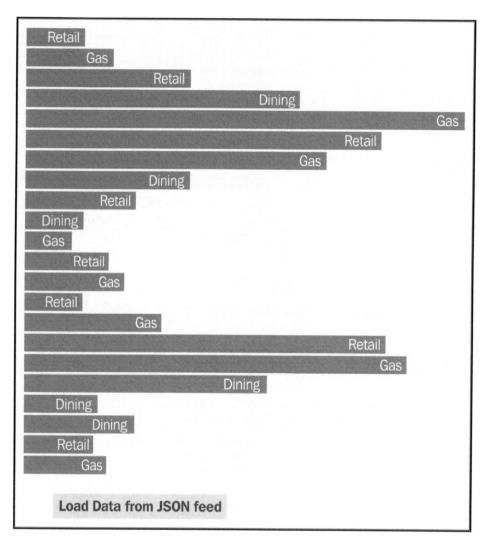

Data Loading from server

How it works...

In this recipe, we created a `render` function to generate a horizontal bar-based visualization very similar to what we did in the last couple of recipes. The `load` function is defined on line C that responds to the user's click on the **Load Data from JSON feed** button, which loads the data from a separate file (`data.json`) served by the server. This is achieved using the `d3.json` function as shown on line F:

```
function load(){ // <-C
    d3.json("data.json", function(error, json){ // <-D
        render(json);
    });
}
```

Since loading a remote dataset from a JSON file could take some time, it is performed asynchronously. Once loaded, the dataset will be passed to the given anonymous callback function defined on line D. In this function, we simply pass the newly loaded dataset to the `render` function in order to generate the visualization.

Similar functions are also provided by D3 to make the loading of CSV, TSV, TXT, HTML, and XML data a simple task.

If a more customized and specific control is required, the `d3.request` function can be used to further customize the MIME type and request headers. Behind the scenes, `d3.json` and `d3.csv` both use `d3.request` to generate the actual request.

MIME media type are a two part identifier for file format transmitted on the internet. The common registered top-level types are: application, text, audio, image, video.

Of course, this is by no means the only way to load remote data from the server. D3 does not dictate how data should be loaded from the remote server. You are free to use your favorite JavaScript libraries, such as jQuery or Zepto.js, to issue an Ajax request and load a remote dataset.

Asynchronous data loading using queue

In this recipe, we will demonstrate another very useful technique commonly used to process or generate data in large data visualization projects. It is usually necessary in complex visualization project to load and merge multiple datasets from different sources before proceeding to visualizing. The challenge in this kind of asynchronous loading is the difficulty in waiting to know when all datasets have been successfully loaded since only then the visualization can begin. D3 provides a very convenient queue interface to help organize these types of asynchronous tasks and helps you coordinate among them, which is the focus of this recipe.

Getting ready

Open your local copy of the following file in your web browser:

```
https://github.com/NickQiZhu/d3-cookbook-
v2/blob/master/src/chapter3/queue.html.
```

How to do it...

In the code example of the queue.html file, we will simulate loading and merging multiple data points using the setTimeout function. The setTimeout function executes the given function after a set period of delay; in our case, we set the delay to 500 milliseconds:

```
<div id="chart"></div>

<script type="text/javascript">
    function render(data) {
        var bars = d3.select("#chart").selectAll("div.h-bar") // <-B
                .data(data);
        bars.enter().append("div") // <-C
                .attr("class", "h-bar")
                .style("width", function (d) {
                    return (d.number) + "px";
                })
                .append("span")
                .text(function (d) {
                    return d.number;
                });
    }
    function generateDatum(callback) {
        setInterval(function(){
```

```
                callback(null, {number: Math.ceil(Math.random() * 500)}); // <-
D
        }, 500);
    }
    function load() { // <-E
        var q = d3.queue(); // <-F
        for (var i = 0; i < 10; i++)
            q.defer(generateDatum); // <-G
        q.awaitAll(function (error, data) { // <-H
            render(data); // <- I
        });
    }
</script>

<div class="control-group">
    <button onclick="load()">Generate Data Set</button>
</div>
```

This recipe generates the following output after clicking on the **Generate Data Set** button:

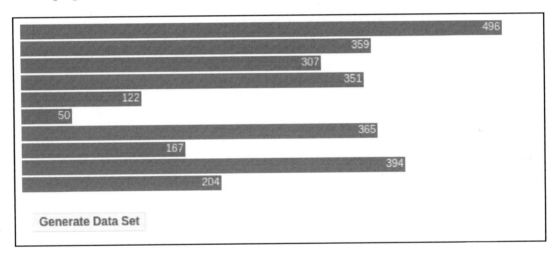

Asynchronous Data Generation using D3 Queue

How it works...

In this recipe, we have a pretty standard `render` function that generates horizontal bar visualization using the standard enter-update-exit pattern shown on lines B and C. This pattern by now should be very familiar to you. However, the data generation part, which is also our focus here, is a bit different in this recipe. On line D, we have a simple random datum generation function called `generateDatum(callback)`, which receives a single parameter callback. This is a very standard template for task function in D3 queue interface, as shown in the following code snippet:

```
function generateDatum(callback) {
        setInterval(function(){
            callback(null, {number: Math.ceil(Math.random() * 500)}); // <-
D
        }, 500);
}
```

In this function, we use the `setInterval` function to simulate asynchronous data generation with a 500 milliseconds delay. Each task function can perform arbitrary logic and calculation in its body, for example, loading data or computing results asynchronously. However, once the task is done, it has to invoke the callback function to notify the queue that it has finished its task and pass back the result as shown on line D. The callback function takes two parameters: error and result; in this case, we pass `null` as error signaling since it has completed successfully with the random number in second parameter. On line E, we have the `load` function defined that leverages `d3.queue` to execute the tasks. Let's take a closer look at the `load` function:

```
function load() { // <-E
    var q = d3.queue(); // <-F
    for (var i = 0; i < 10; i++)
        q.defer(generateDatum); // <-G
        q.awaitAll(function (error, data) { // <-H
        render(data); // <- I
    });
}
```

D3 Queue can be instantiated using the `d3.queue` function as shown on line F. Once created, it can register any number of tasks using the `defer` function as shown on line G. In our case, we used a `for` loop to register 10 asynchronous random datum generation tasks in our queue as shown on line G.

D3 Queue does not provide multithreading internally as **Web Worker** offers. All tasks are handled synchronously; however, the task function can perform, and typically is designed to perform, asynchronous task as we demonstrated here. For more information on Web Worker, refer to `https://developer.mozilla.org/en-US/docs/Web/API/Web_Workers_API` `/Using_web_workers`.

The `d3.queue.awaitAll` function shown on line `H` is used to wait for all tasks to be completed. This callback function passed to the `awaitAll` function will only be invoked once all tasks are completed or when an error occurs (only the first error is captured and passed to the callback). In our example, we have to wait till all the 10 random data points are successfully produced before calling the render function to generate the visualization on line `I`.

The `d3.queue` function also takes a parameter to define the maximum concurrency allowed when executing tasks. If not provided, it puts no limitation on concurrency.

In this chapter we covered the fundamental aspect of using D3 – binding data with the visual elements and how to keep them in synchronization. On top of that we have also covered various topics on data loading and manipulation. In next chapter we will introduce another fundamental concept in D3 to our readers – scales which powers many other higher level D3 features such as animation and shape generator for example.

4

Tipping the Scales

In this chapter, we will cover:

- Using continuous scales
- Using the time scale
- Using the ordinal scale
- Interpolating a string
- Interpolating colors
- Interpolating compound objects

Introduction

As a data visualization developer, one of the key tasks that you will need to perform over and over is to map values from your data domain to your visual domain; for example, mapping your most recent purchase of a fancy tablet of $453.00 to a 653-px-long bar, and your last night's pub bill of $23.59 to a 34-px-long bar. In a sense, this is what data visualization is all about, mapping data elements to their visual metaphor in an efficient and accurate manner. Because this is an absolutely essential task in data visualization and animation (animation will be discussed in `Chapter 6`, *Transition with Style*, in detail), D3 provides rich and robust support on this topic, which is the focus of this chapter.

What are scales?

D3 provides various constructs called *scales* to help you perform this kind of mapping. A proper understanding of these constructs conceptually is crucial to become an effective visualization developer. This is because scales are used not only to perform the mapping we mentioned previously, but also to serve as fundamental building blocks for many other D3 constructs, such as transition and axes.

What are these scales anyway? In short, scales can be thought of as mathematical *functions*. Mathematical functions differ from functions defined in imperative programming languages, such as JavaScript functions. In mathematics, a function is defined as mapping between two sets:

> *Let A and B be nonempty sets. A function f from A to B is an assignment of exactly one element of B to each element of A. We write f(a) = b if b is the unique element of B assigned by the function f to the element a of A.*

> -*Rosen K. H. 2007*

Despite the dryness of this definition, you still can not help but notice how nicely it fits the task we need to perform, mapping elements from the data domain to the visual domain.

Another fundamentally important concept we will need to illustrate here is the *domain* and *range* of a given function.

> *If f is a function from A to B, we say that A is the domain of f and B is the codomain of f. If f(a) = b, we say that b is the image of a and a is a preimage of b. The range, or image, of f is the set of all images of elements of A. Also, if f is a function from A to B, we say that f maps A to B.*

> -*Rosen K. H. 2007*

To help us understand this concept, let's take a look at the following illustration:

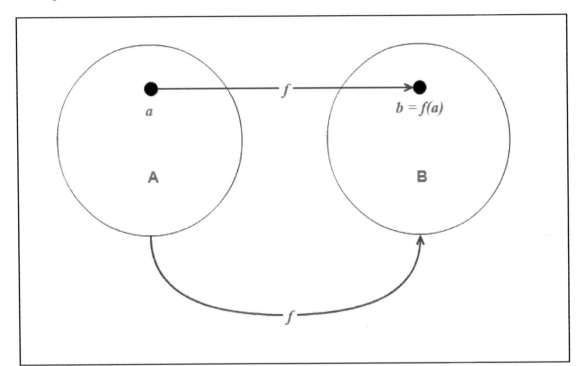

Function f maps A to B

As we can clearly see now, in the preceding illustration for function **f**, the domain is set **A** and the range is set **B**. Imagine if set **A** represents our data domain and **B** represents the visual domain, then a function **f** defined here is essentially a scale in D3 that maps elements from set **A** to set **B**.

 For the mathematically inclined readers, scale functions in data visualization are usually one-to-one, but not *onto* functions. This is a useful insight to know but not critical to the purpose of this book. Therefore, we will not discuss it further here.

Now that we discussed the conceptual definition of scale functions in D3, let's take a look at how it can be used to help us develop our visualization project.

Using continuous scales

In this recipe, we will examine the most commonly used scales provided by D3: the continuous scales that map a continuous quantitative domain to a continuous range, including linear, power, logarithmic, and time scales.

Getting ready

Open your local copy of the following file in your web browser:

```
https://github.com/NickQiZhu/d3-cookbook-v2/blob/master/src/chapter4/continuous
-scales.html.
```

How to do it...

Let's take a look at the following code example:

```
<div id="linear" class="clear"><span>n</span></div>
<div id="linear-capped" class="clear">
    <span>1 &lt;= a*n + b &lt;= 20</span>
</div>
<div id="pow" class="clear"><span>n^2</span></div>
<div id="pow-capped" class="clear">
    <span>1 &lt;= a*n^2 + b &lt;= 10</span>
</div>
<div id="log" class="clear"><span>log(n)</span></div>
<div id="log-capped" class="clear">
    <span>1 &lt;= a*log(n) + b &lt;= 10</span>
</div>

<script type="text/javascript">
    var max = 11, data = [];
    for (var i = 1; i < max; ++i) data.push(i);

    var linear = d3.scaleLinear() // <-A
        .domain([1, 10]) // <-B
        .range([1, 10]); // <-C
    var linearCapped = d3.scaleLinear()
        .domain([1, 10])
        .range([1, 20]); // <-D
    var pow = d3.scalePow().exponent(2); // <-E
    var powCapped = d3.scalePow() // <-F
        .exponent(2)
        .domain([1, 10])
```

```
            .rangeRound([1, 10]); // <-G
    var log = d3.scaleLog(); // <-H
    var logCapped = d3.scaleLog() // <-I
        .domain([1, 10])
        .rangeRound([1, 10]);


    function render(data, scale, selector) {
        d3.select(selector).selectAll("div")
                    .data(data)
                .enter()
                .append("div")
                    .classed("cell", true)
                    .style("display", "inline-block")
                    .text(function (d) {
                        return d3.format(".2")(scale(d), 2);
                    });
    }

    render(data, linear, "#linear");
    render(data, linearCapped, "#linear-capped");
    render(data, pow, "#pow");
    render(data, powCapped, "#pow-capped");
    render(data, log, "#log");
    render(data, logCapped, "#log-capped");
</script>
```

The preceding code generates the following output in your browser:

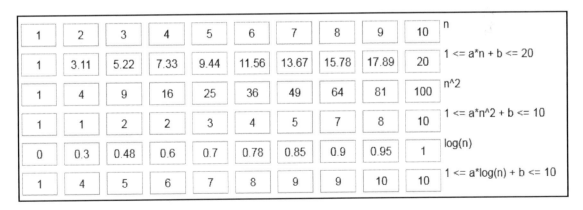

Quantitative scale output

How it works...

In this recipe, we demonstrated some of the most common scales provided by D3.

Linear scale

In the preceding code example, we have our data array filled with integers from 1 to 10, as shown by the for loop above line A. We created a *linear scale* by calling the d3.scaleLinear() function. This returns a linear quantitative scale function with the default domain set to [0, 1] and the default range set to [0, 1]. Thus, the default scale is essentially the *identity function* for numbers. Therefore, this default function is not that useful to us, but typically needs to be further customized using its domain and range functions on lines B and C. In this case, we set them both to [1, 10]. This scale basically defines the function $f(n) = n$ as shown in the following code snippet:

```
var linear = d3.scaleLinear() // <-A
    .domain([1, 10]) // <-B
    .range([1, 10]); // <-C
```

| 1 | 2 | 3 | 4 | 5 | 6 | 7 | 8 | 9 | 10 | n |

Identity scale

The second linear scale is a little bit more interesting and illustrates the mapping between the two sets better. On line D, we set the range as [1, 20], which is different from its domain. Hence, now this function essentially represents the following equations:

- $f(n) = a * n + b$
- $1 <= f(n) <= 20$

This is by far the most common case when using D3 scales because your dataset will be an identical match of your visual set:

```
var linearCapped = d3.scaleLinear()
    .domain([1, 10])
    .range([1, 20]); // <-D
```

| 1 | 3.11 | 5.22 | 7.33 | 9.44 | 11.56 | 13.67 | 15.78 | 17.89 | 20 | $1 <= a*n + b <= 20$ |

Linear scale

In this second scale, D3 will automatically calculate and assign the value of constants a and b to satisfy the equation.

> Some basic algebraic calculation will tell you that a is approximately 2.11 and b is -1.11, as in the previous example.

Power scale

The second scale we created is a *power scale*. On line E, we defined a power scale with exponent of 2. The d3.scalePow() function returns a default power scale function with its exponent set as 1. This scale effectively defines the function $f(n) = n\verb|^|2$:

```
var pow = d3.scalePow().exponent(2); // <-E
```

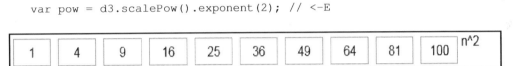

Simple power scale

On line F, a second power scale was defined, this time with a different range set on line G with rounding; the rangeRound() function works pretty much the same as the range() function, which sets the range for a scale. However, the rangeRound function rounds the output number so that there are no decimal fractions. This is very handy since scales are commonly used to map elements from the data domain to the visual domain. So, the output of a scale is very likely to be a number that describes some visual characteristics, for example, the number of pixels. Avoiding sub-pixel numbers is a useful technique that prevents anti-alias in rendering.

The second power scale defines the following function, which is demonstrated in the code after the function:

$f(n) = a*n\verb|^|2 + b, 1 <= f(n) <= 10$

```
var powCapped = d3.scalePow() // <-F
    .exponent(2)
    .domain([1, 10])
    .rangeRound([1, 10]); // <-G
```

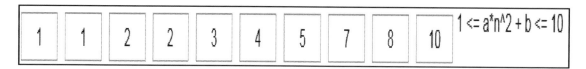

Power scale

Similar to the linear scale, D3 will automatically find the suitable constants a and b to satisfy the constraints defined by `domain` and `range` on a power scale.

Log scale

On line H, a third kind of quantitative scale was created using the `d3.scaleLog()` function. The default log scale has a `base` of `10`. Line H essentially defines the following mathematical function $f(n) = log(n)$, as follows:

```
var log = d3.scale.log(); // <-H
```

Simple log scale

On line I, we customized the log scale to have a domain of [1, 10] and a rounded range of [1, 10], which defines the following constrained mathematical function $f(n) = a*log(n) + b, 1 <= f(n) <= 10$.

```
var logCapped = d3.scaleLog() // <-I
    .domain([1, 10])
    .rangeRound([1, 10]);
```

Log scale

Using the time scale

Often, we will need to create visualization on a dataset that has time and date dimensions; therefore, D3 provides a built-in time scale to help perform this type of mapping. In this recipe, we will learn how to use the D3 time scale.

Getting ready

Open your local copy of the following file in your web browser:

`https://github.com/NickQiZhu/d3-cookbook-v2/blob/master/src/chapter4/time-scale.html`.

How to do it...

First, let's take a look at the following code example:

```html
<div id="time" class="clear">
    <span>Linear Time Progression<br></span>
    <span>Mapping [01/01/2016, 12/31/2016] to [0, 1200]<br></span>
</div>

<script type="text/javascript">
    var start = new Date(2016, 0, 1), // <-A
        end = new Date(2016, 11, 31),
        range = [0, 1200],
        time = d3.scaleTime().domain([start, end]) // <-B
            .rangeRound(range), // <-C
        max = 12,
        data = [];

    for (var i = 0; i < max; ++i){ // <-D
        var date = new Date(start.getTime());
        date.setMonth(start.getMonth() + i);
        data.push(date);
    }

    function render(data, scale, selector) { // <-E
        d3.select(selector).selectAll("div.fixed-cell")
                    .data(data)
                .enter()
                    .append("div")
                        .classed("fixed-cell", true)
                        .style("margin-left", function(d){ // <-F
                            return scale(d) + "px";
                        })
                        .html(function (d) { // <-G
                            var format = d3.timeFormat("%x"); // <-H
                            return format(d) + "<br>" + scale(d) + "px";
                        });
    }
```

```
        render(data, time, "#time");
</script>
```

This recipe generates the following visual output:

Linear Time Progression Mapping [01/01/2013, 12/31/2013] to [0, 900]											
01/01/2013	02/01/2013	03/01/2013	04/01/2013	05/01/2013	06/01/2013	07/01/2013	08/01/2013	09/01/2013	10/01/2013	11/01/2013	12/01/2013
0	102	195	297	395	498	597	699	801	900	1002	1101

Time scale

How it works...

In this recipe, we have a `Date` range between January 1, 2016 and December 31, 2016 defined on line A.

```
var start = new Date(2016, 0, 1), // <-A
        end = new Date(2016, 11, 31),
        range = [0, 1200],
        time = d3.scaleTime().domain([start, end]) // <-B
            .rangeRound(range), // <-C
```

The JavaScript `Date` object starts its month from 0 and day from 1. Therefore, `new Date(2016, 0, 1)` will present January 1, 2016, while `new Date(2016, 0, 0)` actually will present December 31, 2015.

This range was then used to create a D3 *time scale* on line B using the `d3.scaleTime` function. Similar to other continuous scales, time scale also supports separate `domain` and `range` definition, which is used to map date- and time-based data points to visual range. In this example, we set the range of the scale to `[0, 900]`. This effectively defines a mapping from any date and time value in the time range between January 1, 2016 and December 31, 2016 to a number between 0 and 900.

With the time scale defined, we can now map any given `Date` object by calling the scale function, for example, `time(new Date(2016, 4, 1))` will return `395`, `time(new Date(2016, 11, 15))` will return `1147`, and so on.

In the following code, on line D, we created our data array that consists of 12 months from January to December in 2013, as shown in the following code snippet:

```
for (var i = 0; i < max; ++i){ // <-D
    var date = new Date(start.getTime());
```

```
        date.setMonth(start.getMonth() + i);
        data.push(date);
    }
```

Then we created 12 cells that represent each month in a year using the `render` function.

To spread the cells horizontally, line F performs a mapping from the month to the `margin-left` CSS style using the time scale we defined:

```
.style("margin-left", function(d){ // <-F
    return scale(d) + "px";
})
```

Line G generates the label that demonstrates what the scale-based mapping produces in this example:

```
.html(function (d) { // <-G
    var format = d3.timeFormat("%x"); // <-H
    return format(d) + "<br>" + scale(d) + "px";
});
```

To generate human-readable strings from a JavaScript `Date` object, we used a D3 time formatter on line H, which is an alias to the `d3.locale.format` function. D3 ships with a powerful and flexible time-formatting library as part of locale format libraries, which is extremely useful when dealing with the `Date` object.

There's more...

The following are some of the most useful `d3.locale.format` patterns:

- `%a`: This is the abbreviated weekday name
- `%A`: This is the full weekday name
- `%b`: This is the abbreviated month name
- `%B`: This is the full month name
- `%d`: This is the zero-padded day of the month as a decimal number [01,31]
- `%e`: This is the space-padded day of the month as a decimal number [1,31]
- `%H`: This is the hour (24-hour clock) as a decimal number [00,23]
- `%I`: This is the hour (12-hour clock) as a decimal number [01,12]
- `%j`: This is the day of the year as a decimal number [001,366]
- `%m`: This is the month as a decimal number [01,12]
- `%M`: This is the minute as a decimal number [00,59]

- `%L`: This is the milliseconds as a decimal number [000, 999]
- `%p`: This is either AM or PM
- `%S`: This is the time in seconds as a decimal number [00,61]
- `%x`: This is the date, as `%m/%d/%Y`
- `%X`: This is the time, as `%H:%M:%S`
- `%y`: This is the year without century as a decimal number [00,99]
- `%Y`: This is the year with century as a decimal number

See also

- For the complete reference on D3 locale format pattern, visit the following link – `https://github.com/d3/d3-time-format/blob/master/README.md#locale_form at`.

Using the ordinal scale

In some cases, we may need to map our data to some ordinal values, for example, `["a", "b", "c"]` or `["#1f77b4", "#ff7f0e", "#2ca02c"]`. So, how can we perform this kind of mapping using D3 scales? This recipe is dedicated to answer this question.

Getting ready

Open your local copy of the following file in your web browser:

`https://github.com/NickQiZhu/d3-cookbook-v2/blob/master/src/chapter4/ordinal-sc ale.html`.

How to do it...

This kind of ordinal mapping is quite common in data visualization. For example, you may want to map certain data points through categorization into some textual value or perhaps into RGB color code, which in turn can be used in CSS styling. D3 offers a specialized scale implementation to handle this kind of mapping. We will explore its usage here. The following is the code of the `ordinal-scale.html` file:

```
<div id="alphabet" class="clear">
    <span>Ordinal Scale with Alphabet<br></span>
    <span>Mapping [1..10] to ["a".."j"]<br></span>
</div>
<div id="category10" class="clear">
    <span>Ordinal Color Scale Category 10<br></span>
    <span>Mapping [1..10] to category 10 colors<br></span>
</div>
<div id="category20" class="clear">
    <span>Ordinal Color Scale Category 20<br></span>
    <span>Mapping [1..10] to category 20 colors<br></span>
</div>
<div id="category20b" class="clear">
    <span>Ordinal Color Scale Category 20b<br></span>
    <span>Mapping [1..10] to category 20b colors<br></span>
</div>
<div id="category20c" class="clear">
    <span>Ordinal Color Scale Category 20c<br></span>
    <span>Mapping [1..10] to category 20c colors<br></span>
</div>

<script type="text/javascript">
    var max = 10, data = [];

    for (var i = 1; i <= max; ++i) data.push(i); // <-A
    var alphabet = d3.scaleOrdinal() // <-B
        .domain(data)
        .range(["a", "b", "c", "d", "e", "f", "g", "h", "i", "j"]);
    function render(data, scale, selector) { // <-C
        var cells  = d3.select(selector).selectAll("div.cell")
                .data(data);

        cells.enter()
                .append("div")
                    .classed("cell", true)
                    .style("display", "inline-block")
                    .style("background-color", function(d){  // <-D
                        return scale(d).indexOf("#") >=0 ?
                                            scale(d) : "white";
                    })
                    .text(function (d) { // <-E
                        return scale(d);
                    });
    }

    render(data, alphabet, "#alphabet"); // <-F
render(data, d3.scaleOrdinal(d3.schemeCategory10),
                            "#category10");
```

```
render(data, d3.scaleOrdinal(d3.schemeCategory20),
                            "#category20");
render(data, d3.scaleOrdinal(d3.schemeCategory20b),
                            "#category20b");
render(data, d3.scaleOrdinal(d3.schemeCategory20c),
                            "#category20c"); // <-G
</script>
```

The preceding code outputs the following in your browser:

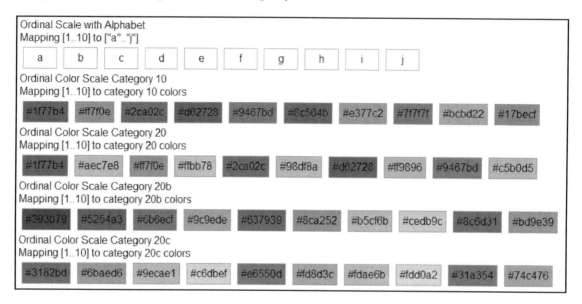

Ordinal scale

How it works...

In the preceding code example, a simple data array containing integers from 0 to 9 was defined on line A:

```
for (var i = 0; i < max; ++i) data.push(i); // <-A
var alphabet = d3.scaleOrdinal() // <-B
    .domain(data)
.range(["a", "b", "c", "d", "e", "f", "g", "h", "i", "j"]);
```

Then, an ordinal scale was created using the d3.scaleOrdinal function on line B. The domain of this scale was set to our integer array data, whereas range was set to a list of alphabets from a to j.

With this scale defined, we can perform the mapping by simply invoking the scale function, for example, `alphabet(0)` will return a, `alphabet(4)` will return e, and so on.

On line C, the `render` function was defined to generate a number of `div` elements on the page to represent the 10 elements in a data array. Each `div` element has its `background-color` attribute set to the scale function's output or `white` if the output is not an RGB color string:

```
.style("background-color", function(d){   // <-D
    return scale(d).indexOf("#")>=0 ? scale(d) : "white";
})
```

On line E, we also set the text of each cell to display the scale function's output:

```
.text(function (d) { // <-E
    return scale(d);
});
```

Now, with all the structures in place, from line F to G, the `render` function was repetitively called with different ordinal scales to produce different visual outputs. On line F, calling `render` with the `alphabet` ordinal scale produces the following output:

Alphabetic ordinal scale

While on line G, calling the `render` function with the built-in `d3.scaleOrdinal(d3.schemeCategory20c)` ordinal color category scheme produces the following output:

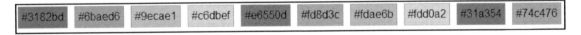

Color ordinal scale

As assigning different colors to different elements in visualization is a common task, for example, assigning different colors in pie and bubble charts, D3 provides a number of different built-in ordinal color scales as we saw in this recipe.

It is quite easy to build your own simple custom ordinal color scale. Just create an ordinal scale with the range set to the colors you want to use, as shown in the following example:

```
d3.scaleOrdinal()
    .range(["#1f77b4", "#ff7f0e", "#2ca02c"]);
```

Interpolating a string

In some cases, you might need to interpolate numbers embedded in a string; perhaps a CSS style for font, for example.

In this recipe, we will examine how you can do that using D3 scale and interpolation. However, before we jump right into string interpolation, a bit of background knowledge on interpolator is due, and the following section will cover the basics of what interpolation is and how D3 implements interpolator functions.

Interpolator

In the first three recipes, we went over three different D3 scale implementations; now it is time to delve a little deeper into D3 scales. You are probably already asking the question, *How do different scales know what value to use for different inputs?* In fact, this question can be generalized through the following definition of interpolator:

> *We are given the values of a function f(x) at different points x0, x1, ... ,xn. We want to find approximate values of the function f(x) for "new" x's that lie between these points. This process is called interpolation.*

> -*Kreyszig E and Kreyszig H, and Norminton E. J. (2010)*

Interpolation is not only important in scale implementation but also essential to many other core D3 capabilities, for example, animation and layout management. It is because of this essential role that D3 has designed a separate and reusable construct called *interpolator* so that this common cross-functional concern can be addressed in a centralized and consistent fashion. Let's take a simple interpolator as an example:

```
var interpolate = d3.interpolateNumber(0, 100);
interpolate(0.1); // => 10
interpolate(0.99); //=> 99
```

In this simple example, we created a D3 number interpolator with a range of [0, 100]. The d3.interpolateNumber function returns an interpolate function, which we can use to perform number-based interpolations. The interpolate function is equivalent to the following code:

```
function interpolate(t) {
    return a * (1 - t) + b * t;
}
```

In this function, a represents the start of the range and b represents the end of the range. The parameter t passed into the interpolate() function is a float-point number, ranging from 0 to 1, and it signifies how far the return value is from a.

D3 provides a number of built-in interpolators. Due to limited scope in this book, we will focus on some of the more interesting interpolators for the next few recipes; we will end our discussion on simple number interpolation here. Nevertheless, the fundamental approach and mechanism will remain the same, whether it is a number or an RGB color code interpolator.

> For more details on number and round interpolation, please refer to the D3 reference documents at
> https://github.com/d3/d3/blob/master/API.md#interpolators-d3-int
> erpolate.

Now, with general interpolation concepts behind us, let's take a look at how string interpolator works in D3.

Getting ready

Open your local copy of the following file in your web browser:

https://github.com/NickQiZhu/d3-cookbook-v2/blob/master/src/chapter4/string-int
erpolation.html.

How to do it...

String interpolator finds the numbers embedded in the string, and then performs interpolation using D3 number interpolator:

```
<div id="font" class="clear">
    <span>Font Interpolation<br></span>
</div>
```

```
<script type="text/javascript">
    var max = 11, data = [];

    var sizeScale = d3.scaleLinear() // <-A
        .domain([0, max])
        .range([  // <-B
            "italic bold 12px/30px Georgia, serif",
            "italic bold 120px/180px Georgia, serif"
        ]);

    for (var i = 0; i < max; ++i) data.push(i);

    function render(data, scale, selector) { // <-C
        var cells = d3.select(selector).selectAll("div.cell")
                .data(data);

        cells.enter()
            .append("div")
                .classed("cell", true)
                .style("display", "inline-block")
            .append("span")
                .style("font", function(d,i){
                    return scale(d); // <-D
                })
                .text(function(d,i){return i;}); // <-E
    }

    render(data, sizeScale, "#font");
</script>
```

The preceding code produces the following output:

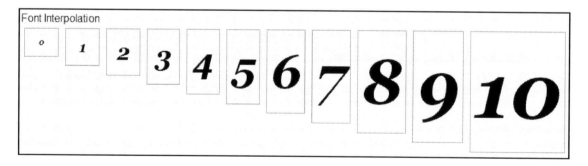

String interpolation

How it works...

In this example, we created a linear scale on line A with a range specified between two strings that represent the start and end `font` styles:

```
var sizeScale = d3.scale.linear() // <-A
        .domain([0, max])
        .range([   // <-B
            "italic bold 12px/30px Georgia, serif",
            "italic bold 120px/180px Georgia, serif"
        ]);
```

As you can see in the code of the `string-interpolation.html` file, the `font` style strings contain `font-size` numbers `12px/30px` and `120px/180px`, which we want to interpolate in this recipe. At this point, you might be asking how the linear scale function can map a number domain to these arbitrary font CSS styles. By default, linear scale uses the `d3.interpolateString` function to handle string-based range. The `d3.interpolateString` function will try to identify embedded numbers in a given string, in our case, the font-size numbers, and apply interpolation on those numbers only. Therefore, in this recipe, we essentially mapped our domain to the font sizes using a linear scale.

On line C, the `render()` function simply creates 10 cells containing each cell's index numbers (line E) styled using the interpolated `font` style string calculated on line D.

```
.style("font", function(d,i){
    return scale(d); // <-D
})
.text(function(d,i){return i;}); // <-E
```

As we can see, simply setting the font style to the output of `scale(d)` is enough since the function output is a complete font CSS style string with transformed embedded numbers.

 If you inspect the output of this recipe, you will notice the output CSS style is actually longer than the original style string we used. The output looks like this:

font-style: italic; font-variant: normal; font-weight: bold; font-stretch: normal; font-size: 90.5455px; line-height: 139.091px; font-family: Georgia, serif;

This is because D3 CSS transformation parses CSS styles first and then uses browser-computed fully qualified CSS string for interpolation. This is done to avoid some subtle bugs that could otherwise be caused by direct interpolation.

There's more...

Though we demonstrated string interpolation in D3 using a CSS font style as an example, D3 string interpolator is not only limited to handling CSS styles. It can basically handle any string and interpolates the embedded number as long as the number matches the following **Regex** pattern:

```
/[-+]?(?:\d+\.?\d*|\.?\d+)(?:[eE][-+]?\d+)?/g
```

When you generate a string using interpolation, very small values, when stringified, may get converted to scientific notation, for example, 1e-7. To avoid this particular conversion, you will need to keep your value larger than 1e-6

Interpolating colors

It is sometimes necessary to interpolate colors when you interpolate values that do not contain numbers but rather RGB or HSL color code. This recipe addresses the question *how can you define scales for color codes and perform interpolation on them?*

Getting ready

Open your local copy of the following file in your web browser:

```
https://github.com/NickQiZhu/d3-cookbook-v2/blob/master/src/chapter4/color-inte
rpolation.html.
```

How to do it...

Color interpolation is such a common operation in visualization that D3 actually provides a number of different kinds of interpolators dedicated to color supporting, for example, **RGB**, **HSL**, **L*a*b***, **HCL**, and **Cubehelix** color space. In this recipe, we will demonstrate how color interpolation can be performed in RGB color space. However, all other color interpolators work in the same way.

D3 color interpolate function always returns the interpolated color in RGB space, no matter what the original color space is, since not all browsers support HSL or L*a*b* color spaces.

Here is what the code for this recipe looks like:

```
<div id="color" class="clear">
    <span>Linear Color Interpolation<br></span>
</div>
<div id="color-diverge" class="clear">
    <span>Poly-Linear Color Interpolation<br></span>
</div>

<script type="text/javascript">
    var max = 21, data = [];

    var colorScale = d3.scaleLinear() // <-A
        .domain([0, max])
        .range(["white", "#4169e1"]);

    var divergingScale = function(pivot) { // <-B
        return d3.scaleLinear()
                .domain([0, pivot, max]) // <-C
                .range(["white", "#4169e1", "white"])
    };

    for (var i = 0; i < max; ++i) data.push(i);

    function render(data, scale, selector) { // <-D
        var cells = d3.select(selector).selectAll("div.cell")
                .data(data);

        cells.enter()
            .append("div").merge(cells)
                .classed("cell", true)
                .style("display", "inline-block")
                .style("background-color", function(d){
                    return scale(d); // <-E
                })
                .text(function(d,i){return i;});
    }

    render(data, colorScale, "#color");
    render(data, divergingScale(5), "#color-diverge");
</script>

<div class="control-group clear">
    <button onclick="render(data, divergingScale(5), '#color-
diverge')">Pivot at 5</button>
    <button onclick="render(data, divergingScale(10), '#color-
diverge')">Pivot at 10</button>
    <button onclick="render(data, divergingScale(15), '#color-
```

```
diverge')">Pivot at 15</button>
    <button onclick="render(data, divergingScale(20), '#color-
diverge')">Pivot at 20</button>
</div>
```

The preceding code produces the following visual output:

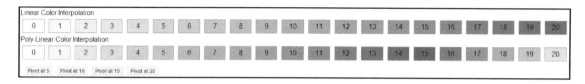

Color interpolation

How it works...

The first step in this recipe is to define a linear color scale on line A with its range set as
["white", "#4169e1"]:

```
var colorScale = d3.scaleLinear() // <-A
    .domain([0, max])
    .range(["white", "#4169e1"]);
```

 As we demonstrated earlier, D3 color interpolator is pretty smart when it comes to color space. Similar to your browser, it understands both color keywords and hexadecimal values.

One new technique used in this recipe, that we haven't encountered yet, is the *poly-linear scale*, which is defined in the divergingScale function on line B, as follows:

```
var divergingScale = function(pivot) { // <-B
    return d3.scaleLinear()
            .domain([0, pivot, max]) // <-C
            .range(["white", "#4169e1", "white"])
};
```

A poly-linear scale is a scale with a non-uniformed linear progression. It is achieved by providing a poly-linear domain on a linear scale as we can see on line C. You can think of a poly-linear scale as a scale that stitches two linear scales with different domains together. Hence, this poly-linear color scale is effectively the two following linear scales combined together:

```
d3.scaleLinear()
```

```
      .domain([0, pivot]).range(["white", "#4169e1"]);
  d3.scaleLinear()
      .domain([pivot, max]).range(["#4169e1", "white "]);
```

No surprise in the rest of the recipe. The `render()` function defined on line D generates 20 cells that are numbered by its index and colored using the output of two color scales we defined earlier. Clicking on the buttons on the web page (such as **Pivot at 5**) will show you the effect of pivoting at different positions in a poly-linear color scale.

See also

- For a complete list of supported color keywords in CSS3, please refer to the W3C official reference at `https://www.w3.org/TR/css3-color/#html4`.

Interpolating compound objects

There will be cases when what you need to interpolate in your visualization is not a simple value but rather an object consisting of multiple and different values, for example, a rectangular object with width, height, and color attributes. Fortunately, D3 has a built-in support for this type of compound object interpolation.

Getting ready

Open your local copy of the following file in your web browser:

`https://github.com/NickQiZhu/d3-cookbook-v2/blob/master/src/chapter4/compound-interpolation.html`.

How to do it...

In this recipe, we will examine how compound object interpolation is performed in D3. The code for the `compound-interpolation.html` file is as follows:

```
<div id="compound" class="clear">
    <span>Compound Interpolation<br></span>
</div>

<script type="text/javascript">
    var max = 21, data = [];
```

```
    var compoundScale = d3.scalePow()
            .exponent(2)
            .domain([0, max])
            .range([
                {color:"#add8e6", height:"15px"}, // <-A
                {color:"#4169e1", height:"150px"} // <-B
            ]);

    for (var i = 0; i < max; ++i) data.push(i);

    function render(data, scale, selector) { // <-C
        var bars = d3.select(selector).selectAll("div.v-bar")
                .data(data);
        bars.enter()
                .append("div")
                .classed("v-bar", true)
                .style("height", function(d){ // <-D
                    return scale(d).height;
                })
                .style("background-color", function(d){ // <-E
                    return scale(d).color;
                })
                .text(function(d,i){return i;});
    }

    render(data, compoundScale, "#compound");
</script>
```

The preceding code generates the following visual output:

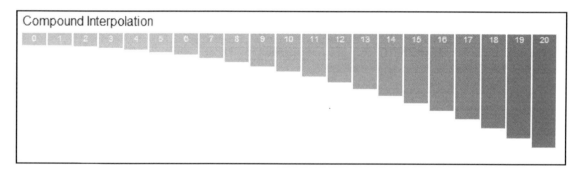

Compound object interpolation

How it works...

This recipe is different from the previous recipes in this chapter by the fact that the scale we will use in this recipe has a range defined using two objects rather than simple primitive data types:

```
var compoundScale = d3.scalePow()
            .exponent(2)
            .domain([0, max])
            .range([
                {color:"#add8e6", height:"15px"}, // <-A
                {color:"#4169e1", height:"150px"} // <-B
            ]);
```

We can see on lines A and B that the start and the end of the scale range are two objects that contain two different kinds of values: one for RGB color and the other one for CSS height style. When you interpolate this kind of a scale containing compound range, D3 will iterate through each of the fields inside an object and recursively apply interpolation rules on each one of them. In other words, for this example, D3 will interpolate the color field using color interpolation from #add8e6 to #4169e1 while using string interpolation on height field from 15px to 150px.

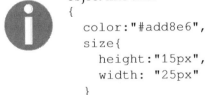

Internally, D3 uses the d3.interpolateObject function to recursively interpolate an object; the recursive nature of this algorithm allows D3 to interpolate even on nested objects. Therefore, you can interpolate on an object like this:

```
{
  color:"#add8e6",
  size{
    height:"15px",
    width: "25px"
  }
}
```

A compound scale function, when invoked, returns a compound object that matches the given range definition:

```
.style("height", function(d){
  return scale(d).height; // <-D
})
.style("background-color", function(d){
  return scale(d).color; // <-E
})
```

As we can see on lines D and E, the returned value is a compound object, and this is why, we can access its attribute to retrieve the interpolated values.

> Though it is not a common case, if the start and end of your compound scale range do not have identical attributes, D3 won't complain but rather it will just treat the missing attribute as a constant. The following scale will render the height to be 15px for all the div elements:

```
var compoundScale = d3.scalePow()
        .exponent(2)
        .domain([0, max])
            range([
            {color:"#add8e6", height:"15px"}, // <-A
            {color:"#4169e1"} // <-B
    ]);
```

In this chapter we have covered an important fundamental concept in D3 – scales. In next chapter we will move on to the first visualization component in this book that is actually built on top of scales – Axes.

5
Playing with Axes

In this chapter, we will cover:

- Working with basic axes
- Customizing ticks
- Drawing grid lines
- Dynamic rescaling of axes

Introduction

D3 was initially released without the built-in support of the Axis component. This situation did not last long since axes are the universal building blocks in many Cartesian coordinate system-based visualization projects and one of the most tedious tasks to build from scratch by hand. It quickly became clear that D3 needs to provide built-in support for axes. Therefore, it was introduced quite early on and is continuously being enhanced ever since it was released. In this chapter, we will explore the usage of the Axis component and some related techniques.

Working with basic axes

In this recipe, we will focus on introducing the basic concepts and supports of the Axis component in D3 while we cover different types and features of Axis as well as their SVG structures.

Getting ready

Open your local copy of the following file in your web browser:

```
https://github.com/NickQiZhu/d3-cookbook-v2/blob/master/src/chapter5/basic-axes
.html
```

How to do it...

Let's first take a look at the following code sample:

```html
<div class="control-group">
    <button onclick="renderAll(d3.axisBottom)">
        horizontal bottom
    </button>
    <button onclick="renderAll(d3.axisTop)">
        horizontal top
    </button>
    <button onclick="renderAll(d3.axisLeft)">
        vertical left
    </button>
    <button onclick="renderAll(d3.axisRight)">
        vertical right
    </button>
</div>

<script type="text/javascript">
    var height = 500,
        width = 500,
        margin = 25,
        offset = 50,
        axisWidth = width - 2 * margin,
        svg;
    function createSvg(){ // <-A
        svg = d3.select("body").append("svg") // <-B
            .attr("class", "axis") // <-C
            .attr("width", width)
            .attr("height", height);
    }
    function renderAxis(fn, scale, i){
        var axis = fn() // <-D
            .scale(scale) // <-E
            .ticks(5); // <-G
        svg.append("g")
            .attr("transform", function(){ // <-H
                if([d3.axisTop, d3.axisBottom].indexOf(fn) >= 0)
```

```
                    return "translate(" + margin + "," +
                                        i * offset + ")";
                else
                    return "translate(" + i * offset + ", " +
                                        margin + ")";
            })
            .call(axis); // <-I
    }
    function renderAll(fn){
        if(svg) svg.remove();
        createSvg();
        renderAxis(fn, d3.scaleLinear()
                    .domain([0, 1000])
                    .range([0, axisWidth]), 1);
        renderAxis(fn, d3.scalePow()
                    .exponent(2)
                    .domain([0, 1000])
                    .range([0, axisWidth]), 2);
        renderAxis(fn, d3.scaleTime()
                    .domain([new Date(2016, 0, 1),
                            new Date(2017, 0, 1)])
                    .range([0, axisWidth]), 3);
    }
</script>
```

The preceding code produces a visual output with only the four buttons shown in the following screenshot; when you click on **horizontal bottom**, it will show you the following:

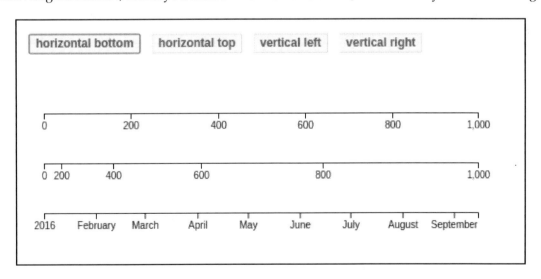

Horizontal axis

The following screenshot shows what it looks like when you click the **vertical right** button:

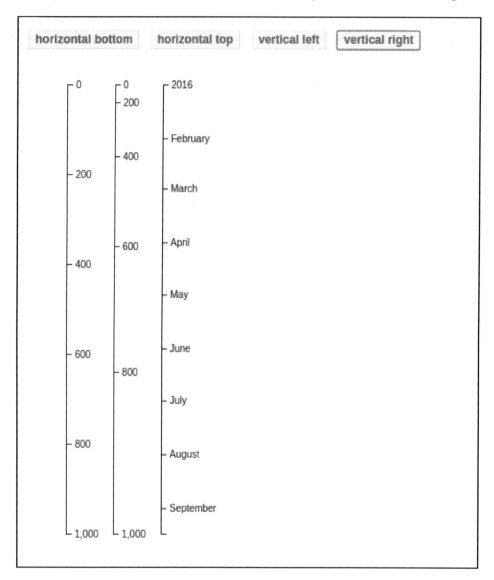

Vertical axis

How it works...

The first step in this recipe is to create the `svg` element, which will be used to render our axes. This is done using the `createSvg` function, which is defined on line A, and the D3 `append` and `attr` modifier functions, shown on lines B and C.

 This is the first recipe in this book that uses SVG instead of HTML element since D3 Axis component supports only SVG. If you are not familiar with SVG standard, don't worry, we will cover it in detail in `Chapter 7`, *Getting into Shape*. Although, for the purpose of this chapter, some of the basic and limited SVG concepts will be introduced when used by the D3 Axis component.

Let's take a look at how we created the SVG canvas in the following code snippet:

```
var height = 500,
  width = 500,
  margin = 25,
  offset = 50,
  axisWidth = width - 2 * margin,
  svg;
function createSvg(){ // <-A
    svg = d3.select("body").append("svg") // <-B
      .attr("class", "axis") // <-C
      .attr("width", width)
      .attr("height", height);
}
```

Now, we are ready to render the axes on this `svg` canvas. The `renderAxis` function is designed to do exactly just that. On line D, we first create an Axis component using the given D3 axis generator function. D3 version 4.x is shipped with four built-in axis generators for different orientations. Orientation tells D3 how a given axis will be placed, and therefore, how it should be rendered; for example, whether horizontally or vertically. The four axis orientations that D3 supports out of box are as follows:

- `d3.axisTop`: A horizontal axis with labels placed on top of the axis
- `d3.axisBottom`: A horizontal axis with labels placed at the bottom of the axis
- `d3.axisLeft`: A vertical axis with labels placed on the left-hand side of the axis
- `d3.axisRight`: A vertical axis with labels placed on the right-hand side of the axis

You can see in the following code snippet that these are indeed the functions that get passed to the `renderAll` function when you click on the specified buttons:

```
<div class="control-group">
    <button onclick="renderAll(d3.axisBottom)">
        horizontal bottom
    </button>
    <button onclick="renderAll(d3.axisTop)">
        horizontal top
    </button>
    <button onclick="renderAll(d3.axisLeft)">
        vertical left
    </button>
    <button onclick="renderAll(d3.axisRight)">
        vertical right
    </button>
</div>
...
function renderAxis(fn, scale, i){
        var axis = fn() // <-D
            .scale(scale) // <-E
            .ticks(5); // <-G
...
```

D3 Axis is designed to work out of the box with D3 scales. The axis scale is provided using the `scale()` function (refer to line E). In this example, we render three different axes with the following scales:

```
d3.scaleLinear().domain([0, 1000]).range([0, axisWidth])
d3.scalePow().exponent(2).domain([0, 1000]).range([0, axisWidth])
d3.scaleTime()
  .domain([new Date(2016, 0, 1), new Date()])
  .range([0, axisWidth])
```

On line G, we set the number of ticks, the small marks on the axes, to 5. This tells D3 ideally how many ticks we want to render for this axis; however, D3 might choose to render slightly more or less ticks based on the available space and its own calculation. We will explore the Axis ticks' configuration in detail in the next recipe.

Once the axis is defined, the final step in this creation process is to create an `svg:g` container element, which will then be used to host all SVG structures that are required to render an axis:

```
svg.append("g")
  .attr("transform", function(){ // <-H
    if(["top", "bottom"].indexOf(orient) >= 0)
      return "translate(" + margin + ","+ i * offset + ")";
```

```
  else
    return "translate(" + i * offset + ", " + margin + ")";
})
.call(axis); // <-I
```

 Having a g container group element to contain all SVG elements related to an axis is not only a good practice but also a requirement of the D3 axis component.

Most of the logic in this code snippet is related to the calculation of where to draw the axis on the svg canvas using the transform attribute (refer to line H). In the preceding code example, to shift the axis using offsets, we used the translate SVG transformation, which allows us to shift an element using a distance parameter that is defined with the coordinates in *x* and *y*.

 SVG transformation will be discussed in detail in Chapter 7, *Getting into Shape*, or you can refer to the following URL for more information on this topic:
https://www.w3.org/TR/SVG/coords.html#TranslationDefined

The more relevant part of this code is on line I, where the d3.selection.call function is used with the axis object being passed in as the parameter. The d3.selection.call function invokes the given function (in our case, the axis object) with the current selection passed in as an argument. In other words, the function being passed into the d3.selection.call function should have the following form:

```
function foo(selection) {
  ...
}
```

 The d3.selection.call function also allows you to pass in additional arguments to the invoking function. For more information, visit the following link:
https://github.com/d3/d3-selection/blob/master/README.md#selection_call

Once the D3 Axis component is called, it will take care of the rest and automatically create all necessary SVG elements for an axis (refer to line I). For example, the horizontal-bottom time axis in the example shown in this recipe has the following complicated SVG structure automatically generated, which we don't really need to know much about:

```
▼<g transform="translate(25,50)" fill="none" font-size="10" font-family="sans-serif" text-anchor="middle">
    <path class="domain" stroke="#000" d="M0.5,6V0.5H450.5V6"></path>
  ▼<g class="tick" opacity="1" transform="translate(0,0)">
      <line stroke="#000" y2="6" x1="0.5" x2="0.5"></line>
      <text fill="#000" y="9" x="0.5" dy="0.71em">0</text>
    </g>
  ►<g class="tick" opacity="1" transform="translate(90,0)">…</g>
  ►<g class="tick" opacity="1" transform="translate(180,0)">…</g>
  ►<g class="tick" opacity="1" transform="translate(270,0)">…</g>
  ►<g class="tick" opacity="1" transform="translate(360,0)">…</g>
  ▼<g class="tick" opacity="1" transform="translate(450,0)">
      <line stroke="#000" y2="6" x1="0.5" x2="0.5"></line>
      <text fill="#000" y="9" x="0.5" dy="0.71em">1,000</text>
    </g>
</g>
```

Horizontal bottom time Axis SVG structure

Customizing ticks

We already saw how to use the `ticks` function in the previous recipe. This is the simplest ticks-related customization you can do on a D3 axis. In this recipe, we will cover some of the most common and useful ticks-related customizations with D3 axis.

Getting ready

Open your local copy of the following file in your web browser:

`https://github.com/NickQiZhu/d3-cookbook-v2/blob/master/src/chapter5/ticks.html`

How to do it...

In the following code example, we will customize the ticks, padding, and formatting of its label. Let's take a look at the code snippet first:

```
<script type="text/javascript">
    var height = 500,
        width = 500,
        margin = 25,
```

```
        axisWidth = width - 2 * margin;
    var svg = d3.select("body").append("svg")
            .attr("class", "axis")
            .attr("width", width)
            .attr("height", height);
    var scale = d3.scaleLinear()
            .domain([0, 1]).range([0, axisWidth]);
    var axis = d3.axisBottom()
            .scale(scale)
            .ticks(10)
            .tickSize(12) // <-A
            .tickPadding(10) // <-B
            .tickFormat(d3.format(".0%")); // <-C

    svg.append("g")
        .attr("transform", function(){
            return "translate(" + margin +
                    "," + margin + ")";
        })
        .call(axis);
</script>
```

The preceding code generates the following visual output:

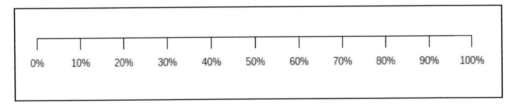

Customized axis ticks

How it works...

The focus of this recipe is the highlighted lines after the `ticks` function. As we have mentioned before, the `ticks` function provides D3 a hint on how many ticks an axis should contain. After setting the number of ticks, in this recipe, we continue to customize the ticks through further function calls. On line A, the `tickSize` function is used to customize the size of the ticks. The default tick size provided by D3 is 6px, whereas we set it to 12px in this example. Then, on line B, the `tickPadding` function was used to specify the amount of space (in pixels) between tick labels and the axis.

Finally, a custom format was used with the `tickFormat` function on line C to convert the tick value into percentage. D3 axis' `tickFormat` function can also take a function as a formatter for more customization, and therefore, the formatter used in this recipe is the same as passing, in the following custom format function:

```
.tickFormat(function(v){ // <-C
    return Math.floor(v * 100) + "%";
});
```

For more information on the aforementioned functions and other ticks-related customizations, visit the D3 Wiki at the following URL:
`https://github.com/d3/d3-axis/blob/master/README.md#_axis`

Drawing grid lines

Quite often, we will need horizontal and vertical grid lines to be drawn in consistency with the ticks on both *x* and *y* axes. As we have shown in the previous recipe, typically, we don't have, or don't want to have, precise control of how ticks are rendered on D3 axes. Therefore, we might not know how many ticks are present and their values, before they are rendered. This is especially true if you are building a reusable visualization library, where it is impossible to know the tick configuration ahead of its time. In this recipe, we will explore some useful techniques for drawing consistent grid lines on Axis without actually needing to know the tick values.

Getting ready

Open your local copy of the following file in your web browser:

`https://github.com/NickQiZhu/d3-cookbook-v2/blob/master/src/chapter5/grid-line.html`

How to do it...

First, let's take a look at how we draw grid lines in the following code:

```
<script type="text/javascript">
    var height = 500,
        width = 500,
        margin = 25;
```

```
var svg = d3.select("body").append("svg")
        .attr("class", "axis")
        .attr("width", width)
        .attr("height", height);
function renderXAxis(){
    var axisLength = width - 2 * margin;
    var scale = d3.scaleLinear()
                    .domain([0, 100])
                    .range([0, axisLength]);
    var xAxis = d3.axisBottom()
            .scale(scale);
    svg.append("g")
        .attr("class", "x-axis")
        .attr("transform", function(){ // <-A
            return "translate(" + margin + "," +
                            (height - margin) + ")";
        })
        .call(xAxis);
    d3.selectAll("g.x-axis g.tick") // <-B
        .append("line") // <-C
            .classed("grid-line", true)
            .attr("x1", 0) // <-D
            .attr("y1", 0)
            .attr("x2", 0)
            .attr("y2", - (height - 2 * margin));  // <-E
}
function renderYAxis(){
    var axisLength = height - 2 * margin;
    var scale = d3.scaleLinear()
                    .domain([100, 0])
                    .range([0, axisLength]);
    var yAxis = d3.axisLeft()
            .scale(scale);

    svg.append("g")
        .attr("class", "y-axis")
        .attr("transform", function(){
            return "translate(" + margin + "," +
                                        margin + ")";
        })
        .call(yAxis);
    d3.selectAll("g.y-axis g.tick")
        .append("line")
            .classed("grid-line", true)
            .attr("x1", 0)
            .attr("y1", 0)
            .attr("x2", axisLength) // <-F
            .attr("y2", 0);
```

```
    }
    renderYAxis();
    renderXAxis();
</script>
```

The previous code generates the following visual output:

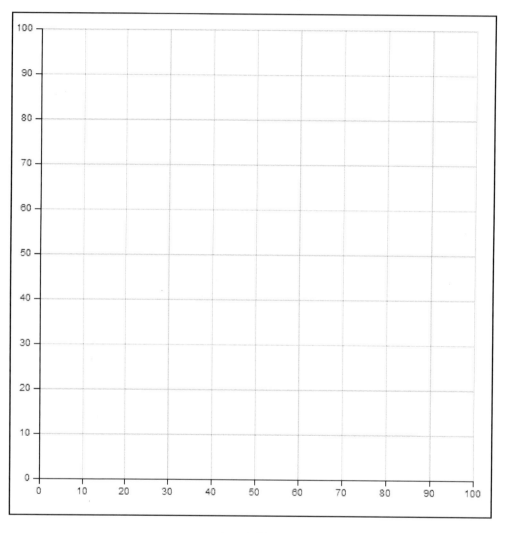

Axes and grid lines

How it works...

In this recipe, two axes–*x* and *y*–were created in the `renderXAxis` and `renderYAxis` functions, respectively. Let's take a look at how the x axis was rendered.

Once you understand how to render the *x* axis and its grid lines, the logic used to render the *y* axis can be easily understood since the logic used is almost identical. The *x* axis and its scale were defined without complications, as we have already demonstrated them a number of times throughout this chapter. An `svg:g` element was created to contain the *x* axis structures. This `svg:g` element was placed at the bottom of the chart using a translate transformation, as shown on line A:

```
.attr("transform", function(){ // <-A
  return "translate(" + margin + "," + (height - margin) + ")";
})
```

It is important to remember that the translate transformation changes the frame of reference for coordinates when it comes to any of its subelements. For example, within this `svg:g` element, if we create a point with its coordinates set as `(0, 0)`, then when we draw this point on the SVG canvas, it will be actually placed as `(margin, height - margin)`. This is because all subelements within the `svg:g` element are automatically transformed to this base coordinate, and hence leading to the shift of the frame of reference. Equipped with this understanding, let's take a look at how dynamic grid lines can be generated after the axis is rendered through the following code snippet:

```
d3.selectAll("g.x-axis g.tick") // <-B
            .append("line") // <-C
              .classed("grid-line", true)
              .attr("x1", 0) // <-D
              .attr("y1", 0)
              .attr("x2", 0)
              .attr("y2", - (height - 2 * margin));  // <-E
```

Once the axis is rendered, we can select all the ticks elements on an axis by selecting the `g.tick`, since each of them is grouped by its own `svg:g` element (refer to line B). Then, on line C, we append a new `svg:line` element to each of the `svg:g` tick element. SVG line element is the simplest shape provided by the SVG standard. It has the following four main attributes:

- `x1` and `y1` attributes define the point of origin of this line
- `x2` and `y2` attributes define the point of destination

In our case, we simply will need to set x1, y1, and x2 to 0 since each g.tick element is already translated to its position on the axis, and therefore, we only need to change the y2 attribute in order to draw a vertical grid line. The y2 attribute is set to -(height - 2 * margin). The reason why the coordinate is negative was because the entire g.x-axis has been shifted down to (height - margin), as mentioned in the previous code. Therefore, in absolute coordinate terms, y2 = (height - margin) - (height - 2 * margin) = margin, which is the top of the vertical grid line we want to draw from the *x* axis.

 In SVG coordinates, (0, 0) denotes the top-left corner of the SVG canvas.

This is what the *x* axis in the SVG structure with an associated grid line looks like:

```
▼<g class="x-axis" transform="translate(25,475)" fill="none" font-size="10" font-family="sans-serif" text-anchor="middle">
  <path class="domain" stroke="#000" d="M0.5,6V0.5H450.5V6"></path>
  ▼<g class="tick" opacity="1" transform="translate(0,0)">
    <line stroke="#000" y2="6" x1="0.5" x2="0.5"></line>
    <text fill="#000" y="9" x="0.5" dy="0.71em">0</text>
    <line class="grid-line" x1="0" y1="0" x2="0" y2="-450"></line>
  </g>
  ▼<g class="tick" opacity="1" transform="translate(45,0)">
    <line stroke="#000" y2="6" x1="0.5" x2="0.5"></line>
    <text fill="#000" y="9" x="0.5" dy="0.71em">10</text>
    <line class="grid-line" x1="0" y1="0" x2="0" y2="-450"></line>
  </g>
  ▶<g class="tick" opacity="1" transform="translate(90,0)">…</g>
  ▶<g class="tick" opacity="1" transform="translate(135,0)">…</g>
  ▶<g class="tick" opacity="1" transform="translate(180,0)">…</g>
  ▶<g class="tick" opacity="1" transform="translate(225,0)">…</g>
  ▶<g class="tick" opacity="1" transform="translate(270,0)">…</g>
  ▶<g class="tick" opacity="1" transform="translate(315,0)">…</g>
  ▶<g class="tick" opacity="1" transform="translate(360,0)">…</g>
  ▶<g class="tick" opacity="1" transform="translate(405,0)">…</g>
  ▶<g class="tick" opacity="1" transform="translate(450,0)">…</g>
</g>
```

X-axis with grid lines SVG structure

As we can see in the preceding screenshot, an svg:line element representing the grid line was added into the g.ticksvg:g container element as discussed earlier in this section.

The *y* axis grid lines are generated using the *identical technique*; the only difference is that instead of setting the y2 attribute on the grid lines, as we did for the *x* axis, we change the x2 attribute since the lines are horizontal (refer to line F):

```
d3.selectAll("g.y-axis g.tick")
            .append("line")
                .classed("grid-line", true)
                .attr("x1", 0)
```

```
                    .attr("y1", 0)
                    .attr("x2", axisLength) // <-F
                    .attr("y2", 0);
```

Dynamic rescaling of axes

In some cases, the scale used by axes might change when triggered by user interaction or changes from data feeds. For example, a user may change the time range for the visualization. This kind of change also needs to be reflected by rescaling the axes. In this recipe, we will explore how this can be achieved dynamically while also redrawing the grid lines associated with each tick.

Getting ready

Open your local copy of the following file in your web browser:

```
https://github.com/NickQiZhu/d3-cookbook-v2/blob/master/src/chapter5/rescaling.
html
```

How to do it...

The following is the code that shows how to perform dynamic rescaling:

```
<script type="text/javascript">
    var height = 500,
        width = 500,
        margin = 25,
        xAxis, yAxis, xAxisLength, yAxisLength;
    var svg = d3.select("body").append("svg")
            .attr("class", "axis")
            .attr("width", width)
            .attr("height", height);
    function renderXAxis(){
        xAxisLength = width - 2 * margin;
            var scale = d3.scaleLinear()
                        .domain([0, 100])
                        .range([0, xAxisLength]);
        xAxis = d3.axisBottom()
                .scale(scale);
        svg.append("g")
            .attr("class", "x-axis")
            .attr("transform", function(){
```

```
                    return "translate(" + margin + "," +
                                    (height - margin) + ")";
            })
            .call(xAxis);
    }
    ...
    function rescale(){ // <-A
        var max = Math.round(Math.random() * 100);
        xAxis.scale().domain([0, max]); // <-B
        svg.select("g.x-axis")
            .transition()
            .call(xAxis); // <-C
        yAxis.scale().domain([max, 0]);
        svg.select("g.y-axis")
            .transition()
            .call(yAxis);
        renderXGridlines();
        renderYGridlines();
    }
    function renderXGridlines(){
        d3.selectAll("g.x-axis g.tick")
                .select("line.grid-line")
                .remove(); // <-D
        d3.selectAll("g.x-axis g.tick")
                .append("line")
                    .classed("grid-line", true)
                    .attr("x1", 0)
                    .attr("y1", 0)
                    .attr("x2", 0)
                    .attr("y2", - yAxisLength);
    }
    ...
    renderXAxis();
    renderXGridlines();
    ...
</script>
```

The preceding code generates the following effects:

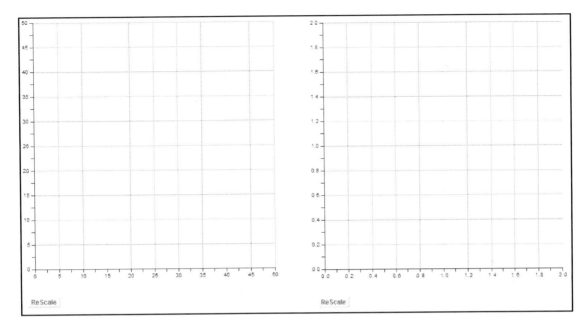

Dynamic axes rescaling

 Due to the limited space in this book, the *y* axis-related code is omitted from the code example in this recipe. Refer to the code example available online for a complete reference.

How it works...

As soon as you click on the **ReScale** button on the screen, you will notice both the axes rescale while all the ticks and grid lines get redrawn accompanied by a smooth transition effect. In this section, we will focus on how this rescaling works and leave the transition effect for the next chapter, *Transition with Style*. Most of the heavy lifting in this recipe is done by the `rescale` function defined on line A:

```
function rescale(){ // <-A
  var max = Math.round(Math.random() * 100);
  xAxis.scale().domain([0, max]); // <-B
  svg.select("g.x-axis")
    .transition()
    .call(xAxis); // <-C
  renderXGridlines();
}
```

To rescale an axis, we simply will change its domain (refer to line B). If you recall, the scale domain represents the data domain, whereas its range corresponds to visual domain. Therefore, visual range should remain constant since we are not resizing the SVG canvas. Once this is updated, we call the axis function xAxis again by passing in the svg:g element for the *x* axis (refer to line C); this simple call will take care of the axis updating, and hence, our job with the axis is done. In the next step, we will also need to update and redraw all the grid lines since the domain change will also change all the ticks:

```
function renderXGridlines(){
        d3.selectAll("g.x-axis g.tick")
                .select("line.grid-line")
                .remove(); // <-D
        d3.selectAll("g.x-axis g.tick")
                .append("line")
                    .classed("grid-line", true)
                    .attr("x1", 0)
                    .attr("y1", 0)
                    .attr("x2", 0)
                    .attr("y2", - yAxisLength);
    }
```

This is achieved by removing every grid line by calling the remove() function, as shown on line D, and then recreating the grid lines for all the new ticks on the rescaled axes. This approach effectively keeps all grid lines consistent with the ticks during rescaling.

6
Transition with Style

The preceding code produces the following visual output where a box appears with In this chapter, we will cover:

- Animating a single element
- Animating multiple elements
- Using ease
- Using tweening
- Using transition chaining
- Using transition filter
- Listening to transitional events
- Working with timer

Introduction

"A picture is worth a thousand words."

This age-old wisdom is arguably one of the most important cornerstones of data visualization. Animation, on the other hand, is generated using a series of still images in quick succession. Human eye-and-brain complex, through positive afterimage, phi phenomenon, and beta movement, is able to create an illusion of continuous imagery. As Rick Parent put it perfectly in his brilliant work *Computer Animation Algorithms and Techniques*:

> *Images can quickly convey a large amount of information because the human visual system is a sophisticated information processor. It follows, then, that moving images have the potential to convey even more information in a short time. Indeed, the human visual system has evolved to provide for survival in an ever-changing world; it is designed to notice and interpret movement.*

-Parent R. 2012

This is in fact the main goal of animation used in data visualization projects. In this chapter, we will focus on the mechanics of *D3 transition*, covering topics from the basics to more advanced ones, such as custom interpolation and timer-based transition. Mastering transition is not only going to add many bells and whistles to your visualization but will also provide a powerful toolset to your visualization and otherwise hard-to-visualize attributes, such as trending and differences.

What is Transition?

D3 transition offers the ability to create computer animation with HTML and SVG elements on a web page. D3 transition implements an animation called *Interpolation-based Animation*. Computers are especially well equipped for value interpolation, and therefore, most of the computer animations are interpolation based. As its name suggests, the foundation for such animation capability is value interpolation.

If you recall, we have already covered D3 interpolators and interpolation functions in detail in `Chapter 4`, *Tipping the Scales*. Transition is built on top of interpolation and scales to provide the ability to change values over time, which powers animation. Each transition can be defined using a start and end value (also called *key frames* in animation), while different algorithms and interpolators will fill in the intermediate values frame by frame (also called "in-betweening" or simply "tweening"). At the first glance, if you are not already familiar with animation algorithms and techniques, this seems to be a somewhat less controlled way of creating an animation. However, it is quite the opposite in reality; interpolation-based transitions can provide direct and specific expectations about the motion produced down to each and every frame, thus offering tremendous control to the animator with simplicity. In fact, D3 transition API is so well designed that, in most cases, only a couple of lines of code are enough to implement the animations you need in a data visualization project. Now, let's get our hands dirty and try out some transitions to further improve our understanding on this topic.

Animating a single element

In this recipe, we will first take a look at the simplest case of transition-interpolating attributes on a single element over time to produce a simple animation.

Getting ready

Open your local copy of the following file in your web browser:

`https://github.com/NickQiZhu/d3-cookbook-v2/blob/master/src/chapter6/single-ele ment-transition.html`

How to do it...

The code necessary to perform this simple transition is extremely short; good news for any animator:

```
<script type="text/javascript">
var body = d3.select("body"),
duration = 5000;

body.append("div") // <-A
        .classed("box", true)
        .style("background-color", "#e9967a") // <-B
      .transition() // <-C
      .duration(duration) // <-D
        .style("background-color", "#add8e6") // <-E
        .style("margin-left", "600px") // <-F
        .style("width", "100px")
        .style("height", "100px");
</script>
```

The preceding code produces a moving, shrinking, and color-changing square, as shown in the following screenshot:

Single element transition

How it works...

You might be surprised to see that the extra code we added to enable this animation is only on lines C and D, as shown in the following code snippet:

```
body.append("div") // <-A
            .classed("box", true)
            .style("background-color", "#e9967a") // <-B
            .transition() // <-C
            .duration(duration) // <-D
```

First, on line C, we call the `d3.selection.transition` function to define a transition. Then, the `transition` function returns a transition-bound selection that still represents the same element(s) in the current selection. However, now, it is equipped with additional functions and allows further customization of the transitional behavior.

On line D, we set the duration of the transition to `5000` milliseconds using the `duration()` function. This function also returns the current transition-bound selection, thus allowing function chaining. As we mentioned at the start of this chapter, interpolation-based animations usually only require you to specify the start and end values while it lets interpolators and algorithms fill the intermediate values over time. D3 transition treats all values that are set before calling the `transition` function as start values, with values set after the `transition` function call as end values. Hence, in our example, we have the following:

```
.style("background-color", "#e9967a") // <-B
```

The `background-color` style defined on line B is treated as the start value for transition. All styles set in the following lines are treated as end values:

```
.style("background-color", "#add8e6") // <-E
.style("margin-left", "600px") // <-F
.style("width", "100px")
.style("height", "100px");
```

At this point, you might be asking, *why these start and end values are not symmetric?* D3 transition does not require every interpolated value to have explicit start and end values. If the start value is missing, then it will try to use the computed style, and if the end value is missing, then the value will be treated as a constant. Once the transition starts, D3 will automatically pick the most suitable built-in interpolator for each value. In our example, an RGB color interpolator will be used in line E, while a string interpolator-which internally uses number interpolators to interpolate embedded numbers-will be used for the rest of the style values. Here, we will list the interpolated style values with their start and end values:

- background-color: The start value-#e9967a-is greater than the end value-#add8e6
- margin-left: The start value is a computed style and greater than the end value 600px
- width: The start value is a computed style and greater than the end value 100px
- height: The start value is a computed style and greater than the end value 100px

Animating multiple elements

More elaborate data visualization requires animating multiple elements instead of a single element, as demonstrated in the previous recipe. More importantly, these transitions often need to be driven by data and coordinated with other elements within the same visualization. In this recipe, we will see how a data-driven multi-element transition can be created to generate a moving bar chart. New bars are added over time, while the chart shifts from right to left with a smooth transition.

Getting ready

Open your local copy of the following file in your web browser:

https://github.com/NickQiZhu/d3-cookbook-v2/blob/master/src/chapter6/multi-elem ent-transition.html

How to do it...

As expected, this recipe is slightly larger than the previous one, however, not by that much. Let's take a look at the following code:

```
<script type="text/javascript">
var id= 0,
data = [],
duration = 500,
chartHeight = 100,
chartWidth = 680;

for(vari = 0; i< 20; i++) push(data);

function render(data) {
        var selection = d3.select("body")
```

```
                        .selectAll("div.v-bar")
                          .data(data, function(d){return d.id;}); // <-A

              // enter
              selection.enter()
                      .append("div")
                      .attr("class", "v-bar")
                      .style("z-index", "0")
                      .style("position", "fixed")
                      .style("top", chartHeight + "px")
                       .style("left", function(d, i){
                          return barLeft(i+1) + "px"; // <-B
                      })
                      .style("height", "0px") // <-C
                      .append("span");

              // update
              selection
                  .transition().duration(duration) // <-D
                      .style("top", function (d) {
                              return chartHeight - barHeight(d) + "px";
                      })
                      .style("left", function(d, i){
                          return barLeft(i) + "px";
                      })
                      .style("height", function (d) {
                          return barHeight(d) + "px";
                      })
                      .select("span")
                      .text(function (d) {return d.value;});

              // exit
              selection.exit()
                      .transition().duration(duration) // <-E
                      .style("left", function(d, i){
                          return barLeft(-1) + "px"; //<-F
                      })
                      .remove(); // <-G
      }

function push(data) {
    data.push({
        id: ++id,
        value: Math.round(Math.random() * chartHeight)
    });
}

functionbarLeft(i) {
```

```
    return i * (30 + 2);
}

functionbarHeight(d) {
    returnd.value;
}

setInterval(function () {
                data.shift();
                push(data);
                render(data);
    }, 2000);

render(data);

d3.select("body")
        .append("div")
            .attr("class", "baseline")
            .style("position", "fixed")
            .style("z-index", "1")
            .style("top", chartHeight + "px")
            .style("left", "0px")
            .style("width", chartWidth + "px");
</script>
```

The preceding code generates a sliding bar chart in your web browser, as shown in the following screenshot:

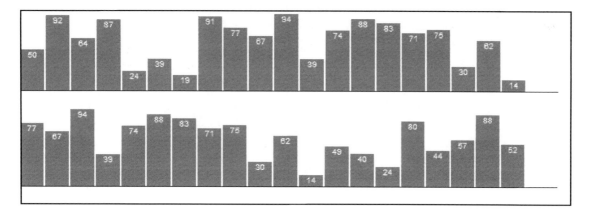

Sliding bar chart

How it works...

On the surface, this example seems to be quite complex with complicated effects. Every second a new bar needs to be created and animated while the rest of the bars need to slide over precisely. The beauty of D3 set-oriented functional API is that it works exactly the same way no matter how many elements you manipulate; therefore, once you understand the mechanics, you will realize this recipe is not so much different than the previous one.

As the first step, we created a data-bound selection for a number of vertical bars (on line A), which can then be used in a classic enter-update-exit D3 pattern:

```
var selection = d3.select("body")
                .selectAll("div.v-bar")
                .data(data, function(d){return d.id;}); // <-A
```

One thing we have not touched so far is the second parameter in the `d3.selection.data` function. This function is called an *object-identity function*. The purpose of using this function is to provide object constancy. What it means in simple terms is that we want the binding between data and visual element to be stable. In order to achieve object constancy, each data needs to have a unique identifier. Once the ID is provided, D3 will ensure that a `div` element is bound to `{id: 3, value: 45}`; the next time the update selection is computed, the same `div` element will be used for the data with the same index `id`, although this time, the value may be changed, for example, to `{id: 3, value: 12}`. Object constancy is crucial in this recipe; without object constancy, the sliding effect will not work.

If you are interested to know more about object constancy, please check out this excellent writing by Mike Bostock, the creator of D3, at the following link: `https://bost.ocks.org/mike/constancy/`

The second step is to create these vertical bars with the `d3.selection.enter` function and compute the `left` position for each bar based on the index number (refer to line B):

```
// enter
selection.enter()
                .append("div")
                .attr("class", "v-bar")
                .style("z-index", "0")
                .style("position", "fixed")
                .style("top", chartHeight + "px")
                .style("left", function(d, i){
returnbarLeft(i+1) + "px"; // <-B
                })
                .style("height", "0px") // <-C
                .append("span");
```

Another point worth mentioning here is that in the `enter` section, we have not called the transition yet, which means any value we specify here will be used as the start value in a transition. If you notice on line C, bar `height` is set to `0px`. This enables the animation of bars to increase from zero height to the target `height`. At the same time, the same logic is applied to the `left` position of the bar (refer to line B) and was set to `barLeft(i+1)`, thus enabling the sliding transition we desired:

```
// update
selection
                .transition().duration(duration) // <-D
                    .style("top", function (d) {
returnchartHeight - barHeight(d) + "px";
                    })
                    .style("left", function(d, i){
returnbarLeft(i) + "px";
                    })
                    .style("height", function (d) {
returnbarHeight(d) + "px";
                    })
                    .select("span")
                        .text(function (d) {return d.value;});
```

After completing the `enter` section, we can now take care of the `update` section, where the transition is defined. First of all, we want to introduce transition for all updates, and therefore, we invoke the `transition` function before any style change is applied (refer to line D). Once the transition-bound selection is created, we applied the following style transitions:

- top: `chartHeight + "px"` >`chartHeight - barHeight(d)+"px"`
- left: `barLeft(i+1) + "px"` >`barLeft(i) + "px"`
- height: `"0px"` >`barHeight(d) + "px"`

The aforementioned three style transitions are all you need to do to handle new bars and every existing bars and their sliding effect. Finally, the last case we will need to handle here is the `exit` case, when a bar is no longer needed. So, we want to keep the number of bars constant on the page. This is handled in the `exit` section:

```
// exit
selection.exit()
                  .transition().duration(duration) // <-E
                  .style("left", function(d, i){
returnbarLeft(-1) + "px"; // <-F
                  })
                  .remove(); // <-G
```

So far in this book, prior to this chapter, we have always called the `remove()` function immediately after the `d3.selection.exit` function. This immediately removes the elements that are no longer needed. In fact, the `exit()` function also returns a selection, and therefore, can be animated before calling the `remove()` function. This is exactly what we did here: we started a transition on line E using the `exit` selection, and then, we animated the left value with the following transition change:

```
left: barLeft(i) + "px" >barLeft(i-1) + "px"
```

Since we always remove the left-most bar, this transition moves the bar left and out of the SVG canvas, and then removes it.

> The `exit` transition is not necessarily limited to simple transitions, such as the one we have shown in this recipe. In some visualization, it could be as elaborate as the `update` transition.

Once the `render` function is in place with the defined transition, all that is left is to simply update the data and rerender our bar chart every second using the `setInterval` function. Now this completes our example.

Using ease

Transition can be thought of as a function of time. It is a function that maps time progression into numeric value progression, which then results in object motion (if the numeric value is used for positioning) or morphing (if the value is used to describe other visual attributes). Time always travels at a constant pace; in other words, time progression is uniform (unless you are doing visualization near a black hole, of course); however, the resulting value progression does not need to be uniform. *Easing* is a standard technique to provide flexibility and control to this kind of mapping. When a transition generates a uniform value progression, it is called *linear easing*. D3 provides support for different types of easing capabilities, and in this recipe, we will explore different built-in D3 easing functions, as well as how to implement custom easing functions with D3 transition.

Getting Ready

Open your local copy of the following file in your web browser:

```
https://github.com/NickQiZhu/d3-cookbook-v2/blob/master/src/chapter6/easing.htm
l
```

How to do it...

In the following code example, we will demonstrate how transition easing can be customized on an element-by-element basis:

```
<script type="text/javascript">
var data = [ // <-A
            {name: 'Linear', fn: d3.easeLinear},
            {name: 'Cubic', fn: d3.easeCubic},
            {name: 'CubicIn', fn: d3.easeCubicIn},
            {name: 'Sin', fn: d3.easeSin},
            {name: 'SinIn', fn: d3.easeSinIn},
            {name: 'Exp', fn: d3.easeExp},
            {name: 'Circle', fn: d3.easeCircle},
            {name: 'Back', fn: d3.easeBack},
            {name: 'Bounce', fn: d3.easeBounce},
            {name: 'Elastic', fn: d3.easeElastic},
            {name: 'Custom', fn: function(t){ return t * t; }}]// <-B
    ],
colors = d3.scaleOrdinal(d3.schemeCategory20);

d3.select("body").selectAll("div")
            .data(data) // <-C
        .enter()
        .append("div")
            .attr("class", "fixed-cell")
            .style("top", function (d, i) {
            returni * 40 + "px";
            })
            .style("background-color", function (d, i) {
            return colors(i);
            })
            .style("color", "white")
            .style("left", "500px")
            .text(function (d) {
            return d.name;
            });

d3.selectAll("div").each(function(d){
d3.select(this)
        .transition().ease(d.fn) // <-D
        .duration(1500)
        .style("left", "10px");
    });
</script>
```

The preceding code produces a set of moving boxes with different easing effects. The following screenshot is captured at the time the easing effect takes place:

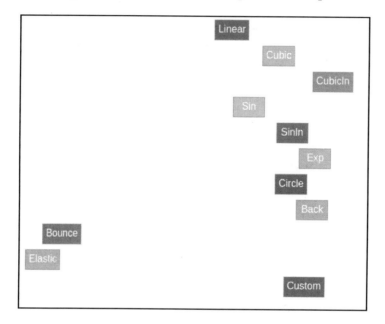

Different easing effects

How it works...

In this recipe, we have shown a number of different built-in D3 ease functions and their effects on transition. Let's take a look at how it is done; first, we created an array to store different ease modes we want to demonstrate:

```
var data = [ // <-A
            {name: 'Linear', fn: d3.easeLinear},
            {name: 'Cubic', fn: d3.easeCubic},
            {name: 'CubicIn', fn: d3.easeCubicIn},
            {name: 'Sin', fn: d3.easeSin},
            {name: 'SinIn', fn: d3.easeSinIn},
            {name: 'Exp', fn: d3.easeExp},
            {name: 'Circle', fn: d3.easeCircle},
            {name: 'Back', fn: d3.easeBack},
            {name: 'Bounce', fn: d3.easeBounce},
            {name: 'Elastic', fn: d3.easeElastic},
            {name: 'Custom', fn: function(t){ return t * t; }}// <-B
        ],
```

```
colors = d3.scaleOrdinal(d3.schemeCategory20);
```

While all the built-in ease functions are defined simply using their name, the last element of this array is a custom easing function (*quadric easing*). Then, afterward, a set of `div` elements created using this data array and a transition with different easing functions were created for each of the `div` element, respectively, moving them from (`"left"`, `"500px"`) to (`"left"`, `"10px"`), as follows:

```
d3.selectAll("div").each(function(d){
d3.select(this)
    .transition().ease(d.fn) // <-D
    .duration(1500)
    .style("left", "10px");
});
```

At this point, you might be asking, Why did we not just specify easing using a function as we normally would have done for any other D3 attributes?

```
d3.selectAll("div").transition().ease(d.fn) // does not work
        .duration(1500)
        .style("left", "10px");
```

The reason is that it does not work on the `ease()` function. What we showed on line D is a workaround of this limitation; though in real-world projects, it is fairly rare that you will need to customize easing behavior on a per-element basis.

 Another way to get around this limitation is using custom tweening, which we will cover in the next recipe.

As seen on line D, specifying different ease function for D3 transition is very straightforward; all you need to do is call the `ease()` function on a transition-bound selection. D3 also provides ease mode modifiers that you can combine with any ease function to achieve additional effects, for example, sin-out or quad-out-in. The following are the available ease mode modifiers:

- **In**: default
- **Out**: reversed
- **InOut**: reflected
- **OutIn**: reversed and reflected

The default ease effect used by D3 is `easeCubic()`.
For the list of supported D3 ease functions, please refer to the following link:
`https://github.com/d3/d3-ease`
For anyone who wants to explore different kind of built-in ease modes visually, you can check out this visual ease explorer built by D3's creator:
`http://bl.ocks.org/mbostock/248bac3b8e354a9103c4`

When a custom ease function is used, the function is expected to take the current parametric time value as its parameter in the range of [0, 1] as shown in the following function.

```
function(t){ // <-B
    return t * t;
}
```

In our example, we implemented a simple quadric easing function, which is actually available as a built-in D3 ease function and is named quad.

For more information on easing and Penner's equations (most of the modern JavaScript framework implementations including D3 and jQuery), check out the following link:
`http://www.robertpenner.com/easing/`

Using tweening

Tween comes from the word *inbetween*, which is a common practice performed in the traditional animation where after key frames were created by the master animator, less experienced animators were used to generate frames in between the key frames. This phrase is borrowed in modern computer-generated animation and refers to the technique or algorithm that controls how the *inbetween* frames are generated. In this recipe, we will examine how the D3 transition supports tweening.

Getting ready

Open your local copy of the following file in your web browser:

`https://github.com/NickQiZhu/d3-cookbook-v2/blob/master/src/chapter6/tweening.html`

How to do it...

In the following code example, we will create a custom tweening function to animate a button label through nine discrete integral numbers:

```
<script type="text/javascript">
var body = d3.select("body"), duration = 5000;

body.append("div").append("input")
        .attr("type", "button")
        .attr("class", "countdown")
        .attr("value", "0")
        .style("width", "150px")
        .transition().duration(duration).ease(d3.easeLinear)
            .style("width", "400px")
            .attr("value", "9");

body.append("div").append("input")
        .attr("type", "button")
        .attr("class", "countdown")
        .attr("value", "0")
        .transition().duration(duration).ease(d3.easeLinear)
.styleTween("width", widthTween) // <- A
            .attrTween("value", valueTween); // <- B


functionwidthTween(a){
var interpolate = d3.scaleQuantize()
            .domain([0, 1])
            .range([150, 200, 250, 350, 400]);

            return function(t){
            return interpolate(t) + "px";
        };
    }

functionvalueTween(){
var interpolate = d3.scaleQuantize() // <-C
            .domain([0, 1])
            .range([1, 2, 3, 4, 5, 6, 7, 8, 9]);

            return function(t){ // <-D
            return interpolate(t);
        };
    }
</script>
```

The preceding code generates two buttons morphing at a very different rate, and the following screenshot was taken while this process was going on:

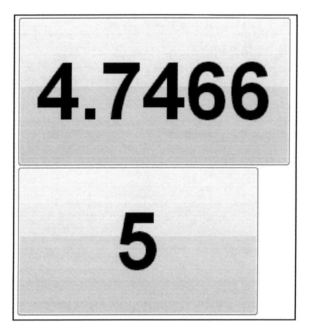

Tweening

How it works...

In this recipe, the first button was created using simple transition with linear easing:

```
body.append("div").append("input")
        .attr("type", "button")
        .attr("class", "countdown")
        .attr("value", "0")
        .style("width", "150px")
        .transition().duration(duration).ease(d3.easeLinear)
            .style("width", "400px")
            .attr("value", "9");
```

The transition changes the button's width from `150px` to `400px`, while changing its value from 0 to 9. As expected, this transition simply relies on continuous linear interpolation of these values using the D3 string interpolator. In comparison, the second button has the effect of changing these values in chunks, moving from 1 to 2, then to 3, and so on up to 9. This is achieved using D3 tweening support with the `attrTween` and `styleTween` functions. Let's first take a look at how the button value tweening works:

```
.transition().duration(duration).ease(d3.easeLinear)
        .styleTween("width", widthTween) // <- A
        .attrTween("value", valueTween); // <- B
```

In the preceding code snippet, we can see that instead of setting the end value for the value attribute as we did in the case of the first button, we used the `attrTween` function and offered a pair of tweening functions `widthTween` and `valueTween`, which are implemented as follows:

```
functionwidthTween(a){
var interpolate = d3.scaleQuantize()
            .domain([0, 1])
            .range([150, 200, 250, 350, 400]);

return function(t){
return interpolate(t) + "px";
        };
    }

functionvalueTween(){
var interpolate = d3.scaleQuantize() // <-C
            .domain([0, 1])
            .range([1, 2, 3, 4, 5, 6, 7, 8, 9]);

return function(t){ // <-D
return interpolate(t);
        };
    }
```

In D3, a tween function is expected to be a factory function, which constructs the actual function that will be used to perform the tweening. In this case, we defined a `quantize` scale that maps the domain [0, 1] to a discrete integral range of [1, 9], on line C. The actual tweening function defined on line D simply interpolates the parametric time value using the quantize scale, which generates the jumping integer effect.

Quantize scales are a variant of linear scale with a discrete range rather than a continuous one. For more information on quantize scales, please visit the following link:
`https://github.com/d3/d3/blob/master/API.md#quantize-scales`

There's more...

At this point, we have touched upon all three concepts related to transition: ease, tween, and interpolation. Typically, D3 transition is defined and driven through all the three levels shown in the following sequence diagram:

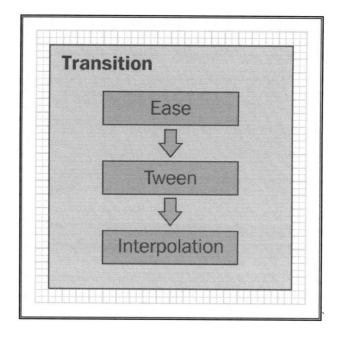

Drivers of transition

As we have shown through multiple recipes, D3 transition supports customization in all three levels. This gives us tremendous flexibility to customize the transition behavior exactly the way we want.

Though custom tween is usually implemented using interpolation, there is no limit to what you can do in your own tween function. It is entirely possible to generate custom tween without using D3 interpolator at all.

We used linear easing in this recipe to highlight the effect of tweening; however, D3 fully supports *eased tweening*, which means that you can combine any of the ease functions that are demonstrated in the previous recipe with your custom tween to generate even more complex transition effects.

Using transition chaining

The first four recipes in this chapter are focused on single transition controls in D3, including custom easing and tweening functions. However, sometimes, regardless of how much easing or tweening you do, a single transition is just not enough; for instance, you would want to simulate teleporting a `div` element by first squeezing the `div` element into a beam, then passing the beam to a different position on the web page, and finally restoring the `div` to its original size. In this recipe, we will see exactly how this type of transition can be achieved using *transition chaining*.

Getting ready

Open your local copy of the following file in your web browser:

```
https://raw.githubusercontent.com/NickQiZhu/d3-cookbook-v2/master/src/chapter6/
chaining.html
```

How to do it...

Our simple teleportation transition code is surprisingly short:

```
<script type="text/javascript">
var body = d3.select("body");

function teleport(s){
s.transition().duration(1000) // <-A
        .style("width", "200px")
        .style("height", "1px")
    .transition().duration(500) // <-B
        .style("left", "600px")
```

```
            .transition().duration(1000) // <-C
                .style("left", "800px")
                .style("height", "80px")
                .style("width", "80px");
    }

body.append("div")
            .style("position", "fixed")
            .style("background-color", "steelblue")
            .style("left", "10px")
            .style("width", "80px")
            .style("height", "80px")
            .call(teleport); // <-D
</script>
```

The preceding code performs a div teleportation:

DIV teleportation using transition chaining

How it works...

This simple teleportation effect was achieved by chaining a few transitions together. In D3,
when transitions are chained, they are guaranteed to be executed only after the previous
transition reaches its completion state. Now, let's take a look at how this is done in the
following code:

```
function teleport(s){
s.transition().duration(1000) // <-A
        .style("width", "200px")
        .style("height", "1px")
    .transition().duration(500) // <-B
        .style("left", "600px")
    .transition().duration(1000) // <-C
        .style("left", "800px")
        .style("height", "80px")
```

```
          .style("width", "80px");
    };
```

The first transition was defined and initiated on line A (compression); then, on line B, a second transition (beaming) was created; and finally, the third transition is chained on line C (restoration). Transition chaining is a powerful yet simple technique to orchestrate a complex transition effect by stitching simple transitions together. Finally, in this recipe, we have also shown a basic example on reusable composite transition effect by wrapping the teleportation transition in a function and then applying it on a selection using the `d3.selection.call` function (refer to line D). Reusable transition effect is essential to following the DRY principle, especially when the animation in your visualization becomes more elaborate.

Using transition filter

Under some circumstances, you might find it necessary to selectively apply transition to a subset of a certain selection. In this recipe, we will explore this effect using data-driven transition filtering techniques.

Getting ready

Open your local copy of the following file in your web browser:

```
https://github.com/NickQiZhu/d3-cookbook-v2/blob/master/src/chapter6/filtering.
html
```

How to do it...

In this recipe, we will move a set of `div` elements (or boxes) across the web page from right to left. After moving all the boxes to the left, we will selectively move only the boxes that are marked as **Cat** back, so they won't fight each other. Let's take a look at the following code:

```
<script type="text/javascript">
var data = ["Cat", "Dog", "Cat", "Dog", "Cat", "Dog", "Cat", "Dog"],
    duration = 1500;

d3.select("body").selectAll("div")
            .data(data)
        .enter()
```

```
            .append("div")
                .attr("class", "fixed-cell")
                .style("top", function (d, i) {
                return i * 40 + "px";
                })
                .style("background-color", "steelblue")
                .style("color", "white")
                .style("left", "500px")
                .text(function (d) {
    return d;
                })
                .transition() // <- A
                    .duration(duration)
                        .style("left", "10px")
                .filter(function(d){return d == "Cat";}) // <- B
                    .transition() // <- C
                    .duration(duration)
                        .style("left", "500px");
</script>
```

Here is what the page looks like after the transition:

Transition filtering

How it works...

The initial setup of this recipe is quite simple since we want to keep the plumbing as minimal as possible in order to help you focus on the core of the technique. We have a data array containing interlaced strings of Cat and Dog. Then, a set of div boxes was created for the data and a transition was created (refer to line A) to move all the boxes across the web page to the left-hand side. So far, it is a simple example of a multi-element transition with no surprises yet:

```
.transition() // <- A
.duration(duration)
    .style("left", "10px")
.filter(function(d){return d == "Cat";}) // <- B
.transition() // <- C
.duration(duration)
    .style("left", "500px");
```

Then, on line B, the d3.selection.filter function was used to generate a subselection that contains only the *cat* boxes. Remember, D3 transition is still a selection (transition-bound selection); therefore, the d3.selection.filter function works exactly the same way as on a regular selection. Once the subselection is generated by the filter function, we can apply a secondary transition (refer to line C) to this subselection alone. The filter function returns a transition-bound selection; therefore, the second transition created on line C is actually generating a transition chain. It will only be triggered after the first transition reaches its completion. Using combinations of transition chaining and filtering, we can generate some really interesting data-driven animations; it is a useful tool to have in any data visualizer's toolset.

See also

- For recipes on D3 data-driven selection filtering, please see the *Filtering with data* recipe Chapter 3, *Dealing with Data*
- Read about API doc for the selection.filter function at https://github.com/d3/d3-selection/blob/master/README.md#selection_filter

Listening to transitional events

Transition chaining gives you the ability to trigger secondary transitions after the initial transition reach its completion state; however, sometimes you might need to trigger certain action other than a transition, or maybe do something else during the transition. This is what transition event listeners are designed for, they are the topic of this recipe.

Getting ready

Open your local copy of the following file in your web browser:

```
https://github.com/NickQiZhu/d3-cookbook-v2/blob/master/src/chapter6/events.htm
l
```

How to do it...

In this recipe, we will demonstrate how to display different captions on an animated `div` element based on its transition state. Obviously, this example can easily be extended to perform more meaningful tasks using the same technique:

```
<script type="text/javascript">
var body = d3.select("body"), duration = 3000;

var div = body.append("div")
            .classed("box", true)
            .style("background-color", "steelblue")
            .style("color", "white")
.text("waiting") // <-A
        .transition().duration(duration) // <-B
              .delay(1000) // <-C
              .on("start", function(){ // <-D
              d3.select(this).text(function (d, i) {
              return "transitioning";
                  });
              })
              .on("end", function(){ // <-E
              d3.select(this).text(function (d, i) {
              return "done";
                  });
              })
            .style("margin-left", "600px");
</script>
```

The preceding code produces the following visual output where a box appears with **waiting** label; it moves to the right with the label changed to **transitioning** and when it's done, it stops moving and changes its label to **done**:

Transition event handling

How it works...

In this recipe, we constructed a single `div` element with a simple horizontal-movement transition, which, when initiated, also changes the label based on what transition state it is in. Let's first take a look at how we manage to display the **waiting** label:

```
var div = body.append("div")
            .classed("box", true)
            .style("background-color", "steelblue")
            .style("color", "white")
            .text("waiting") // <-A
        .transition().duration(duration) // <-B
            .delay(1000) // <-C
```

The **waiting** label is set on line A before the transition is defined on line B, however, we also specified a delay for the transition thus showing the **waiting** label before the transition is initiated. Next, let's find out how we were able to display the **transitioning** label during the transition:

```
.on("start", function(){ // <-D
d3.select(this).text(function (d, i) {
  return "transitioning";
    });
})
```

This is achieved by calling the `on()` function and selecting its first parameter set as `"start"` event name with an event listener function passed in as the second parameter. The `this` reference of the event listener function points to the current selected element, hence, can be wrapped by D3 and further manipulated. The transition `"end"` event is handled in an identical manner:

```
.on("end", function(){ // <-E
d3.select(this).text(function (d, i) {
  return "done";
    });
})
```

The only difference here is that the event name is passed into the `on()` function.

Working with timer

So far in this chapter we have discussed various topics on D3 transition. At this point you might be asking the question, *What is powering D3 transition that is generating the animated frames?*

In this recipe, we will explore a low-level D3 timer function that you can leverage to create your own custom animation from scratch.

Getting ready

Open your local copy of the following file in your web browser:

```
https://github.com/NickQiZhu/d3-cookbook-v2/blob/master/src/chapter6/timer.html
```

How to do it...

In this recipe, we will create a custom animation that does not rely on D3 transition or interpolation at all; essentially a custom animation created from scratch. Let's look at the following code:

```
<script type="text/javascript">
var body = d3.select("body");

var countdown = body.append("div").append("input");

countdown.attr("type", "button")
```

```
            .attr("class", "countdown")
            .attr("value", "0");

    functioncountUp(target){ // <-A
      var t = d3.timer(function(){ // <-B
      var value = countdown.attr("value");
        if( value == target ) {
            t.stop();
               return true;
    }  // <-C
    countdown.attr("value", ++value); // <-D
            });
        }

    function reset(){
        countdown.attr("value", 0);
    }
    </script>

    <div class="control-group">
    <button onclick="countUp(100)">
            Start
    </button>
    <button onclick="reset()">
            Clear
    </button>
    </div>
```

The preceding code generates a box where a timer is set to **0**, and when you click on **Start**, the time increases until it reaches **100** and stops, as shown in the following:

Custom timer-based animation

How it works...

In this example, we constructed a custom animation that moves integer from 0 to 100. For such a simple animation, of course, we could have accomplished it using D3 transition and tweening. However, a simple example like this avoids any distraction from the technique itself. Additionally, even in this simple example, the timer-based solution is arguably simpler and more flexible than a typical transition-based solution. The power of this animation lies in the countUp function (refer to line A):

```
functioncountUp(target){ // <-A
    var t = d3.timer(function(){ // <-B
        var value = countdown.attr("value");
        if( value == target ) {
            t.stop();
            return true;
        }  // <-C
        countdown.attr("value", ++value); // <-D
    });
}
```

As we have shown in this example, the key to understanding this recipe lies in the d3.timer function. This d3.timer(function, [delay], [mark]) starts a custom timer function and invokes the given function repeatedly, until the function returns true or when the timer is stopped. Before D3 v4, there was no way to stop the timer once it is started, so the programmer must make sure that the function eventually returns true; with the latest D3 release, timer object now offers an explicit stop() function. However, it is still recommended that the function returns true from a timer function once it has completed its task, as seen on line C. Optionally, you can also specify a *delay* or a *mark*. The delay starts from the mark and when the mark is not specified, Date.now will be used as the mark. The following illustration shows the temporal relationship we discussed here:

In our implementation, the custom timer function increases button caption by one every time it is called (refer to line D) and stops when the value reaches 100 (refer to line C).

Internally, D3 transition uses the same timer function to generate its animation. At this point, you might be asking what is the difference between using d3.timer versus Using the animation frame directly. The answer is that the d3.timer function actually uses animation frame if the browser supports it; otherwise, it is smart enough to fallback to use the setTimeout function, thus freeing you from worrying about your browser's support.

See also

- For more information on d3.timer, please visit its API at the following link: `https://github.com/d3/d3-timer/blob/master/README.md#timer`

7
Getting into Shape

In this chapter, we will cover:

- Creating simple shapes
- Using a line generator
- Using line curve
- Changing line tension
- Using an area generator
- Using area curve
- Using an arc generator
- Implementing arc transition

Introduction

Scalable Vector Graphics (SVG) is a mature **World Wide Web Consortium (W3C)** standard designed for user-interactive graphics on the Web and Mobile platform. Similar to HTML, SVG can coexist happily with other technologies, such as CSS and JavaScript, in modern browsers and forms the backbone of many Web applications. In today's Web, you can see use cases of SVG everywhere, from digital map to data visualization. So far, in this book, we covered most of the recipes using HTML elements alone; however, in real-world projects, SVG is the *de facto* standard for data visualization; it is also where D3's strength really shines. In this chapter, we will cover the basic concept of SVG and D3's support for SVG shape generation. SVG is a very rich topic. Volumes of books can be, and have been, devoted to this topic alone; hence, we will not plan or even try to cover all SVG-related topics, rather we'll focus on D3 and data visualization-related techniques and features.

What is SVG?

As its name suggests, SVG is about graphics. It is a way to describe graphical image with scalable vectors. Let's take a look at the following two of the main SVG advantages:

Vector

SVG image is based on vectors instead of pixels. With the pixel-based approach, an image is composed of a bitmap with x and y as its coordinates filled with color pigmentations. Whereas, with the vector-based approach, each image consists of a set of geometric shapes described using simple and relative formulae filled with certain texture. As you can imagine, this latter approach fits naturally with our data visualization requirement. It is much simpler to visualize your data with lines, bar, and circles in SVG rather than trying to manipulate color pigmentations in a bitmap.

Scalability

The second signature capability of SVG is scalability. Since SVG graphic is a group of geometric shapes described using relative formulas, it can be rendered and re-rendered

with different sizes and zoom levels without losing precision. On the other hand, when

bitmap-based images are resized to a large resolution, they suffer the effect of pixelation, which occurs when the individual pixels become visible, while SVG does not have this drawback. Refer to the following figure to get a better picture of what we just read:

SVG versus bitmap pixelation

As a data visualizer, using SVG gives you the benefit of being able to display your visualization on any resolution without losing the crispiness of your eye-catching creation. On top of that, SVG offers you some additional advantages such as the following:

- **Readability**: SVG is based on XML, a human-readable markup language.
- **Open standard**: SVG was created by W3C and is not a proprietary vendor standard.
- **Adoption**: All modern browsers support SVG standard, even on mobile platform.
- **Interoperability**: SVG works well with other Web technologies, such as CSS and JavaScript; D3 itself is a perfect demonstration of this capability.
- **Lightweight**: Compared to bitmap-based images, SVG is a lot lighter and takes up much less space.

Because of all these capabilities we have mentioned so far, SVG has become the *de facto* standard for data visualization on the Web. From this chapter onward, all recipes in this book will be illustrated using SVG as its most important part, with which the true power of D3 can be professed.

 Some older browsers do not support SVG natively. If your target users are using legacy browsers, please check the SVG compatibility before deciding whether SVG is the right choice for your visualization project. Here is a link that you can visit to check your browser's compatibility:
`http://caniuse.com/#feat=svg`

Creating simple shapes

In this recipe, we will explore a few simple built-in SVG shape formulas and their attributes. These simple shapes are quite easy to generate and are usually created manually using D3 when necessary. Though these simple shapes are not the most useful shape generator to know when working with D3, occasionally, they could be handy when drawing peripheral shapes in your visualization project.

Getting ready

Open your local copy of the following file in your web browser:

`https://github.com/NickQiZhu/d3-cookbook-v2/blob/master/src/chapter7/simple-shapes.html`

How to do it...

In this recipe, we will draw four different shapes in four different colors using native SVG shape elements:

```
<script type="text/javascript">
    var width = 600,
        height = 500;

    var svg = d3.select("body").append("svg");

    svg.attr("height", height)
        .attr("width", width);

    svg.append("line") // <-A
        .attr("x1", 0)
        .attr("y1", 200)
        .attr("x2", 100)
        .attr("y2", 100);

    svg.append("circle") // <-B
        .attr("cx", 200)
        .attr("cy", 150)
        .attr("r", 50);

    svg.append("rect")
        .attr("x", 300) // <-C
        .attr("y", 100)
        .attr("width", 100) // <-D
        .attr("height", 100)
        .attr("rx", 5); // <-E

    svg.append("polygon")
        .attr("points", "450,200 500,100 550,200"); // <-F
</script>
```

The preceding code generates the following visual output:

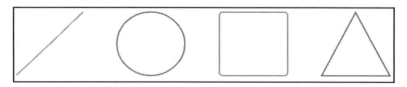

Simple SVG shapes

How it works...

We have drawn four different shapes-a line, a circle, a rectangle, and a triangle-in this example using SVG built-in shape elements, which can be described as follows:

A little refresher on SVG coordinate system
SVG *x* and *y* coordinate system originates from the top-left corner (0, 0) of the canvas and ends on the lower-right corner (`<width>`, `<height>`).

- `line`: A line element creates a simple straight line with coordinate attributes x1 and y1 as its start point and x2, y2 as its endpoint (refer to line A).
- `circle`: The `append()` function draws a circle with coordinate attributes cx and cy defining the center of the circle, whereas the attribute r defines the radius of the circle (refer to line B).
- `rect`: The `append()` function draws a rectangle with coordinate attributes x and y that define the top-left corner of the rectangular (refer to line C), attributes width and height that control the size of the rectangle, and the attributes rx and ry that introduce rounded corners. The attributes rx and ry control the *x* and *y* axes radius of the ellipse used to round off the corners of the rectangle (refer to line E).
- `polygon`: To draw a polygon, a set of points that makes up the polygon need to be defined using a `points` attribute (refer to line F). The `points` attribute accepts a list of point coordinates that are separated by space, as shown in the following code snippet:

```
svg.append("polygon")
    .attr("points", "450,200 500,100 550,200"); // <-F
```

All SVG shapes can be styled using style attributes directly or through CSS similar to HTML elements. Furthermore, they can be transformed and filtered using SVG transformation and filter support; however, due to the limited scope of this book, we will not cover these topics in detail. In the rest of this chapter, we will focus on D3-specific supports on SVG shape generation instead.

There's more...

SVG also supports the `ellipse` and `polyline` elements; however, due to their similarity to `circle` and `polygon`, we will not cover them in detail in this book. For more information on SVG shape elements, please visit `https://www.w3.org/TR/SVG/shapes.html`.

D3 SVG shape generators

The *swiss army knife* among SVG shape elements is `svg:path`. A path defines the outline of any shape, which can then be filled, stroked, or clipped. Every shape we have discussed so far can be mathematically defined using `svg:path` alone. The SVG `path` is a very powerful construct and has its own mini-language and grammar. The `svg:path` mini-language is used to set the `d` attribute on an `svg:path` element, which consists of the following commands:

- **moveto**: M (absolute)/m (relative) moveto (x y)+
- **closepath**: Z (absolute)/z (relative) closepath
- **lineto**: L (absolute)/l (relative) lineto (x y)+, H (absolute)/h (relative) horizontal lineto x+, V(absolute)/v(relative) vertical lineto y+
- **Cubic Bezier**: C(absolute)/c(relative) curve to (x1 y1 x2 y2 x y)+, S(absolute)/s(relative) shorthand curve to (x2 y2 x y)+
- **Quadratic Bezier curve**: Q (absolute)/q (relative) quadratic Bezier curve to (x1 y1 x y)+, T (absolute)/t (relative) shorthand Quadratic Bezier curve to (x y)+
- **Elliptical curve**: A (absolute)/a (relative) elliptical arc (rx ry x-axis-rotation large-arc-flag sweep-flag x y)+

As directly using paths is not a very pleasant method due to its cryptic language, in most cases, some kind of software, for example, Adobe Illustrator or Inkscape, is required to assist us in creating the SVG `path` element visually. Similarly, D3 ships with a set of SVG shape generator functions that can be used to generate data-driven path formulas; this is how D3 truly revolutionizes the field of data visualization by combining the power of SVG with intuitive data-driven approach. This will be our focus for the rest of this chapter.

See also

- Please refer to `https://www.w3.org/TR/SVG/Overview.html` for more information on SVG-related topics
- For a complete reference on SVG path formula language and its grammar, please visit `https://www.w3.org/TR/SVG/paths.html`

Using a line generator

D3 line generator is probably one of the most versatile generators. Although it is called a line generator, it has little to do with the svg:line element. In contrast, it is implemented using the svg:path element. Similar to svg:path, D3 line generator is so flexible that you can effectively draw any shape using line alone; however, to make your life easier, D3 also provides other more specialized shape generators, which will be covered in later recipes in this chapter. In this recipe, we will draw multiple data-driven lines using the d3.svg.line generator.

Getting ready

Open your local copy of the following file in your web browser:

https://github.com/NickQiZhu/d3-cookbook/blob/master/src/chapter7/line.html

How to do it...

Now, let's take a look at the following line generator in action:

```
<script type="text/javascript">
    var width = 500,
        height = 500,
        margin = 50,
        x = d3.scaleLinear() // <-A
            .domain([0, 10])
            .range([margin, width - margin]),
        y = d3.scaleLinear() // <-B
            .domain([0, 10])
            .range([height - margin, margin]);

    var data = [ // <-C
        [
            {x: 0, y: 5},{x: 1, y: 9},{x: 2, y: 7},
            {x: 3, y: 5},{x: 4, y: 3},{x: 6, y: 4},
            {x: 7, y: 2},{x: 8, y: 3},{x: 9, y: 2}
        ],

        d3.range(10).map(function(i){
            return {x: i, y: Math.sin(i) + 5};
        })
    ];
```

```
var line = d3.line() // <-D
            .x(function(d){return x(d.x);})
            .y(function(d){return y(d.y);});

    var svg = d3.select("body").append("svg");

    svg.attr("height", height)
        .attr("width", width);

    svg.selectAll("path.line")
            .data(data)
          .enter()
            .append("path") // <-E
            .attr("class", "line")
            .attr("d", function(d){return line(d);}); // <-F

    // Axes related code omitted
    ...
</script>
```

The preceding code draws multiple lines along with the *x* and *y* axes:

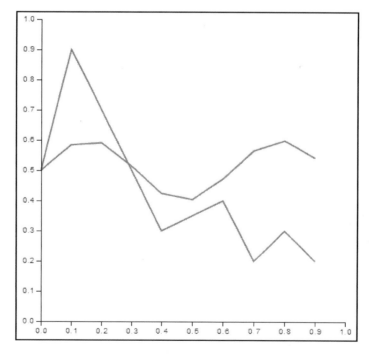

D3 line generator

How it works…

In this recipe, the data we used to draw the lines is defined in a two-dimensional array:

```
var data = [ // <-C
        [
            {x: 0, y: 5},{x: 1, y: 9},{x: 2, y: 7},
            {x: 3, y: 5},{x: 4, y: 3},{x: 6, y: 4},
            {x: 7, y: 2},{x: 8, y: 3},{x: 9, y: 2}
        ],

        d3.range(10).map(function(i){
            return {x: i, y: Math.sin(i) + 5};
        })
    ];
```

The first data series is defined manually and explicitly, whereas the second series is generated using a mathematical formula. Both of these cases are quite common in data visualization projects. Once the data is defined, in order to map data points to their visual representation, the following two scales were created for the *x* and *y* coordinates:

x = d3.scaleLinear() // <-A .domain([0, 10]) .range([margin, width – margin]), y = d3.scaleLinear() // <-B
.domain([0, 10]) .range([height – margin, margin]);

Note that the domains for these scales were set to be large enough to include all data points in both the series, while the ranges were set to represent the canvas area without including the margins. The *y* axis range is inverted since we want our point of origin at the lower-left corner of the canvas instead of the SVG-standard upper-left corner. Once both data and scales are set, all we need to do is generate the lines to define our generator using the d3.line function:

```
var line = d3.line() // <-D
            .x(function(d){return x(d.x);})
            .y(function(d){return y(d.y);});
```

The d3.line function returns a D3 line generator function, which you can further customize. In our example, we simply stated for this particular line generator the *x* coordinate, which will be calculated using the *x* scale mapping, while the *y* coordinate will be mapped by the *y* scale. Using D3 scales, to map coordinates, is not only convenient but also a widely accepted best practice (separation of concerns). Though, technically, you can implement these functions using any approach you prefer. Now the only thing left for you to do is the actual creation of the svg:path elements as follows:

```
svg.selectAll("path.line")
            .data(data)
```

```
    .enter()
        .append("path") // <-E
        .attr("class", "line")
        .attr("d", function(d){return line(d);}); // <-F
```

Path creation process in the preceding code was very straightforward. Two `svg:path` elements were created using the data array we defined (on line E). Then, the d attribute for each path element was set using the `line` generator we created previously by passing in the data d as its input parameter. The following screenshot shows what the generated `svg:path` elements look like:

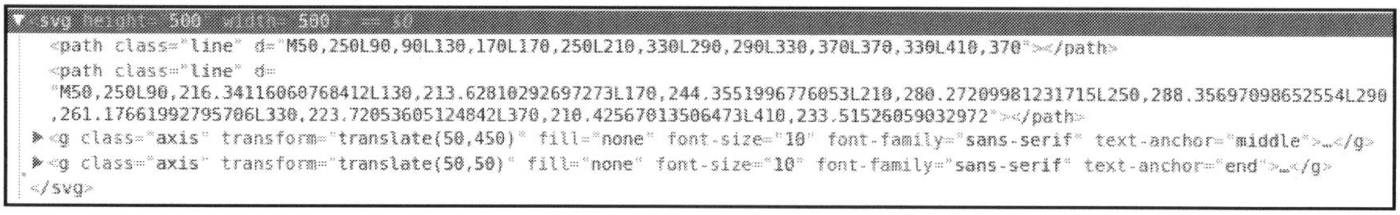

```
▼<svg height="500" width="500" == $0
   <path class="line" d="M50,250L90,90L130,170L170,250L210,330L290,290L330,370L370,330L410,370"></path>
   <path class="line" d=
   "M50,250L90,216.34116060768412L130,213.62810292697273L170,244.3551996776053L210,280.27209981231715L250,288.35697098652554L290
   ,261.17661992795706L330,223.72053605124842L370,210.42567013506473L410,233.51526059032972"></path>
 ▶<g class="axis" transform="translate(50,450)" fill="none" font-size="10" font-family="sans-serif" text-anchor="middle">…</g>
 ▶<g class="axis" transform="translate(50,50)" fill="none" font-size="10" font-family="sans-serif" text-anchor="end">…</g>
 </svg>
```

Generated SVG path elements

Finally, two axes were created using the same *x* and *y* scales we defined earlier. Due to limited space in this book, we have omitted the axes-related code in this recipe and in the rest of this chapter since they don't really change and also are not the focus of this chapter.

See also

For detailed information on D3 axes support, please refer to `Chapter 5`, *Playing with Axes*.

Using line curve

By default, the D3 line generator uses the *linear curve* mode; however, D3 supports a number of different curve factories. The curve function determines how data points will be connected, for example, by a straight line (*linear*) or a curved line (**B-spline**). In this recipe, we will show you how these curve modes can be set along with their effects.

Getting ready

Open your local copy of the following file in your web browser:

```
https://github.com/NickQiZhu/d3-cookbook-v2/blob/master/src/chapter7/line-curve
.html
```

This recipe is built on top of what we did in the previous recipe, so if you are not

yet familiar with basic line generator functions, please refer to the previous recipe first

before proceeding.

How to do it...

Now, let's take a look at how different line interpolation modes can be used:

```javascript
<script type="text/javascript">
var width = 500,
        height = 500,
        margin = 30,
        x = d3.scaleLinear()
            .domain([0, 10])
            .range([margin, width - margin]),
        y = d3.scaleLinear()
            .domain([0, 10])
            .range([height - margin, margin]);

    var data = [
        [
            {x: 0, y: 5},{x: 1, y: 9},{x: 2, y: 7},
            {x: 3, y: 5},{x: 4, y: 3},{x: 6, y: 4},
            {x: 7, y: 2},{x: 8, y: 3},{x: 9, y: 2}
        ],
        d3.range(10).map(function(i){
            return {x: i, y: Math.sin(i) + 5};
        })
    ];

    var svg = d3.select("body").append("svg");

    svg.attr("height", height)
        .attr("width", width);

    renderAxes(svg);

    render(d3.curveLinear);

    renderDots(svg);

    function render(mode){
        var line = d3.line()
                .x(function(d){return x(d.x);})
```

```
                .y(function(d){return y(d.y);})
                .curve(mode); // <-A

        svg.selectAll("path.line")
                .data(data)
            .enter()
                .append("path")
                .attr("class", "line");

        svg.selectAll("path.line")
                .data(data)
            .attr("d", function(d){return line(d);});
    }

    function renderDots(svg){ // <-B
        data.forEach(function(list){
            svg.append("g").selectAll("circle")
                .data(list)
              .enter().append("circle") // <-C
                .attr("class", "dot")
                .attr("cx", function(d) { return x(d.x); })
                .attr("cy", function(d) { return y(d.y); })
                .attr("r", 4.5);
        });
    }
// Axes related code omitted
...
</script>

<h4>Interpolation Mode:</h4>
<div class="control-group">
<button onclick="render(d3.curveLinear)">linear</button>
<button onclick="render(d3.curveLinearClosed)">linear closed</button>
<button onclick="render(d3.curveStepBefore)">step before</button>
<button onclick="render(d3.curveStepAfter)">step after</button>
<button onclick="render(d3.curveBasis)">basis</button>
<button onclick="render(d3.curveBasisOpen)">basis open</button>
</div>
...
```

The preceding code generates the following line chart in your browser with configurable interpolation modes:

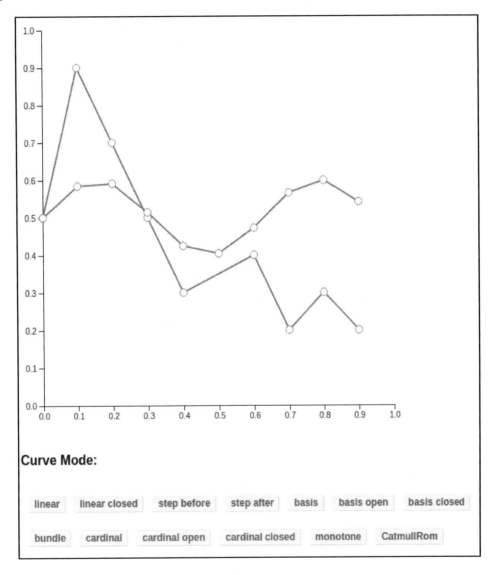

Line curve

How it works...

Overall, this recipe is similar to the previous one. Two lines are generated using predefined dataset. However, in this recipe, you will allow the user to select a specific line interpolation mode, which is then set using the `interpolate` function on line generator (refer to line A) in the following code snippet:

```
var line = d3.line()
            .x(function(d){return x(d.x);})
            .y(function(d){return y(d.y);})
            .curve(mode); // <-A
```

The following interpolation modes are supported by D3:

- `d3.curveLinear`: Linear segments, that is, polyline
- `d3.curveLinearClosed`: Closed linear segments, that is, polygon
- `d3.curveStepBefore`: Alternated between the vertical and horizontal segments, as in a step function
- `d3.curveStepAfter`: Alternated between the horizontal and vertical segments, as in a step function
- `d3.curveBasis`: It is a B-spline, with control point duplication on the ends
- `d3.curveBasisOpen`: An open B-spline; may not intersect the start or end
- `d3.curveBasisClosed`: A closed B-spline, as in a loop
- `d3.curveBundle`: Equivalent to basis, except the tension parameter is used to straighten the spline
- `d3.curveCardinal`: A cardinal spline, with control point duplication on the ends.
- `d3.curveCardinalOpen`: An open cardinal spline; may not intersect the start or end, but will intersect other control points
- `d3.curveCardinalClosed`: A closed cardinal spline, as in a loop
- `d3.curveMonotoneY`: Cubic interpolation that preserves monotonicity in y
- `d3.curveCatmullRom`: A cubic catmull-Rom spline.

Additionally, in the `renderDots` function (refer to line B), we have also created a small circle for each data point to serve as reference points. These dots are created using the `svg:circle` elements, as shown on line C of the following code snippet:

```
function renderDots(svg){ // <-B
        data.forEach(function(set){
            svg.append("g").selectAll("circle")
                .data(set)
```

```
            .enter().append("circle") // <-C
              .attr("class", "dot")
              .attr("cx", function(d) { return x(d.x); })
              .attr("cy", function(d) { return y(d.y); })
              .attr("r", 4.5);
        });
    }
```

See Also

- For detailed listing and API document for all D3 curve factories, please refer to `https://github.com/d3/d3-shape#curves`

Changing line tension

If Cardinal interpolation mode (cardinal, cardinal-open, or cardinal-closed) is used, then the line can be further modified using tension settings. In this recipe, you will see how tension can be modified and its effect on line interpolation.

Getting ready

Open your local copy of the following file in your web browser:

`https://github.com/NickQiZhu/d3-cookbook-v2/blob/master/src/chapter7/line-tension.html`

How to do it...

Now, let's take a look at how line tension can be changed and what effect it has on line generation:

```
<script type="text/javascript">
    var width = 500,
        height = 500,
        margin = 30,
        duration = 500,
        x = d3.scaleLinear()
            .domain([0, 10])
            .range([margin, width - margin]),
        y = d3.scaleLinear()
```

```
            .domain([0, 1])
            .range([height - margin, margin]);

var data = d3.range(10).map(function(i){
        return {x: i, y: (Math.sin(i * 3) + 1) / 2};
    });

    var svg = d3.select("body").append("svg");

    svg.attr("height", height)
        .attr("width", width);

    renderAxes(svg);

    render(1);

    function render(tension){
        var line = d3.line()
                .curve(d3.curveCardinal.tension(tension)) // <-A
                .x(function(d){return x(d.x);})
                .y(function(d){return y(d.y);});

        svg.selectAll("path.line")
                .data([tension])
            .enter()
                .append("path")
                .attr("class", "line");

svg.selectAll("path.line")
                .data([tension])
            .transition().duration(duration)
                .ease(d3.easeLinear) // <-B
            .attr("d", function(d){
                return line(data); // <-C
            });

        svg.selectAll("circle")
            .data(data)
          .enter().append("circle")
            .attr("class", "dot")
            .attr("cx", function(d) { return x(d.x); })
            .attr("cy", function(d) { return y(d.y); })
            .attr("r", 4.5);
    }
// Axes related code omitted
    ...
</script>
<h4>Line Tension:</h4>
```

```
<div class="control-group">
<button onclick="render(0)">0</button>
<button onclick="render(0.2)">0.2</button>
<button onclick="render(0.4)">0.4</button>
<button onclick="render(0.6)">0.6</button>
<button onclick="render(0.8)">0.8</button>
<button onclick="render(1)">1</button>
</div>
```

The preceding code generates a cardinal line chart with configurable tension:

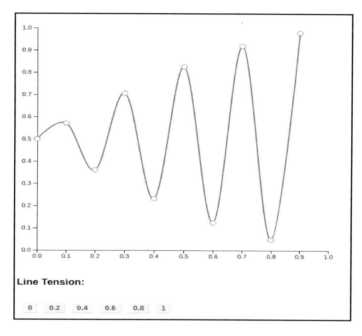

Line Tension

How it works...

Tension sets the Cardinal spline interpolation tension to a specific number in the range of [0, 1]. Tension can be set using the `tension` function on line generator (refer to line C):

```
var line = d3.line()
            .curve(d3.curveCardinal.tension(tension)) // <-A
            .x(function(d){return x(d.x);})
            .y(function(d){return y(d.y);});
```

Additionally, we also initiated a transition on line B to highlight the tension effect on line interpolation. The tension in cardinal curve essentially determines the length of the tangents. At tension one, it is the same as curve linear while at zero it produces uniform Catmull-Rom spline. If the tension is not set explicitly, Cardinal interpolation sets tension to 0 by default.

Using an area generator

Using D3 line generator, we can technically generate an outline of any shape; however, even with a different curve support, directly drawing an area using line (as in an area chart) is not an easy task. This is why D3 also provides a separate shape generator function specifically designed for drawing area.

Getting ready

Open your local copy of the following file in your web browser:

`https://github.com/NickQiZhu/d3-cookbook-v2/blob/master/src/chapter7/area.html`

How to do it...

In this recipe, we will add a filled area to a pseudo line chart, effectively turning it into an area chart:

```
<script type="text/javascript">
    var width = 500,
        height = 500,
        margin = 30,
        duration = 500,
        x = d3.scaleLinear() // <-A
            .domain([0, 10])
            .range([margin, width - margin]),
        y = d3.scaleLinear()
            .domain([0, 10])
            .range([height - margin, margin]);

    var data = d3.range(11).map(function(i){ // <-B
            return {x: i, y: Math.sin(i)*3 + 5};
        });
```

```
    var svg = d3.select("body").append("svg");

    svg.attr("height", height)
        .attr("width", width);

    renderAxes(svg);

    render();

    renderDots(svg);

    function render(){
        var line = d3.line()
                .x(function(d){return x(d.x);})
                .y(function(d){return y(d.y);});

        svg.selectAll("path.line")
                .data([data])
            .enter()
                .append("path")
                .attr("class", "line");

        svg.selectAll("path.line")
                .data([data])
            .attr("d", function(d){return line(d);});

        var area = d3.area() // <-C
            .x(function(d) { return x(d.x); }) // <-D
            .y0(y(0)) // <-E
            .y1(function(d) { return y(d.y); }); // <-F

        svg.selectAll("path.area") // <-G
                .data([data])
            .enter()
                .append("path")
                .attr("class", "area")
                .attr("d", function(d){return area(d);}); // <-H
    }

    // Dots rendering code omitted

    // Axes related code omitted
    ...
</script>
```

The preceding code generates the following visual output:

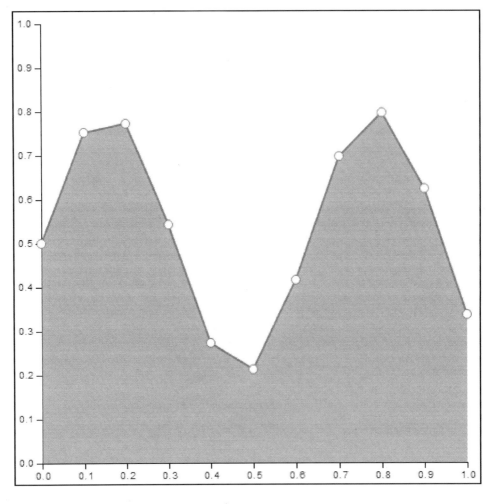

Area generator

How it works...

Similar to the earlier given *Using a line generator* recipe, we have two scales defined in this recipe to map data to visual domain on *x* and *y* coordinates (refer to line A) as given in the following code snippet:

```
x = d3.scaleLinear() // <-A
    .domain([0, 10])
```

```
            .range([margin, width - margin]),
      y = d3.scaleLinear()
            .domain([0, 10])
            .range([height - margin, margin]);

   var data = d3.range(11).map(function(i){ // <-B
            return {x: i, y: Math.sin(i)*3 + 5};
      });
```

On line B, data is generated by a mathematical formula. Area generator is then created using the d3.area function (refer to line C):

```
   var area = d3.area() // <-C
                .x(function(d) { return x(d.x); }) // <-D
                .y0(y(0)) // <-E
                .y1(function(d) { return y(d.y); }); // <-F
```

As you can see, D3 area generator is-similar to the line generator-designed to work in a 2D Cartesian coordinate system. The x function defines an accessor function for the *x* coordinate (refer to line D), which simply maps data to the visual coordinate using the x scale we defined earlier. For the *y* coordinate, we provided the area generator with two different accessors: one for the lower bound (y0) and the other for the higher bound (y1) coordinates. This is the crucial difference between area and line generator. D3 area generator supports higher and lower bound on both *x* and *y* axes (x0, x1, y0, y1) and supports the shorthand accessors (x and y) if the higher and lower bounds are the same. Once the area generator is defined, the method of creating an area is almost identical to the line generator:

```
   svg.selectAll("path.area") // <-G
                .data([data])
            .enter()
                .append("path")
                .attr("class", "area")
                .attr("d", function(d){return area(d);}); // <-H
```

Area is also implemented using the svg:path element (refer to line G). D3 area generator is used to generate the d formula for the svg:path element on line H with data d as its input parameter.

Using area curve

Similar to the D3 line generator, area generator also supports identical interpolation mode, and hence, it can be used in combination with the line generator in every mode.

Getting ready

Open your local copy of the following file in your web browser:

https://github.com/NickQiZhu/d3-cookbook-v2/blob/master/src/chapter7/area-curve
.html

How to do it...

In this recipe, we will show how interpolation mode can be configured on an area generator. This way, the matching interpolated area can then be created with its corresponding line:

```
var width = 500,
        height = 500,
        margin = 30,
        x = d3.scaleLinear()
            .domain([0, 10])
            .range([margin, width - margin]),
        y = d3.scaleLinear()
            .domain([0, 10])
            .range([height - margin, margin]);

var data = d3.range(11).map(function(i){
    return {x: i, y: Math.sin(i)*3 + 5};
});

var svg = d3.select("body").append("svg");

svg.attr("height", height)
    .attr("width", width);

renderAxes(svg);

render(d3.curveLinear);

renderDots(svg);

function render(mode){
```

```
var line = d3.line()
        .x(function(d){return x(d.x);})
        .y(function(d){return y(d.y);})
        .curve(mode); // <-A

svg.selectAll("path.line")
        .data([data])
    .enter()
        .append("path")
        .attr("class", "line");

svg.selectAll("path.line")
        .data([data])
    .attr("d", function(d){return line(d);});

var area = d3.area()
    .x(function(d) { return x(d.x); })
    .y0(y(0))
    .y1(function(d) { return y(d.y); })
    .curve(mode); // <-B

svg.selectAll("path.area")
        .data([data])
    .enter()
        .append("path")
        .attr("class", "area")

svg.selectAll("path.area")
    .data([data])
    .attr("d", function(d){return area(d);});
}
// Dots and Axes related code omitted
```

The preceding code generates the following pseudo area chart with configurable interpolation mode:

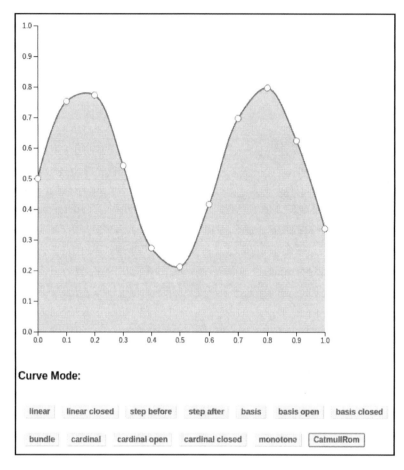

Area curve

How it works...

This recipe is similar to the previous one, except that in this recipe the interpolation mode is passed in based on the user's selection:

```
var line = d3.line()
            .x(function(d){return x(d.x);})
            .y(function(d){return y(d.y);})
            .curve(mode); // <-A
```

```
var area = d3.area()
            .x(function(d) { return x(d.x); })
            .y0(y(0))
            .y1(function(d) { return y(d.y); })
            .curve(mode); // <-B
```

As you can see, the curve mode was configured on both lines along with the area generator through the `curve` function (refer to lines A and B). Since D3 line and area generator supports the same set of curve factories, they can always be counted on to generate matching line and area as seen in this recipe.

There's more...

D3 area generator also supports the same tension configuration when using Cardinal mode; however, since it is identical to the line generator's tension support, and due to limited space in this book, we will not cover area tension here.

See also

- Please refer to `https://github.com/d3/d3/blob/master/API.md#areas` for more information on area generator functions

Using an arc generator

Among the most common shape generators-besides the line and area generator-D3 also provides the *arc generator*. At this point, you might be wondering, *Didn't SVG standard already include circle element? Isn't that enough?*

The simple answer to this is *no*. The D3 arc generator is a lot more versatile than the simple `svg:circle` element. The D3 arc generator is capable of creating not only circles but also annulus (donut), circular sector, and annulus sector, all of which we will learn in this recipe. More importantly, an arc generator is designed to generate, as its name suggests, an arc (in others words, not a full circle or even a sector but rather arcs of arbitrary angle).

Getting ready

Open your local copy of the following file in your web browser:

`https://github.com/NickQiZhu/d3-cookbook-v2/blob/master/src/chapter7/arc.html`

How to do it...

In this recipe, we will use arc generator to generate multi-slice circle, annulus (donut), circular sectors, and annulus sectors as follows:

```
<script type="text/javascript">
    var width = 400,
        height = 400,
        fullAngle = 2 * Math.PI, // <-A
        colors =  d3.scaleOrdinal(d3.schemeCategory20);

    var svg = d3.select("body").append("svg")
                .attr("class", "pie")
                .attr("height", height)
                .attr("width", width);

    function render(innerRadius, endAngle){
        if(!endAngle) endAngle = fullAngle;

        var data = [ // <-B
            {startAngle: 0, endAngle: 0.1 * endAngle},
            {startAngle: 0.1 * endAngle, endAngle: 0.2 * endAngle},
            {startAngle: 0.2 * endAngle, endAngle: 0.4 * endAngle},
            {startAngle: 0.4 * endAngle, endAngle: 0.6 * endAngle},
            {startAngle: 0.6 * endAngle, endAngle: 0.7 * endAngle},
            {startAngle: 0.7 * endAngle, endAngle: 0.9 * endAngle},
            {startAngle: 0.9 * endAngle, endAngle: endAngle}
        ];

        var arc = d3.arc().outerRadius(200) // <-C
                    .innerRadius(innerRadius);

        svg.select("g").remove();

        svg.append("g")
                .attr("transform", "translate(200,200)")
        .selectAll("path.arc")
                .data(data)
            .enter()
                .append("path")
```

```
                      .attr("class", "arc")
                      .attr("fill", function(d, i){
        return colors(i);
          })
                      .attr("d", function(d, i){
                          return arc(d, i); // <-D
                      });
      }

      render(0);
</script>

<div class="control-group">
<button onclick="render(0)">Circle</button>
<button onclick="render(100)">Annulus(Donut)</button>
<button onclick="render(0, Math.PI)">Circular Sector</button>
<button onclick="render(100, Math.PI)">Annulus Sector</button>
</div>
```

The preceding code produces the following circle, which you can change into an arc, a sector, or an arc sector by clicking on the buttons, for example, **Annulus(Donut)** generates the second shape:

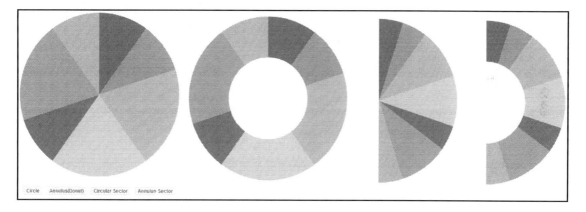

Arc generator

How it works...

The most important part of understanding the D3 arc generator is its data structure. D3 arc generator has very specific requirements when it comes to its data, as shown on line B:

```
var data = [ // <-B
        {startAngle: 0, endAngle: 0.1 * endAngle},
```

```
        {startAngle: 0.1 * endAngle, endAngle: 0.2 * endAngle},
        {startAngle: 0.2 * endAngle, endAngle: 0.4 * endAngle},
        {startAngle: 0.4 * endAngle, endAngle: 0.6 * endAngle},
        {startAngle: 0.6 * endAngle, endAngle: 0.7 * endAngle},
        {startAngle: 0.7 * endAngle, endAngle: 0.9 * endAngle},
        {startAngle: 0.9 * endAngle, endAngle: endAngle}
];
```

Each row of the arc data has to contain two mandatory fields: `startAngle` and `endAngle`. The angles have to be in the range `[0, 2 * Math.PI]` (refer to line A). D3 arc generator will use these angles to generate corresponding slices, as shown earlier in this recipe.

 Along with the start and end angles, arc dataset can contain any number of additional fields, which can then be accessed in D3 functions to drive other visual representation.

If you think that calculating these angles based on the data you have will be a big hassle, you are absolutely correct. This is why D3 provides specific layout manager to help you calculate these angles, and we will cover this in the next chapter. For now, let's focus on understanding the basic mechanism behind the scenes so that when it is time to introduce the layout manager or if you ever need to set the angles manually, you will be well equipped to do so. D3 arc generator is created using the following `d3.arc` function:

```
var arc = d3.arc().outerRadius(200) // <-C
                .innerRadius(innerRadius);
```

The `d3.arc` function optionally has the `outerRadius` and `innerRadius` settings. When `innerRadius` is set, the arc generator will produce an image of annulus (donut) instead of a circle. Finally, the D3 arc is also implemented using the `svg:path` element, and thus similar to the line and area generator, the `d3.arc` generator function can be invoked (refer to line D) to generate the d formula for the `svg:path` element:

```
svg.append("g")
            .attr("transform", "translate(200,200)")
    .selectAll("path.arc")
            .data(data)
        .enter()
            .append("path")
                .attr("class", "arc")
                .attr("fill", function(d, i){return colors(i);})
                .attr("d", function(d, i){
                    return arc(d, i); // <-D
                });
```

One additional element worth mentioning here is the `svg:g` element. This element does not define any shape itself but serves rather as a container element used to group other elements, in this case, the `path.arc` elements. Transformation applied to the `g` element is applied to all the child elements while its attributes are also inherited by its child elements.

See also

- Please refer to `https://github.com/d3/d3/blob/master/API.md#arcs` for more information on arc generator function

Implementing arc transition

One area where arc differs significantly from other shapes, such as line and area, is its transition. For most of the shapes that we covered so far, including simple SVG built-in shapes, you can rely on D3 transition and interpolation to handle their animation. However, this is not the case when dealing with arc. We will explore the arc transition technique in this recipe.

Getting ready

Open your local copy of the following file in your web browser:

```
https://github.com/NickQiZhu/d3-cookbook-v2/blob/master/src/chapter7/arc-transi
tion.html
```

How to do it...

In this recipe, we will animate a multi-slice annulus transitioning with each slice starting from angle 0 to its final desired angle and eventually reaching a full annulus:

```
<script type="text/javascript">
    var width = 400,
            height = 400,
            endAngle = 2 * Math.PI,
            colors = d3.scaleOrdinal(d3.schemeCategory20c);

    var svg = d3.select("body").append("svg")
            .attr("class", "pie")
```

```
            .attr("height", height)
            .attr("width", width);

    function render(innerRadius) {

        var data = [
            {startAngle: 0, endAngle: 0.1 * endAngle},
            {startAngle: 0.1 * endAngle, endAngle: 0.2 * endAngle},
            {startAngle: 0.2 * endAngle, endAngle: 0.4 * endAngle},
            {startAngle: 0.4 * endAngle, endAngle: 0.6 * endAngle},
            {startAngle: 0.6 * endAngle, endAngle: 0.7 * endAngle},
            {startAngle: 0.7 * endAngle, endAngle: 0.9 * endAngle},
            {startAngle: 0.9 * endAngle, endAngle: endAngle}
        ];

        var arc = d3.arc()
                .outerRadius(200).innerRadius(innerRadius);

        svg.select("g").remove();

        svg.append("g")
            .attr("transform", "translate(200,200)")
            .selectAll("path.arc")
                .data(data)
            .enter()
                .append("path")
                .attr("class", "arc")
                .attr("fill", function (d, i) {
                    return colors(i);
                })
                .transition().duration(1000)
                .attrTween("d", function (d) {
                  var start = {startAngle: 0, endAngle: 0}; // <-A
                  var interpolate = d3.interpolate(start, d); // <-B
                  return function (t) {
                      return arc(interpolate(t)); // <-C
                  };
                });
    }

    render(100);
</script>
```

The preceding code generates an arc that starts rotating and eventually becomes a complete annulus as follows:

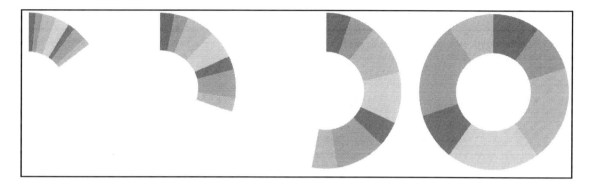

Arc transition with tweening

How it works...

When confronted with the requirement of such transition, your first thought might be using the vanilla D3 transition while relying on built-in interpolations to generate the animation. Here is the code snippet that will do just that:

```
svg.append("g")
        .attr("transform", "translate(200,200)")
        .selectAll("path.arc")
            .data(data)
        .enter()
            .append("path")
            .attr("class", "arc")
            .attr("fill", function (d, i) {
                return colors(i);
            })
            .attr("d", function(d){
                return arc({startAngle: 0, endAngle: 0});
             })
            .transition().duration(1000)
            .attr("d", function(d){return arc(d);});
```

As shown with highlighted lines in the preceding code snippet, with this approach, we initially created slice path with both `startAngle` and `endAngle` set to zero. Then, through transition, we interpolated the path d attribute to its final angle using the arc generator function `arc(d)`. This approach seems to make sense, however, what it generates is the transition shown in the following:

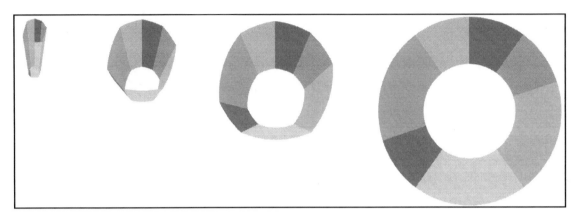

Arc transition without tweening

This is obviously not the animation we want. The reason for this strange transition is that by directly creating a transition on the `svg:path` attribute d, we are instructing D3 to interpolate this string:

```
d="M1.2246063538223773e-14,-200A200,200 0 0,1 1.2246063538223773e-
14,-200L6.123031769111886e-15,-100A100,100 0 0,0
6.123031769111886e-15,-100Z"
```

Then, the preceding string will interpolate to this string linearly:

```
d="M1.2246063538223773e-14,-200A200,200 0 0,1 117.55705045849463,-
161.80339887498948L58.778525229247315,-80.90169943749474A100,100 0
0,0 6.123031769111886e-15,-100Z"
```

Hence, it leads to this particular transition effect.

Though this transition effect is not what we desire in this example, this is still a good showcase of how flexible and powerful built-in D3 transition is.

In order to achieve the transition effect we want, we will need to leverage the D3 attribute tweening (for detailed description on tweening, refer to the *Using tweening* recipe of `Chapter 6, Transition with Style`):

```
svg.append("g")
        .attr("transform", "translate(200,200)")
        .selectAll("path.arc")
            .data(data)
        .enter()
            .append("path")
            .attr("class", "arc")
            .attr("fill", function (d, i) {
                return colors(i);
            })
            .transition().duration(1000)
            .attrTween("d", function (d) { // <-A
                var start = {startAngle: 0, endAngle: 0}; // <-B
                var interpolate = d3.interpolate(start, d); // <-C
                return function (t) {
                    return arc(interpolate(t)); // <-D
                };
            });
```

Here, instead of transitioning the `svg:path` attribute d directly, we created a tweening function on line A. As you can recall, D3 `attrTween` expects a factory function for a tween function. In this case, we started our tweening from angle zero (refer to line B). Then, we created a compound object interpolator on line C, which will interpolate both start and end angles for each slice. Finally, on line D, the arc generator is used to generate a proper `svg:path` formula using the already interpolated angles. This is how a smooth transition of properly angled arcs can be created through custom attribute tweening.

There's more...

D3 also provides support for other shape generators, for example, symbol, chord, and diagonal. However, due to their simplicity and the limited scope of this book, we will not cover them individually here, although we will cover them as parts of other more complex visual constructs in the following chapters. More importantly, with well-grounded understanding of these basic shape generators covered in this chapter, you should be able to pick up other D3 shape generators without much trouble.

See also

- For more information on transition and tweening, refer to the *Using tweening recipe* in `Chapter 6`, *Transition with Style*

8
Chart Them Up

In this chapter, we will cover:

- Creating a line chart
- Creating an area chart
- Creating a scatterplot chart
- Creating a bubble chart
- Creating a bar chart

Introduction

In this chapter, we will turn our attention to one of the oldest and well-trusted companions in data visualization-charts. Charts are well-defined and well-understood graphical representation of data; the following definition expresses it in the simplest terms:

> *(In charts) the data is represented by symbols, such as bars in a bar chart, lines in a line chart, or slices in a pie chart.*

> *Jensen C. & Anderson L. (1991)*

When charts are used in data visualization, their well-understood graphical semantics and syntax relieve the audience of your visualization from the burden of learning the meaning of the graphical metaphor. Hence, they can focus on the data itself and the information generated through visualization. The goal of this chapter is not only to introduce some of the commonly used chart types but also to demonstrate how the various topics and techniques you learned so far can be combined and leveraged in producing sleek, interactive charts using D3.

Recipes in this chapter are much longer than the recipes we encountered so far since they are designed to implement fully functional and reusable charts. I have tried to break these into different segments and with consistent chart structures to ease your reading experience. However, it is still highly recommended to open the companion code examples in your browser and your text editor while you go through this chapter to minimize potential confusion and maximize the benefit.

D3 chart convention

Before you dive into creating your first reusable chart in D3, we need to cover some charting conventions commonly accepted in the D3 community; otherwise, you might risk creating charting libraries that might confuse your user instead of helping them.

 As you would have imagined, D3 charts are most commonly implemented using SVG instead of HTML; however, the convention we will discuss here would also apply to HTML-based charts albeit the implementation details will be somewhat different.

Let's first take a look at the following diagram:

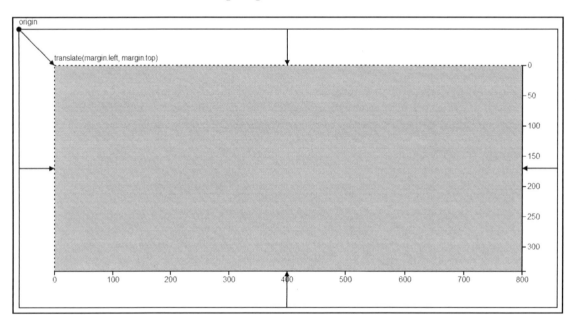

D3 chart convention

As shown in this diagram, the point of origin *(0, 0)* in an SVG image is at its top-leftmost corner as expected; however, the most important aspect of this convention pertains to how chart margins are defined and furthermore where the axes are placed.

- **Margins**: First of all, let's take a look at the most important aspect of this convention-the margins. As you can see, for each chart, there are four different margin settings: left, right, top, and bottom margins. A flexible chart implementation should allow its user to set different values for each of these margins, and we will see in the later recipes how this can be achieved.

- **Coordinate translation**: Secondly, this convention also suggests that the coordinate reference of the chart body (gray area) should be defined using a SVG translate transformation, **translate(margin.left, margin.top)**. This translation effectively moves the chart body area to the desired point; and one additional benefit of this approach is that by shifting the frame of reference for chart body coordinates, it simplifies the job of creating subelements inside the chart body since the margin size becomes irrelevant. For any subelement inside the chart body, its point of origin *(0, 0)* is now the top-leftmost corner of the chart body area.

- **Axes**: Lastly, the final aspect of this convention is regarding how and where chart axes are placed. As shown in the preceding diagram, chart axes are placed inside chart margins instead of being a part of the chart body. This approach has the advantage of treating axes as peripheral elements in a chart, and hence, doesn't convolute the chart body implementation and additionally makes axes rendering logic chart independent and easily reusable.

Now let's create our first reusable D3 chart with all the knowledge and techniques we covered so far.

To see this convention as it was explained by the creator of D3, please visit `http://bl.ocks.org/mbostock/3019563`.

Creating a line chart

Line chart is a common, basic chart type that is widely used in many fields. This chart consists of a series of data points connected by straight line segments. A line chart is also typically bordered by two perpendicular axes: the *x* axis and the *y* axis. In this recipe, we will take a look at how this basic chart can be implemented using D3 as a reusable JavaScript object that can be configured to display multiple data series on a different scale. Besides that, we will also show the technique of implementing a dynamic multi-data-series update with animation.

Getting ready

Open your local copy of the following file in your web browser:

```
https://github.com/NickQiZhu/d3-cookbook-v2/blob/master/src/chapter8/line-chart
.html
```

It is highly recommended that you have the companion code example open while reading this recipe.

How to do it...

Let's take a look at the following code that implements this chart type; due the length of the recipe, we will only show the outline of the code here while diving into the details in the *How it works...* section:

```
<script type="text/javascript">
// First we define the chart object using a functional object

function lineChart() { // <-1A
    ...
    // main render function
    _chart.render = function () { // <-2A
    ...
    };

    // axes rendering function
    functionrenderAxes(svg) {
        ...
    }
    ...
```

```
// function to render chart body
function renderBody(svg) { // <-2D
...
}

// function to render lines
function renderLines() {
...
}

// function to render data points
function renderDots() {

}

return _chart; // <-1E
}
```

This recipe generates the following chart:

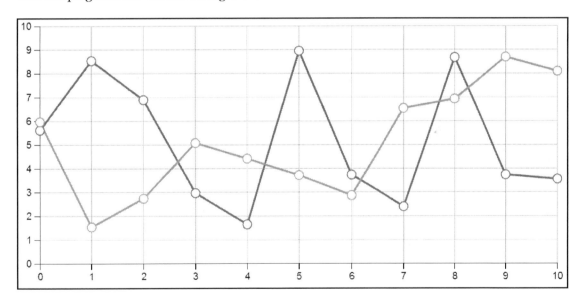

Line chart

How it works...

As you can see, this recipe is significantly more involved than anything we encountered so far; so now, I will break it into multiple detailed sections with different focuses.

Chart object and attributes

First, we will take a look at how this chart object is created and how its associated attributes can be retrieved and set on it in the following code:

```
function lineChart() { // <-1A
    var _chart = {};

    var _width = 600, _height = 300, // <-1B
        _margins = {top: 30, left: 30, right: 30, bottom: 30},
        _x, _y,
        _data = [],
        _colors = d3.scaleOrdinal(d3.schemeCategory10),
        _svg,
        _bodyG,
        _line;

    . . .

    _chart.width = function (w) {
        if (!arguments.length) return _width;
        _width = w;
        return _chart;
    };

    _chart.height = function (h) { // <-1C
        if (!arguments.length) return _height;
        _height = h;
        return _chart;
    };

    _chart.margins = function (m) {
        if (!arguments.length) return _margins;
        _margins = m;
        return _chart;
    };

    . . .

    _chart.addSeries = function (series) { // <-1D
        _data.push(series);
```

```
            return _chart;
        };

        return _chart; // <-1E
    }

    ...

var chart = lineChart()
            .x(d3.scaleLinear().domain([0, 10]))
            .y(d3.scaleLinear().domain([0, 10]));

data.forEach(function (series) {
    chart.addSeries(series);
});

chart.render();
```

As you can see, the chart object is defined using a function called `lineChart` on line 1A, following the functional object pattern we have discussed in the *Understanding D3-Style JavaScript* recipe in `Chapter 1`, *Getting Started with D3.js*. Leveraging the greater flexibility with information hiding offered by the functional object pattern, we have defined a series of internal attributes all named starting with an underscore (line 1B). Some of these attributes are made public by offering an accessor function (line 1C). Publicly accessible attributes are as follows:

- `width`: Chart SVG total width in pixels
- `height`: Chart SVG total height in pixels
- `margins`: Chart margins
- `colors`: Chart ordinal color scale used to differentiate different data series
- x: *x* axis scale
- y: *y* axis scale

The accessor functions are implemented using the technique we introduced in `Chapter 1`, *Getting Started with D3.js*, effectively combining both getter and setter functions in one function, which behave as a getter when no argument is given and a setter when an argument is present (line 1C). Additionally, both `lineChart` function and its accessors return a chart instance, thus allowing function chaining. Finally, the chart object also offers an `addSeries` function, which simply pushes a data array (`series`) into its internal data storage array (_`data`), refer to line 1D.

Chart body frame rendering

After covering the basic chart object and its attributes, the next aspect of this reusable chart implementation is the chart body svg:g element rendering and its clip path generation:

```
_chart.render = function () { // <-2A
  if (!_svg) {
    _svg = d3.select("body").append("svg") // <-2B
      .attr("height", _height)
      .attr("width", _width);

    renderAxes(_svg);

    defineBodyClip(_svg);
  }

  renderBody(_svg);
};
...
function defineBodyClip(svg) { // <-2C
  var padding = 5;

  svg.append("defs")
    .append("clipPath")
    .attr("id", "body-clip")
    .append("rect")
    .attr("x", 0 - padding)
    .attr("y", 0)
    .attr("width", quadrantWidth() + 2 * padding)
    .attr("height", quadrantHeight());
}

function renderBody(svg) { // <-2D
  if (!_bodyG)
    _bodyG = svg.append("g")
      .attr("class", "body")
      .attr("transform", "translate("
        + xStart() + ","
        + yEnd() + ")") // <-2E
      .attr("clip-path", "url(#body-clip)");

  renderLines();

  renderDots();
}
...
```

The `render` function defined on line 2A is responsible for creating the `svg:svg` element and setting its `width` and `height` (line 2B). After that, it creates an `svg:clipPath` element that covers the entire chart body area. The `svg:clipPath` element is used to restrict the region where paint can be applied. In our case, we used it to restrict the line and dots that can be painted (only within the chart body area). This code generates the following SVG element structure that defines the chart body:

```
▼<svg height="300" width="600">
  ▶<g class="axes">…</g>
  ▼<defs>
    ▶<clippath id="body-clip">…</clippath>
    </defs>
  ▶<g class="body" transform="translate(30,30)" clip-path="url(#body-clip)">…</g>
  </svg>
```

For more information on clipping and masking, please visit
`https://www.w3.org/TR/SVG/masking.html`.

The `renderBody` function defined on line 2D generates the `svg:g` element, which wraps all the chart body content with a translation set according to the chart margin convention we have discussed in the previous section (line 2E).

Render axes

Axes are rendered in the `renderAxes` function (line 3A):

```
function renderAxes(svg) { // <-3A
    varaxesG = svg.append("g")
                    .attr("class", "axes");

    renderXAxis(axesG);

    renderYAxis(axesG);
}
```

As discussed in the previous chapter, both the *x* and *y* axes are rendered inside the chart margin area. We will not go into details of axes rendering since we have discussed this topic in much detail in `Chapter 5`, *Playing with Axes*.

Render data series

Everything we discussed so far in this recipe is not unique to this chart type alone but rather it is a shared framework among other Cartesian coordinates-based chart types. Finally, now we can discuss the core of this recipe-how the line segments and dots are created for multiple data series. Let's take a look at the following code fragments that are responsible for data series rendering:

```
function renderLines() {
        _line = d3.line() //<-4A
                        .x(function (d) { return _x(d.x); })
                        .y(function (d) { return _y(d.y); });

        var pathLines = _bodyG.selectAll("path.line")
                        .data(_data);

        pathLines
                .enter() //<-4B
                    .append("path")
                .merge(pathLines)
                    .style("stroke", function (d, i) {
                        return _colors(i); //<-4C
                    })
                    .attr("class", "line")
                .transition() //<-4D
                    .attr("d", function (d) {
                            return _line(d);
                    });
}

function renderDots() {
    _data.forEach(function (list, i) {
        var circle = _bodyG.selectAll("circle._" + i) //<-4E
                .data(list);

        circle.enter()
                .append("circle")
            .merge(circle)
                .attr("class", "dot _" + i)
                .style("stroke", function (d) {
                    return _colors(i); //<-4F
                })
            .transition() //<-4G
                .attr("cx", function (d) { return _x(d.x); })
                .attr("cy", function (d) { return _y(d.y); })
                .attr("r", 4.5);
    });
```

```
}
```

The line segments and dots are generated using techniques we introduced in `Chapter 7`, *Getting into Shape*. The `d3.line` generator was created on line 4A to create `svg:path` that maps the data series. The Enter-and-Update pattern is used to create the data line (line 4B). Line 4C sets a different color for each data line based on its index. Lastly, line 4E sets the transition in the update mode to move the data line smoothly on each update. The `renderDots` function performs a similar rendering logic that generates a set of `svg:circle` elements representing each data point (line 4E), coordinating its color based on the data series index (line 4F), and finally also initiates a transition on line 4G, so the dots can move with the line whenever the data is updated.

As illustrated by this recipe, creating a reusable chart component involves actually quite a bit of work. However, more than two-thirds of the code is required to create peripheral graphical elements and accessors methods. Therefore, in a real-world project, you can extract this logic and reuse a large part of this implementation for other charts; though we did not do this in our recipes in order to reduce the complexity, you can quickly grasp all aspects of chart rendering. Due to limited scope in this book, in later recipes, we will omit all peripheral rendering logic and only focus on the core logic related to each chart type.Feel free to jump back to this recipe if you ever need to double-check the peripheral rendering logic while reading the later recipes in this chapter.

Creating an area chart

An area chart or an area graph is very similar to a line chart and largely implemented based on the line chart. The main difference between an area chart and a line chart is that in the area chart, the area between the axis and the line will be filled with colors or textures. In this recipe, we will explore techniques of implementing a type of area chart known as **Layered Area Chart**.

Getting ready

Open your local copy of the following file in your web browser:

```
https://github.com/NickQiZhu/d3-cookbook-v2/blob/master/src/chapter8/area-chart
.html
```

How to do it...

An area chart implementation is largely based on the line chart implementation and shares a lot of common graphical elements, such as the axes and the clip path; therefore, in this recipe, we will only show the code that concerns the area chart implementation specifics:

```
. . .

function renderBody(svg) {
        if (!_bodyG)
            _bodyG = svg.append("g")
                    .attr("class", "body")
                    .attr("transform", "translate("
                        + xStart() + ","
                        + yEnd() + ")")
                    .attr("clip-path", "url(#body-clip)");

        renderLines();

        renderAreas();

        renderDots();
    }

function renderLines() {
        _line = d3.line()
                            .x(function (d) { return _x(d.x); })
                            .y(function (d) { return _y(d.y); });

        var pathLines = _bodyG.selectAll("path.line")
                .data(_data);

        pathLines.enter()
                    .append("path")
                .merge(pathLines)
                    .style("stroke", function (d, i) {
                        return _colors(i);
                    })
                    .attr("class", "line")
                .transition()
                    .attr("d", function (d) { return _line(d); });
    }

function renderDots() {
        _data.forEach(function (list, i) {
            var circle = _bodyG.selectAll("circle._" + i)
                    .data(list);
```

```
            circle.enter()
                    .append("circle")
                .merge(circle)
                    .attr("class", "dot _" + i)
                    .style("stroke", function (d) {
                        return _colors(i);
                    })
                .transition()
                    .attr("cx", function (d) { return _x(d.x); })
                    .attr("cy", function (d) { return _y(d.y); })
                    .attr("r", 4.5);
        });
    }

    function renderAreas() {
        var area = d3.area() // <-A
                    .x(function(d) { return _x(d.x); })
                    .y0(yStart())
                    .y1(function(d) { return _y(d.y); });

        var pathAreas = _bodyG.selectAll("path.area")
                .data(_data);

        pathAreas.enter() // <-B
                .append("path")
            .merge(pathAreas)
                .style("fill", function (d, i) {
                    return _colors(i);
                })
                .attr("class", "area")
            .transition() // <-D
                .attr("d", function (d) {
                    return area(d); // <-E
                });
    }
...
```

This recipe generates the following layered area chart:

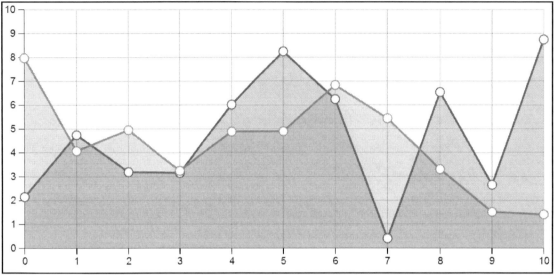

Layered area chart

How it works...

As we mentioned before, since the area chart implementation is based on our line chart implementation, a large part of the implementation is identical to the line chart. In fact, the area chart needs to render the exact line and dots implemented in the line chart. The crucial difference lies in the renderAreas function. In this recipe, we rely on the area generation technique discussed in Chapter 7, *Getting into Shape*. The d3.area generator was created on line A with its upper line created to match the line while its lower line (y0) fixed on x axis.

```
var area = d3.area() // <-A
  .x(function(d) { return _x(d.x); })
  .y0(yStart())
  .y1(function(d) { return _y(d.y); });
```

Once the area generator is defined, a classic Enter-and-Update pattern is employed to create and update the areas. In the Enter case (line B), an svg:path element was created for each data series. On line B2, we merged the pathAreas.enter() and pathAreas; therefore, all following code will be applied to both the enter and update modes; all areas are colored using its series index so it will have matching color with our line and dots (line C):

```
Var pathAreas = _bodyG.selectAll("path.area")
                    .data(_data);

pathAreas.enter() // <-B
.append("path")
.merge(pathAreas) // <-B2
.style("fill", function (d, i) {
    return _colors(i); // <-C
  })
  .attr("class", "area")
.transition() // <-D
  .attr("d", function (d) {
      return area(d); // <-E
  });
```

Whenever the data is updated, as well as for newly created areas, we start a transition (line D) to update the area `svg:path` elements' d attribute to the desired shape (line E).Since we know that the line chart implementation animates both line and dots when updated, our area update transition here effectively allows the areas to be animated and moved in accordance with both lines and dots in our chart.

Finally, we also add the CSS style for `path.area` to decrease its opacity so areas become see-through and `hence allow the layered effect` we want:

```
.area {
  stroke: none;
  fill-opacity: .2;
}
```

Creating a scatterplot chart

A scatterplot or scattergraph is another common type of diagram used to display data points on Cartesian coordinates with two different variables. Scatterplot is especially useful when you're exploring the problem of spreading, clustering, and classification. In this recipe, you will learn how to implement a multi-series scatterplot chart in D3.

Getting ready

Open your local copy of the following file in your web browser:

```
https://github.com/NickQiZhu/d3-cookbook-v2/blob/master/src/chapter8/scatterplo
t-chart.html
```

How to do it...

A scatterplot is another chart that uses Cartesian coordinates. Thus, a large part of its implementation is very similar to the charts we introduced so far; and therefore, the code concerning peripheral graphical elements are again omitted to save space in this book. Please refer to the companion code for the complete implementation. Now let's take a look the implementation of this recipe:

```
. . .

_symbolTypes = d3.scaleOrdinal() // <-A
                  .range([d3.symbolCircle,
                          d3.symbolCross,
                          d3.symbolDiamond,
                          d3.symbolSquare,
                          d3.symbolStar,
                          d3.symbolTriangle,
                          d3.symbolWye
              ]);

. . .

function renderBody(svg) {
    if (!_bodyG)
        _bodyG = svg.append("g")
            .attr("class", "body")
            .attr("transform", "translate("
                        + xStart() + ","
                        + yEnd() + ")")
            .attr("clip-path", "url(#body-clip)");

            renderSymbols();
}

function renderSymbols() { // <-B
    _data.forEach(function (list, i) {
        var symbols = _bodyG.selectAll("path._" + i)
                        .data(list);

        symbols.enter()
                .append("path")
            .merge(symbols)
                .attr("class", "symbol _" + i)
                .classed(_symbolTypes(i), true)
            .transition() // <-C
                .attr("transform", function(d){
                        return "translate(" // <-D
```

```
                            + _x(d.x)
                            + ","
                            + _y(d.y)
                            + ")";
            })
            .attr("d",
                    d3.symbol() // <-E
                        .type(_symbolTypes(i))
            );
        });
    }
    ...
```

This recipe generates the following scatterplot chart:

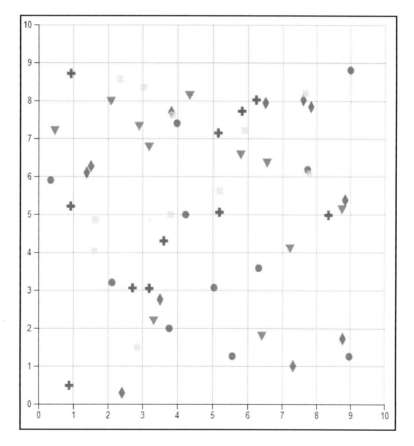

Scatter plot chart

How it works...

The content of the scatterplot chart is mainly rendered by the `renderSymbols` function on line B. You probably may have already noticed that the `renderSymbols` function implementation is very similar to the `renderDots` function we discussed in the *Creating a line chart* recipe. This is not by accident since both try to plot data points on Cartesian coordinates with two variables (x and y). In the case of plotting dots, the `svg:circle` elements were being created, whereas, in scatterplot, you will need to create the `d3.symbol` elements. D3 provides a list of predefined symbols that can be generated easily and rendered using an `svg:path` element. As shown on line A, we defined an ordinal scale to allow mapping of data series index to different symbol types:

```
_symbolTypes = d3.scaleOrdinal() // <-A
                    .range([d3.symbolCircle,
                        d3.symbolCross,
                        d3.symbolDiamond,
                        d3.symbolSquare,
                        d3.symbolStar,
                        d3.symbolTriangle,
                        d3.symbolWye
                    ]);
```

Plotting the data points with symbols is quite straightforward. First, we will loop through the data series array, and for each data series, we will create a set of `svg:path` elements representing each data point in the series as follows:

```
_data.forEach(function (list, i) {
    var symbols = _bodyG.selectAll("path._" + i)
                    .data(list);

    symbols.enter()
            .append("path")
        .merge(symbols)
            .attr("class", "symbol _" + i)
            .classed(_symbolTypes(i), true)
        .transition() // <-C
            .attr("transform", function(d){
                        return "translate(" // <-D
                                + _x(d.x)
                                + ","
                                + _y(d.y)
                                + ")";
            })
            .attr("d",d3.symbol() // <-E
                        .type(_symbolTypes(i))
```

```
        );
    });
```

By merging the `symbols.enter()` and `symbols` selections, we made sure that whenever data series are updated, as well as for newly created symbols, we apply the update with transition (line C), placing them on the right coordinates with an SVG translation transformation (line D). Finally, the d attribute of each `svg:path` element is generated using the `d3.svg.symbol` generator function as shown on line E.

Creating a bubble chart

A bubble chart is a typical visualization capable of displaying three data dimensions. Every data entity with its three data points is visualized as a bubble (or disk) on Cartesian coordinates, with two different variables represented using *x* axis and *y* axis, similar to the `scatterplot` chart, while the third dimension is represented using the radius of the bubble (size of the disk). The bubble chart is particularly useful when it's used to facilitate the understanding of relationships between data entities.

Getting ready

Open your local copy of the following file in your web browser:

```
https://github.com/NickQiZhu/d3-cookbook-v2/blob/master/src/chapter8/bubble-cha
rt.html
```

How to do it...

In this recipe, we will explore techniques and ways of implementing a typical bubble chart using D3. The following code example shows the important implementation aspects of a bubble chart, omitting the accessors and peripheral graphic implementation details:

```
...

var _width = 600, _height = 300,
            _margins = {top: 30, left: 30, right: 30, bottom: 30},
            _x, _y, _r, // <-A
            _data = [],
            _colors = d3.scaleOrdinal(d3.schemeCategory10),
            _svg,
            _bodyG;
```

```
            _chart.render = function () {
                if (!_svg) {
                    _svg = d3.select("body").append("svg")
                            .attr("height", _height)
                            .attr("width", _width);

                    renderAxes(_svg);

                    defineBodyClip(_svg);
                }

                renderBody(_svg);
            };
    ...
    function renderBody(svg) {
            if (!_bodyG)
                _bodyG = svg.append("g")
                        .attr("class", "body")
                        .attr("transform", "translate("
                                + xStart()
                                + ","
                                + yEnd() + ")")
                        .attr("clip-path", "url(#body-clip)");

            renderBubbles();
    }

    function renderBubbles() {
            _r.range([0, 50]); // <-B

            _data.forEach(function (list, i) {
                var bubbles = _bodyG.selectAll("circle._" + i)
                        .data(list);

                bubbles.enter()
                        .append("circle") // <-C
                    .merge(bubbles)
                        .attr("class", "bubble _" + i)
                        .style("stroke", function (d, j) {
                            return _colors(j);
                        })
                        .style("fill", function (d, j) {
                            return _colors(j);
                        })
                    .transition()
                        .attr("cx", function (d) {
                            return _x(d.x); // <-D
                        })
```

```
                            .attr("cy", function (d) {
                                return _y(d.y); // <-E
                            })
                            .attr("r", function (d) {
                                return _r(d.r); // <-F
                            });
                    });
        }
        ...
```

This recipe generates the following visualization:

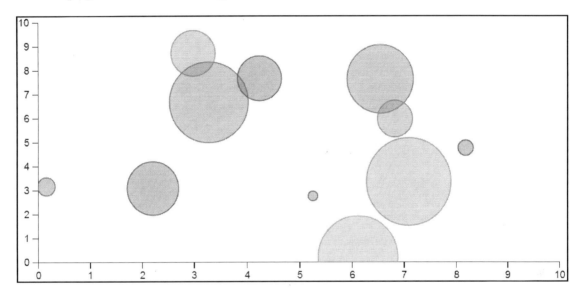

Bubble chart

How it works...

Overall, the bubble chart implementation follows the same pattern as other chart implementations introduced in this chapter so far. However, since we want to visualize three different dimensions (x, y, and radius) instead of two in the bubble chart, a new scale _r was added in this implementation (line A) as follows:

```
var _width = 600, _height = 300,
    _margins = {top: 30, left: 30, right: 30, bottom: 30},
    _x, _y, _r, // <-A
    _data = [],
    _colors = d3.scale.category10(),
```

```
    _svg,
    _bodyG;
```

Most of the bubble chart-related implementation details are handled by the
renderBubbles function. It starts with setting the range on the radius scale (line B). Of
course, we can also make the radius range configurable in our chart implementation;
however, for simplicity, we chose to set it explicitly in the following code:

```
function renderBubbles() {
        _r.range([0, 50]); // <-B

    _data.forEach(function (list, i) {
        var bubbles = _bodyG.selectAll("circle._" + i)
                .data(list);

        bubbles.enter()
                .append("circle") // <-C
            .merge(bubbles)
                .attr("class", "bubble _" + i)
                .style("stroke", function (d, j) {
                    return _colors(j);
                })
                .style("fill", function (d, j) {
                    return _colors(j);
                })
            .transition()
                .attr("cx", function (d) {
                    return _x(d.x); // <-D
                })
                .attr("cy", function (d) {
                    return _y(d.y); // <-E
                })
                .attr("r", function (d) {
                    return _r(d.r); // <-F
                });
    });
}
```

Once the range is set, we iterated through our data series, and for each series, we created a
set of svg:circle elements (line C). Finally, we handled the newly created bubble and its
update in the last section, where the svg:circle elements are colored and placed to the
correct coordinates using its cx and cy attributes (lines D and E). In the end, the bubble size
is controlled using its radius attribute r mapped using the _r scale we defined earlier (line
F).

In some of the bubble chart implementations, the implementer also leverages the color of each bubble to visualize a fourth data dimension, although some believe this kind of visual representation is hard to grasp and superfluous.

Creating a bar chart

A bar chart is a visualization that uses either horizontal (row charts) or vertical (column charts) rectangular bars with length proportional to the values that they represent. In this recipe, we will implement a column chart using D3. A column chart is capable of visually representing two variables at the same time with its y axis; in other words, the bar height and its x axis. The x axis values can be either discrete or continuous (for example, a histogram). In our example, we choose to visualize continuous values on the x axis. However, the same technique can be applied when you work with discrete values.

Getting ready

Open your local copy of the following file in your web browser:

```
https://github.com/NickQiZhu/d3-cookbook-v2/blob/master/src/chapter8/bar-chart.
html
```

How to do it...

The following code example shows the important implementation aspects of a histogram, omitting the accessors and peripheral graphic implementation details:

```
...

var _chart = {};

    var _width = 600, _height = 250,
            _margins = {top: 30, left: 30, right: 30, bottom: 30},
            _x, _y,
            _data = [],
            _colors = d3.scaleOrdinal(d3.schemeCategory10),
            _svg,
            _bodyG;

    _chart.render = function () {
        if (!_svg) {
```

```
                _svg = d3.select("body").append("svg")
                        .attr("height", _height)
                        .attr("width", _width);

                renderAxes(_svg);

                defineBodyClip(_svg);
            }

            renderBody(_svg);
        };
...
function renderBody(svg) {
        if (!_bodyG)
            _bodyG = svg.append("g")
                    .attr("class", "body")
                    .attr("transform", "translate("
                            + xStart()
                            + ","
                            + yEnd() + ")")
                    .attr("clip-path", "url(#body-clip)");

        renderBars();
    }
    function renderBars() {
        var padding = 2; // <-A

        var bars = _bodyG.selectAll("rect.bar")
                .data(_data);
        bars.enter()
                .append("rect") // <-B
            .merge(bars)
                .attr("class", "bar")
            .transition()
                .attr("x", function (d) {
                    return _x(d.x); // <-C
                })
                .attr("y", function (d) {
                    return _y(d.y); // <-D
                })
                .attr("height", function (d) {
                    return yStart() - _y(d.y);
                })
                .attr("width", function(d){
                    return Math.floor(quadrantWidth() /
                            _data.length) - padding;
                });
    }
```

. . .

This recipe generates the following visualization:

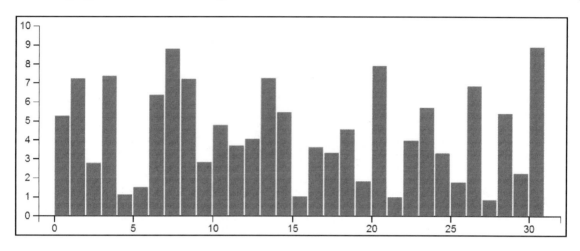

Bar chart (histogram)

How it works...

One major difference here is that the bar chart implementation does not support multiple data series. Therefore, instead of using a 2D array storing multiple data series as we did with other charts so far, in this implementation, the _data array simply stores a single set of data points directly. Main bar chart-related visualization logic resides in the renderBars function:

```
functionrenderBars() {
  var padding = 2; // <-A
  ...
}
```

In the first step, we defined the padding between bars (line A) so that later on we can automatically calculate the width of each bar. After that, we generated an svg:rect element (the bars) for each data point (line B) as follows:

```
var bars = _bodyG.selectAll("rect.bar")
                .data(_data);

        bars.enter()
                .append("rect") // <-B
            .merge(bars)
```

```
                    .attr("class", "bar")
                .transition()
                    .attr("x", function (d) {
                        return _x(d.x); // <-C
                    })
                    .attr("y", function (d) {
                        return _y(d.y); // <-D
                    })
                    .attr("height", function (d) {
                        return yStart() - _y(d.y);
                    })
                    .attr("width", function(d){
                        return Math.floor(quadrantWidth() /
                            _data.length) - padding;
                    });
```

Then, in the update section, we placed each bar at the correct coordinates using its *x* and *y* attributes (lines C and D) and extended each bar all the way down to touch the *x* axis with an adaptive `height` calculated on line E. Finally, we calculated the optimal width for each bar using the number of bars and the padding value we defined earlier:

```
.attr("width", function(d){
    returnMath.floor(quadrantWidth() / _data.length) - padding;
});
```

Of course, in a more flexible implementation, we can make the padding configurable instead of being fixed to 2 pixels.

See also

Before planning to implement your own reusable chart for your next visualization project, make sure that you also check out the following open source reusable chart projects based on D3:

- NVD3: http://nvd3.org/.
- Dimensional Charting: https://dc-js.github.io/dc.js/.
- Rickshaw: http://code.shutterstock.com/rickshaw/.

9
Lay Them Out

In this chapter, we will cover:

- Building a pie chart
- Building a stacked area chart
- Building a treemap
- Building a tree
- Building an enclosure diagram

Introduction

The D3 layout is the focus of this chapter-a concept we have not encountered before. As expected, D3 layouts are algorithms that calculate and generate placement information for a group of elements. However, there are a few critical properties worth mentioning before we dive deeper into the specifics:

- **Layouts are data**: Layouts are purely data centric and data driven; they do not generate any graphical or display-related output directly. This allows them to be used and reused with SVG or canvas or even when there is no graphical output.
- **Abstract and reusable**: Layouts are abstract, allowing a high degree of flexibility and reusability. You can combine and reuse layouts in various different interesting ways.
- **Layouts are different**: Each layout is different. Every layout provided by D3 focuses on a very special graphical requirement and data structure.
- **Stateless**: Layouts are mostly stateless by design to simplify their usage. What statelessness means here is that generally layouts are like functions; they can be called multiple times with different input data and generate different layout output.

Layouts are interesting and powerful concepts in D3. In this chapter, we will explore some of the most commonly used layouts in D3 by creating a fully functional visualization leveraging these layouts.

Building a pie chart

A pie chart or a circle graph is a circular graph that contains multiple sectors used to illustrate numerical proportion. We will explore techniques, involving D3 **pie layout**, to build a fully functional pie chart in this recipe. In Chapter 7, *Getting into Shape*, it became clear that using the D3 arc generator directly is a very tedious job. Each arc generator expects the following data format:

```
var data = [
    {startAngle: 0, endAngle: 0.6283185307179586},
    {startAngle: 0.6283185307179586, endAngle: 1.2566370614359172},
    ...
    {startAngle: 5.654866776461628, endAngle: 6.283185307179586}
];
```

This essentially requires the calculation of the angle partition for each slice out of an entire circle of 2 * Math.PI. Obviously, this process can be automated by an algorithm, which is exactly what d3.pie is designed for. In this recipe, we will see how a pie layout can be used to implement a fully functional pie chart.

Getting ready

Open your local copy of the following file in your web browser:
https://github.com/NickQiZhu/d3-cookbook-v2/blob/master/src/chapter9/pie-chart.html

How to do it...

A pie chart or a circle graph is a circular diagram divided into sectors (slices). Pie charts are popular in many fields and widely used to demonstrate relationships between different entities, though not without criticism. Let's take a look at how a pie chart is implemented using d3.layout first:

```
<script type="text/javascript">
    function pieChart() {
        var _chart = {};
```

```
var _width = 500, _height = 500,
        _data = [],
        _colors = d3.scaleOrdinal(d3.schemeCategory10),
        _svg,
        _bodyG,
        _pieG,
        _radius = 200,
        _innerRadius = 100,
        _duration = 1000;

_chart.render = function () {
    if (!_svg) {
        _svg = d3.select("body").append("svg")
                .attr("height", _height)
                .attr("width", _width);
    }

    renderBody(_svg);
};

function renderBody(svg) {
    if (!_bodyG)
        _bodyG = svg.append("g")
                .attr("class", "body");

    renderPie();
}

function renderPie() {
    var pie = d3.pie() // <-A
            .sort(function (d) {
                return d.id;
            })
            .value(function (d) {
                return d.value;
            });

    var arc = d3.arc()
            .outerRadius(_radius)
            .innerRadius(_innerRadius);

    if (!_pieG)
        _pieG = _bodyG.append("g")
                .attr("class", "pie")
                .attr("transform", "translate("
                    + _radius
                    + ","
                    + _radius + ")");
```

```
            renderSlices(pie, arc);

            renderLabels(pie, arc);
    }

  function renderSlices(pie, arc) {
  // explained in detail in the'how it works...' section
  ...
  }

  function renderLabels(pie, arc) {
  // explained in detail in the 'how it works...' section
  ...
  }
  ...
  return _chart;
}
...
</script>
```

This recipe generates the following pie chart:

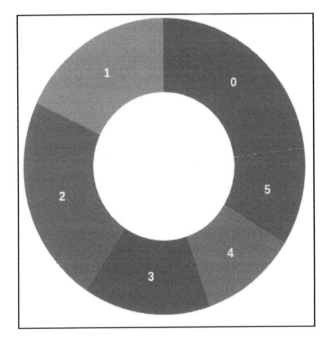

Pie chart

How it works...

This recipe is built over what you have learned in the `Chapter 7`, *Getting into Shape*. One major difference is that you rely on `d3.pie` to transform the raw data into arcs data for us. The pie layout was created on line A with both sort and value accessors specified:

```
var pie = d3.pie() // <-A
            .sort(function (d) {
                return d.id;
            })
            .value(function (d) {
                return d.value;
            });
```

The `sort` function tells the pie layout to sort slices by its ID field, so that we can maintain stable order among slices. Without the sorting, by default, the pie layout will order the slices by value, resulting in the swapping of slices whenever we update the pie chart. The `value` function is used to provide value accessor, which, in our case, returns the `value` field. When rendering slices, now with the pie layout, we directly set the output of the `pie` function call as data (remember, layouts are data) to generate the arc `svg:path` elements (refer to line B):

```
function renderSlices(pie, arc) {
    var slices = _pieG.selectAll("path.arc")
            .data(pie(_data)); // <-B

    slices.enter()
            .append("path")
        .merge(slices)
            .attr("class", "arc")
            .attr("fill", function (d, i) {
                return _colors(i);
            })
        .transition()
            .duration(_duration)
            .attrTween("d", function (d) {
                var currentArc = this.__current__; // <-C

                if (!currentArc)
                    currentArc = {startAngle: 0,
                                  endAngle: 0};

                var interpolate = d3.interpolate(
                                  currentArc, d);
                this.__current__ = interpolate(1);//<-D
                return function (t) {
```

```
            return arc(interpolate(t));
        };
    });
}
```

At this point, you might be wondering what kind of data d3.pie generates. Here is what the output data looks like:

```
▼ [Object, Object, Object, Object, Object, Object] ⬤
  ▼ 0: Object
    ▶ data: Object
      endAngle: 1.3029801277680182
      index: 0
      padAngle: 0
      startAngle: 0
      value: 7.605104422042922
    ▶ __proto__: Object
  ▶ 1: Object
  ▶ 2: Object
```

Pie output data

As we can see clearly, this is exactly what the d3.arc generator expects. This is why we can use this data directly with d3.arc without dealing with any detailed calculation for angles and partitions. The rest of the rendering logic is pretty much the same as what you have learned in Chapter 7, *Getting into Shape*, with one exception that can be seen on line C. On line C, we retrieve the current arc value from the element so the transition can start from the current angle instead of zero. Then, on line D, we reset the current arc value to the latest one; so, the next time when we update the pie chart data, we can repeat the stateful transition.

Technique – stateful visualization

Technique of value injection on a DOM element is a common approach to introduce statefulness to your visualization. In other words, if you need your visualizations to remember what their previous states are, you can save them in DOM elements, as demonstrated on line C in this recipe.

Finally, we also need to render labels on each slice so our user can understand what each slice is representing. This is done by the renderLabels function:

```
function renderLabels(pie, arc) {
        var labels = _pieG.selectAll("text.label")
                .data(pie(_data)); // <-E
```

```
labels.enter()
        .append("text")
    .merge(labels)
        .attr("class", "label")
    .transition()
        .duration(_duration)
        .attr("transform", function (d) {
            return "translate("
                + arc.centroid(d) + ")"; // <-F
        })
        .attr("dy", ".35em")
        .attr("text-anchor", "middle")
        .text(function (d) {
            return d.data.id;
        });
}
```

Once again, we use the output of the `pie` function call as data to generate the `svg:text` elements. The placement of the labels is calculated using `arc.centroid` (refer to line F). Additionally, the label placement is animated through the transition so they can be moved with arcs in unison.

There's more...

Pie charts are very widely used in many different domains. However, they are also widely criticized due to the fact that they are difficult for the human eyes to compare different sections of a given pie chart as well as for their low information density. Therefore, it is highly recommended to limit the number of sections to less than three, with two considered to be ideal. Otherwise, you can always use a bar chart or a small table to replace a pie chart for better precision and communicative power.

See also

- The *Using arc generators* recipe in `Chapter 7`, *Getting into Shape*
- The *Implementing arc transition* recipe in `Chapter 7`, *Getting into Shape*

Building a stacked area chart

In the *Creating an area chart* recipe in `Chapter 8`, *Chart Them Up*, we explored how a basic layered area chart can be implemented using D3. In this recipe, we will build over what we covered in the area chart recipe to implement a stacked area chart. Stacked area chart is a variation of the standard area chart in which different areas are stacked on top of each other giving your audience the ability to compare not only different data series individually but also their relationship to the total in proportion.

Getting ready

Open your local copy of the following file in your web browser:
`https://github.com/NickQiZhu/d3-cookbook-v2/blob/master/src/chapter9/stacked-ar ea-chart.html`

How to do it...

This recipe is built over what we had implemented in `Chapter 8`, *Chart Them Up*; therefore, in the following code example, only the parts that are particularly relevant to the stacked area chart are included:

```
<script type="text/javascript">
function stackedAreaChart() {
    var _chart = {};

    var _width = 900, _height = 450,
            _margins = {top: 30, left: 30, right: 30, bottom: 30},
            _x, _y,
            _data = [],
            _colors = d3.scaleOrdinal(d3.schemeCategory10),
            _svg,
            _bodyG,
            _line;

    _chart.render = function () {
        if (!_svg) {
            _svg = d3.select("body").append("svg")
                    .attr("height", _height)
                    .attr("width", _width);

            renderAxes(_svg);

            defineBodyClip(_svg);
```

```
        }

    renderBody(_svg);
};
...
function renderBody(svg) {
    if (!_bodyG)
        _bodyG = svg.append("g")
                    .attr("class", "body")
                    .attr("transform", "translate("
                            + xStart() + ","
                            + yEnd() + ")")
                    .attr("clip-path", "url(#body-clip)");

    var stack = d3.stack() // <-A
                .keys(['value1', 'value2', 'value3'])
                .offset(d3.stackOffsetNone);

    var series = stack(_data); //<-B

    renderLines(series);

    renderAreas(series);
}

function renderLines(stackedData) {
  // explained in details in the'how it works...' section
...
}

function renderAreas(stackedData) {
  // explained in details in the 'how it works...' section
...
}
...
```

This recipe generates the following visualization:

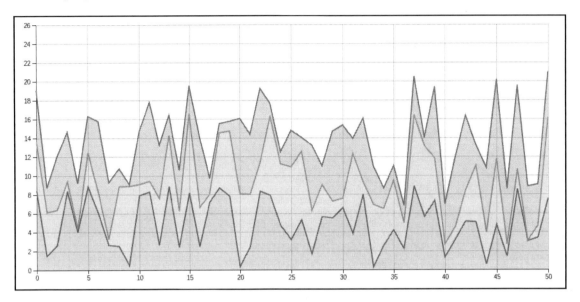

Stacked area chart

How it works...

The main difference between this recipe and the standard area chart is the stacking, which is also the focus of this recipe. The stacking effect as illustrated in this recipe was achieved through d3.stack created on line A:

```
var stack = dn3.stack() // <-A
            .keys(['value1', 'value2', 'value3']) // <-B
            .offset(d3.stackOffsetNone);
...
function update() {
    data = d3.range(numberOfDataPoint).map(function (i) {
        return {value1: randomData(),
                value2: randomData(),
                value3: randomData()};
    });

    chart.data(data).render();
}
```

As we can see in this code snippet, the data points we generated in the `update` function has three different series, `value1`, `value2`, and `value3`. This is why we need to specify their names to the `d3.stack` on line B. The only other customization we have done on stack layout is setting its `offset` to `d3.stackOffsetNone`. D3 stack layout supports a few different offset modes, which determine the stacking algorithm to be used; this is something that we will explore in this and the next recipe. In this case, we use the `zero` offset stacking, which generates a zero base-lined stacking algorithm, which is exactly what we want in this recipe. Next, on line B, we invoked the stack layout on the given data array, which generates the following layout data:

```
▼ [Array[51], Array[51], Array[51]]
  ▶ 0: Array[51]
  ▼ 1: Array[51]
    ▼ 0: Array[2]
        0: 8.562230180873533
        1: 17.34846703856522
      ▶ data: Object
        length: 2
      ▶ __proto__: Array[0]
    ▼ 1: Array[2]
        0: 7.715414689420507
        1: 14.038567272608105
      ▶ data: Object
        length: 2
      ▶ __proto__: Array[0]
  ▶ 2: Array[2]
  ▶ 3: Array[2]
```

Stacked data

As shown, the stack layout automatically calculates a y baseline 0 for each data in our three different data series as well as the y topline 1. Now, with this stacked dataset in hand, we can easily generate stacked lines:

```
function renderLines(series) {
    _line = d3.line()
        .x(function (d, i) {
            return _x(i); //<-C
        })
        .y(function (d) {
            return _y(d[1]); //<-D
        });

    var linePaths = _bodyG.selectAll("path.line")
```

```
            .data(series);

    linePaths.enter()
            .append("path")
        .merge(linePaths)
            .style("stroke", function (d, i) {
                return _colors(i);
            })
            .attr("class", "line")
        .transition()
            .attr("d", function (d) {
                return _line(d);
            });
}
```

A d3.line generator function was created with its index count value i directly mapped to the x (refer to line C) and its y topline value mapped to d[1] (refer to line D). This is all you need to do for line stacking. The rest of the renderLines function is essentially the same as in the basic area chart implementation. The area stacking logic is slightly different:

```
function renderAreas(series) {
    var area = d3.area()
            .x(function (d, i) {
                return _x(i); //<-E
            })
            .y0(function(d){return _y(d[0]);}) //<-F
            .y1(function (d) {
                return _y(d[1]); //<-G
            });

    var areaPaths = _bodyG.selectAll("path.area")
            .data(series);

    areaPaths.enter()
            .append("path")
        .merge(areaPaths)
            .style("fill", function (d, i) {
                return _colors(i);
            })
            .attr("class", "area")
        .transition()
            .attr("d", function (d) {
                return area(d);
            });
}
```

Similar to the line rendering logic when rendering area, the only place we need to change is in the d3.area generator setting. For areas, the x value is still directly mapped to the index count i (line E) with its y0 directly mapped with y baseline d[0] and finally again y1 is the y topline d[1] (line G).

As we saw so far, the D3 stack layout is nicely designed to be compatible with different D3 SVG generator functions. Hence, using it to generate the stacking effect is quite straightforward and convenient.

There's more...
Let's take a look at a couple of variations of the stacked area chart.

Expanded area chart
We have mentioned that d3.stack supports different offset modes. In addition to the d3.stackOffsetNone offset we saw so far, another very useful offset mode for the area chart is called d3.stackOffsetExpand. With the d3.stackOffsetExpand mode, stack layout will normalize different layers to fill the range of [0, 1]. If we change the offset mode in this recipe and the y axis domain to [0, 1], we will get the following expanded (normalized) area chart; this visualization is very useful when your audience care more about the relative proportion of each data series more than their absolution values:

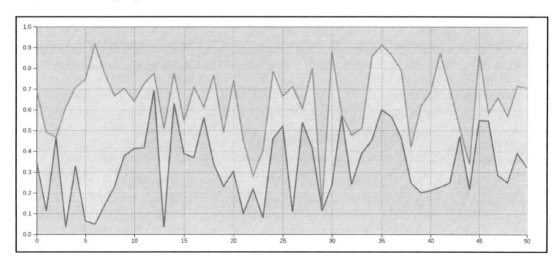

Expanded area chart

For the complete companion code example, visit
`https://github.com/NickQiZhu/d3-cookbook-v2/blob/master/src/chapter9/expanded-a`
`rea-chart.html`.

Streamgraph

Another interesting variation of a stacked area chart is called streamgraph. Streamgraph is a stacked area chart displayed around a central axis, creating a flowing and organic shape. Streamgraph was initially developed by Lee Byron and popularized by its use in a New York Times article on movie box office revenues in 2008. The D3 stack layout has built-in support for this kind of stacking algorithm, and therefore, changing a zero-based stacked area chart to streamgraph is simple. The key difference is that streamgraph uses `d3.stackOffsetWiggle` as its layout offset mode. Stream graph is a useful visualization when you want to highlight the change of data or its trend over time rather than its absolute values.

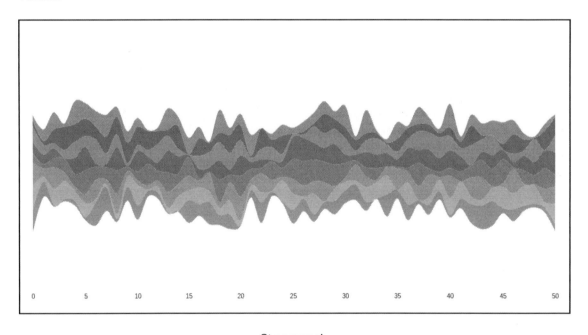

Streamgraph

For the complete companion code example, please visit
`https://github.com/NickQiZhu/d3-cookbook-v2/blob/master/src/chapter9/streamgrap`
`h.html`.

See also

- d3.stack function offers several additional functions to customize its behavior; for more information on stack layout, visit
  https://github.com/d3/d3/blob/master/API.md#stacks
- The Creating an area chart recipe in Chapter 8, *Chart Them Up*

Building a treemap

Treemaps were introduced by Ben Shneiderman in 1991. A treemap displays hierarchical tree-structured data as a set of recursively subdivided rectangles. In other words, it displays each branch of the tree as a large rectangle, which is then tiled with smaller rectangles representing subbranches. This process continuously repeats itself till it reaches the leaves of the tree.

 For more information on treemaps, refer to treemaps for space-constrained visualization of hierarchies by Ben Shneiderman at
http://www.cs.umd.edu/hcil/treemap-history.

Before we dive into the code example, let's first define what we mean by **hierarchical data**. So far, we discussed many types of visualizations capable of representing flat data structure usually stored in one or two dimensional arrays. In the rest of this chapter, we will switch our focus onto another common type of data structure in data visualization-the hierarchical data structure. Instead of using arrays, as in the case of flat data structures, hierarchical data is usually structured as a rooted tree. The following JSON file shows a typical hierarchical data you would expect in a data visualization project:

```
{
  "name": "flare",
  "children": [
  {
    "name": "analytics",
    "children": [
    {
      "name": "cluster",
      "children": [
        {"name": "AgglomerativeCluster", "size": 3938},
        {"name": "CommunityStructure", "size": 3812},
        {"name": "MergeEdge", "size": 743}
      ]
    },
```

```
    {
      "name": "graph",
      "children": [
        {"name": "BetweennessCentrality", "size": 3534},
        {"name": "LinkDistance", "size": 5731}
      ]
    },
    {
      "name": "optimization",
      "children": [
        {"name": "AspectRatioBanker", "size": 7074}
      ]
    }
  ]
  ]
}
```

This is a shortened version of a popular hierarchical dataset used in the D3 community for demonstration purposes. This data is extracted from a popular flash-based data visualization library-`flare`, created by the UC Berkeley Visualization Lab. It shows the size and hierarchical relationship among different packages within the library.

 Refer to the official Flare site for more information on the project at `http://flare.prefuse.org/`.

As we can see quite easily, this particular JSON feed is structured as a typical singly-linked rooted tree with each node having a single parent and multiple child nodes stored in the `children` array. This is a pretty common way to organize your hierarchical data in order to be consumed by the D3 hierarchical layouts. For the rest of this chapter, we will use this particular dataset for exploring different hierarchical data visualization techniques D3 has to offer.

Getting ready

Open your local copy of the following file in your web browser:
`https://github.com/NickQiZhu/d3-cookbook-v2/blob/master/src/chapter9/treemap.html`.

How to do it...

Now let's take a look at how we can use the d3.treemap function to visually represent this kind of hierarchical data:

```
function treemapChart() {
        var _chart = {};

        var _width = 1600, _height = 800,
                _colors = d3.scaleOrdinal(d3.schemeCategory20c),
                _svg,
                _nodes,
                _valueAccessor,
                _treemap,
                _bodyG;

        _chart.render = function () {
            if (!_svg) {
                _svg = d3.select("body").append("svg")
                        .attr("height", _height)
                        .attr("width", _width);
            }

            renderBody(_svg);
        };

        function renderBody(svg) {
            // explained in the 'how it works...' section
            ...

            renderCells(cells);
        }

        function renderCells(cells){
            // explained in the 'how it works...' section
            ...
        }

        // accessors omitted
        ...

        return _chart;
}

d3.json("flare.json", function (nodes) {
  var chart = treemapChart();
  chart.nodes(nodes).render();
});
```

This recipe generates the following `treemap` visualization:

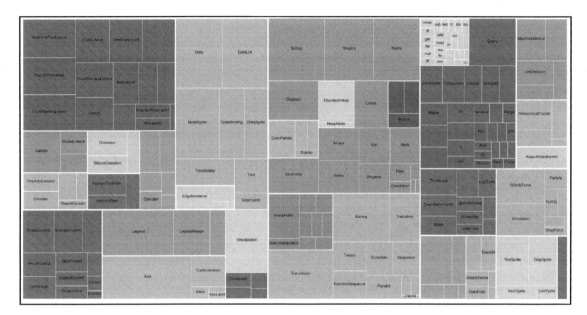

Treemap

How it works...

At this point, you might be surprised to know how little code is needed to implement a complex data visualization like this. This is because most of the heavy lifting is done by the `d3.treemap` and `d3.hierarchy` functions:

```
function renderBody(svg) {
        if (!_bodyG) {
            _bodyG = svg.append("g")
                    .attr("class", "body");

            _treemap = d3.treemap()  //<-A
                    .size([_width, _height])
                    .round(true)
                    .padding(1);
        }

        var root = d3.hierarchy(_nodes) // <-B
                .sum(_valueAccessor)
                .sort(function(a, b) {
                    return b.value - a.value;
```

```
        });

    _treemap(root); //<-C

    var cells = _bodyG.selectAll("g")
            .data(root.leaves()); // <-D

    renderCells(cells);
}
```

The d3.treemap layout was defined on line A with some basic custom settings:

- round(true): When rounding is on, the treemap layout will round to exact pixel boundaries. This is great when you want to avoid antialiasing artifacts in SVG.
- size([_width, _height]): It sets the layout boundary to the size of this SVG.
- padding(1): We set the padding to 1 so the blocks generated in tree map will have some white space padded in between.

The d3.hierarchy function was used in this recipe on line B to restructure the input data into a format that can be consumed by d3.treemap and other D3 hierarchical data functions:

- sum(_valueAccessor): One feature this recipe offers is the ability to switch the treemap value accessor on the fly. Value accessor is used by a d3.hierachy function to access value field on each node. In our case, it can be either one of the following functions:

```
function(d){ return d.size; } // visualize package size
function(d){ return 1; } // visualize package count
```

- sort(function(a, b) { return b.value - a.value; }): We have also instructed d3.hierarch to sort each node in the order of their value, effectively making the treemap arrange each block in the order of their size.

To apply the d3.hierarchy transformation on Flare JSON datafeed, we simply set the nodes on the d3.hierarchy function to the root node in our JSON tree (refer to line B). Then, we store the data after the d3.hierarchy transformation using the variable root. Here is how the data now looks like:

```
▼ Node {data: Object, height: 4, depth: 0, parent: null, children: Array[10]…} ▣
  ▶ children: Array[10]
  ▶ data: Object
    depth: 0
    height: 4
    parent: null
    value: 956129
    x0: 0
    x1: 1600
    y0: 0
    y1: 800
```

Treemap hierarchy transformation

As we can see here, after the transformation, each node now has its value calculated based on the sum of all their children's values and also the depth and size computed, as follows:

- depth: It indicates the depth of the node
- height: It indicates the height of the node in the tree
- value: It indicates the sum of all sub-tree values
- x0: It indicates the cell starting x coordinate
- y0: It indicates the cell starting y coordinate
- x1: It indicates the cell ending x coordinate
- y1: It indicates the cell ending y coordinate

After this transformation, now we can pass the root variable to the _treemap function on line C. Now, we are ready to generate the visualization. On line D, we generate cells using only the leaf nodes from the treemap:

```
var cells = _bodyG.selectAll("g")
                .data(root.leaves()); // <-D
```

This is because firstly d3.selection.data expects flat data array instead of hierarchical tree. Secondly, the tree map actually only render leaf nodes anyway; the sub-tree grouping is visualized using color. If we look at the visualization carefully, it is not hard to see this.

In `renderCells` function, a set of `svg:g` elements were created for the given nodes. The `renderCells` function is then responsible for creating rectangles and their labels:

```
function renderCells(cells) {
      var cellEnter = cells.enter().append("g")
            .attr("class", "cell")
            .attr("transform", function (d) {
                return "translate(" + d.x0 + ","
                                    + d.y0 + ")"; //<-E
            });

      renderRect(cellEnter, cells);

      renderText(cellEnter, cells);

      cells.exit().remove();
   }
```

Each rectangle is placed at its location `(x, y)` that's determined by the layout on line E:

```
function renderRect(cellEnter, cells) {
      cellEnter.append("rect");

      cellEnter.merge(cells)
            .transition()
            .attr("transform", function (d) {
                return "translate(" + d.x0 + "," + d.y0 + ")";
            })
            .select("rect")
            .attr("width", function (d) { //<-F
                return d.x1 - d.x0;
            })
            .attr("height", function (d) {
                return d.y1 - d.y0;
            })
            .style("fill", function (d) {
                return _colors(d.parent.data.name); //<-G
            });
   }
```

Then, in the `renderRect` function, we set its width and height to `d.x1 - d.x0` and `d.y1 - d.y0`, respectively on line F. On line G, we colored every cell using its parent's names, therefore making sure that all children belonging to the same parent are colored the same way. The next step is to render labels:

```
function renderText(cellEnter, cells) {
      cellEnter.append("text");
```

```
cellEnter.merge(cells)
        .select("text") //<-H
        .style("font-size", 11)
        .attr("x", function (d) {
            return (d.x1 - d.x0) / 2;
        })
        .attr("y", function (d) {
            return (d.y1 - d.y0) / 2;
        })
        .attr("text-anchor", "middle")
        .text(function (d) {
            return d.data.name;
        })
        .style("opacity", function (d) {
            d.w = this.getComputedTextLength();
            return d.w < (d.x1 - d.x0) ? 1 : 0; //<-I
        });
}
```

From line H onward, we created the label (svg:text) element for each rectangle and set its text to the node name. One aspect worth mentioning here is that in order to avoid displaying label for the cells that are smaller than the label itself, the opacity of label is set to 0 if the label is larger than the cell width (refer to line I).

Technique – auto-hiding label

What we have seen here on line I is a useful technique in visualization to implement auto-hiding labels. This technique can be considered generally in the following form:

```
.style("opacity", function (d) {
width = this.getComputedTextLength();
return d.dx > width ? 1 : 0;
```

See also

- This recipe is inspired by Mike Bostock's treemap layout example, which you can find at http://mbostock.github.io/d3/talk/20111018/treemap.html.

Building a tree

When working with hierarchical data structures, a tree (tree graph) is probably one of the most natural and common visualizations typically used to demonstrate structural dependencies between different data elements. Tree is an undirected graph in which any two nodes (vertices) are connected by one and only one simple path. In this recipe, we will learn how to implement a tree visualization using D3 tree layout.

Getting ready

Open your local copy of the following file in your web browser:

https://github.com/NickQiZhu/d3-cookbook-v2/blob/master/src/chapter9/tree.html.

How to do it...

Now let's see d3.tree in action:

```
function tree() {
    var _chart = {};

    var _width = 1600, _height = 1600,
            _margins = {top: 30, left: 120, right: 30, bottom: 30},
            _svg,
            _nodes,
            _i = 0,
            _duration = 300,
            _bodyG,
            _root;

    _chart.render = function () {
        if (!_svg) {
            _svg = d3.select("body").append("svg")
                    .attr("height", _height)
                    .attr("width", _width);
        }

        renderBody(_svg);
    };

    function renderBody(svg) {
        if (!_bodyG) {
            _bodyG = svg.append("g")
```

```
                              .attr("class", "body")
                              .attr("transform", function (d) {
                                  return "translate(" + _margins.left
                                          + "," + _margins.top + ")";
                              });
                    }

                    _root = d3.hierarchy(_nodes); // <-A

                    render(_root);
             }

             function render(root) {
                 var tree = d3.tree() // <-B
                              .size([
                                  (_height - _margins.top - _margins.bottom),
                                  (_width - _margins.left - _margins.right)
                              ]);

                 tree(root); // <-C

                 renderNodes(root); // <-D

                 renderLinks(root); // <-E
             }

        function renderNodes(nodes, source) {
          // will be explained in the 'how it works...' section
          ...
        }

        function renderLinks(nodes, source) {
          // will be explained in the 'how it works...' section
          ...
        }

        // accessors omitted
        ...

        return _chart;
    }
```

This recipe generates the following tree visualization:

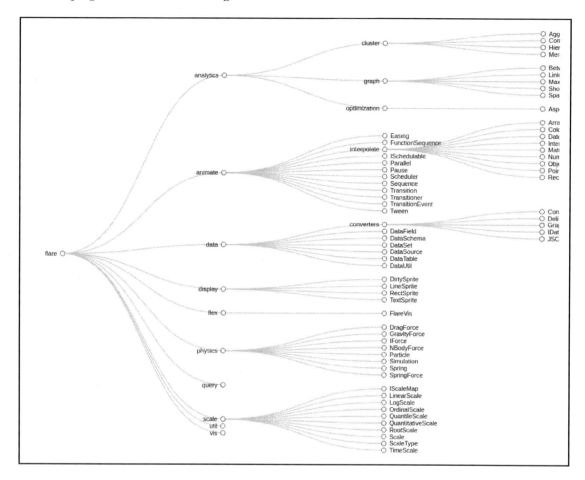

Tree

How it works...

As we have mentioned before, this recipe is built over the D3 tree layout. The `d3.tree` function is specifically designed to convert a hierarchical data structure into a visual layout data suitable for generating a tree graph. However, similar to the *Building a teemap* recipe, the `d3.tree` layout function only accepts structured D3 hierarchical data, meaning before we can use the layout function we need to use `d3.hierachy` to process and format our data first. Again, in this recipe, we are using the same Flare project package data we were using so far in this chapter. The raw JSON data source looks like this:

```
{
 "name": "flare",
 "children": [
  {
   "name": "analytics",
   "children": [
    {
     "name": "cluster",
     "children": [
      {"name": "AgglomerativeCluster", "size": 3938},
      {"name": "CommunityStructure", "size": 3812},
      {"name": "HierarchicalCluster", "size": 6714},
      {"name": "MergeEdge", "size": 743}
     ]
  },
  ...
  }
```

This data is loaded and passed into our chart object in the following function:

```
function flare() {
        d3.json("../../data/flare.json", function (nodes) {
            chart.nodes(nodes).render();
        });
}
```

Once the data is loaded, we first pass the loaded JSON data to d3.hierachy for processing (refer to line A):

```
_root = d3.hierarchy(_nodes); // <-A
```

In this recipe, this is all we need since `d3.tree` layout only cares about the hierarchical relationship between nodes, therefore, there is no need to sum or order the data as we did in the *Build a treemap* recipe. Once processed, we can now create tree layout using the following code:

```
var tree = d3.tree() // <-B
                .size([
                    (_height - _margins.top - _margins.bottom),
                    (_width - _margins.left - _margins.right)
                ]);
```

The only setting we provided here is the size of our visualization, which is the size of our SVG image minus the margins. The d3.tree function will then take care of the rest and calculate every node's position accordingly. To use the tree layout, you simply need to invoke the layout function on line C.

```
tree(root); // <-C
```

If you peek into the nodes layout data, it contains node data that will look like this:

```
▼ Node {data: Object, height: 4, depth: 0, parent: null, children: Array[10]...}
  ▶ children: Array[10]
  ▼ data: Object
    ▶ children: Array[10]
      name: "flare"
    ▶ __proto__: Object
    depth: 0
    height: 4
    id: 1
    parent: null
    x: 624.4383561643835
    y: 0
  ▶ __proto__: Object
```

Tree layout data

Tree nodes are rendered in the renderNode function as follows:

```
function renderNodes(root) {
        var nodes = root.descendants();

        var nodeElements = _bodyG.selectAll("g.node")
                .data(nodes, function (d) {
                        return d.id || (d.id = ++_i);
                    });

        var nodeEnter = nodeElements.enter().append("g")
                .attr("class", "node")
                .attr("transform", function (d) {   // <-F
                    return "translate(" + d.y
```

```
                              + "," + d.x + ")";
                    })
                    .on("click", function (d) { // <-G
                        toggle(d);
                        render(_root);
                    });

            nodeEnter.append("circle") // <-H
                    .attr("r", 4);

            var nodeUpdate = nodeEnter.merge(nodeElements)
                .transition().duration(_duration)
                .attr("transform", function (d) {
                    return "translate(" + d.y + "," + d.x + ")"; // <-I
                });

            nodeUpdate.select('circle')
                .style("fill", function (d) {
                  return d._children ? "lightsteelblue" : "#fff"; // <-J
                });

            var nodeExit = nodeElements.exit()
                    .transition().duration(_duration)
                    .attr("transform", function (d) {
                        return "translate(" + d.y
                                + "," + d.x + ")";
                    })
                    .remove();

            nodeExit.select("circle")
                    .attr("r", 1e-6)
                    .remove();

            renderLabels(nodeEnter, nodeUpdate, nodeExit);
    }
```

In this function, first we generate a set of `g.node` elements bound to `root.descendents()`:

```
    var nodes = root.descendants();
    var nodeElements = _bodyG.selectAll("g.node")
            .data(nodes, function (d) {
                return d.id || (d.id = ++_i);
            });
```

The `root.descendents` function returns all nodes in the hierarchical data. This is different from the `root.leaves` function we used in the *Build a treemap* recipe. The `root.leaves` function returns only the leaf nodes as a JavaScript array; however, with `d3.tree` layout, we not only care about the leaves but also any intermediary nodes in order to visualize the entire tree structure, and thus, we need to use `root.descendents` instead. At this point, we also assign an ID to each node using an index to obtain object constancy; refer to `Chapter 6`, *Transition with Style* for more information on object constancy in case this is a new concept to you;

```
var nodeEnter = nodeElements.enter().append("g")
        .attr("class", "node")
        .attr("transform", function (d) {   // <-F
            return "translate(" + d.y
                    + "," + d.x + ")";
        })
        .on("click", function (d) { // <-G
            toggle(d);
            render(_root);
        });
```

On line F, we created the nodes and moved them to the coordinates of (`d.y`, `d.x`) that the `d3.tree` layout has calculated for us. We switched `x` and `y` in this case since by default the `d3.tree` layout calculates coordinates in portrait mode while we want to render them in the landscape mode in this recipe. On line G, we also created `onClick` event handler to handle user mouse click on tree nodes. The `toggle` function consists of the following code:

```
function toggle(d) {
    if (d.children) {
        d._children = d.children;
        d.children = null;
    } else {
        d.children = d._children;
        d._children = null;
    }
}
```

This function effectively hides the children field on a given data node temporarily. Doing this essentially remove all children from that node in visualization and hence gives the users the sense of collapsing its subtree when they click on a node:

```
nodeEnter.append("circle") // <-H
        .attr("r", 4);

    var nodeUpdate = nodeEnter.merge(nodeElements)
            .transition().duration(_duration)
                .attr("transform", function (d) {
```

```
                        return "translate(" + d.y + "," + d.x + ")"; // <-I
                });

        nodeUpdate.select('circle')
                .style("fill", function (d) {
                        return d._children ? "lightsteelblue" : "#fff"; // <-J
                });
```

On line H, we created SVG circle element to represent each tree node, and again we position them at (d.y, d.x). Finally, on line J, we colored the node with different fill based on whether it is collapsed or open by checking the temporary _children file generated by the toggle function. The rest of the node and label rendering code are quite simple, so we will not cover them line by line here; refer to the source code on GitHub for more details.

The next important function in this recipe is the renderLinks function. This function draws all the links that connect all the tree nodes we just created:

```
function renderLinks(root) {
        var nodes = root.descendants().slice(1);

        var link = _bodyG.selectAll("path.link")
                .data(nodes, function (d) {
                        return d.id || (d.id = ++_i);
                });

        link.enter().insert("path", "g") // <-M
                .attr("class", "link")
                .merge(link)
                .transition().duration(_duration)
                .attr("d", function (d) {
                        return generateLinkPath(d, d.parent); // <-N
                });

        link.exit().remove();
}
```

First, for rendering links, we use root.descendants().slice(1) as its data instead of root.descendants(). This is because for n nodes there are n − 1 links since there is no link pointing to the root node in a tree. Once again, object constancy is used here to make our visualization more stable during re-rendering. Then, on line M, we created path elements to represent each link in our visualization. Now, the interesting part of this function lies in the generateLinkPath function on line N:

```
function generateLinkPath(target, source) {
        var path = d3.path();
        path.moveTo(target.y, target.x);
```

```
path.bezierCurveTo((target.y + source.y) / 2, target.x,
       (target.y + source.y) / 2, source.x, source.y, source.x);
   return path.toString();
}
```

In this function, we use the `d3.path` generator to generate a Bezier curve that connects the source and target nodes. You can probably see that the usage of the `d3.path` generator is almost like describing how the line should be drawn. In this case, we moved the starting point of such line to (`target.y`, `target.x`) and then draw a Bezier curve with the given control points from target to source, as shown in the following illustration:

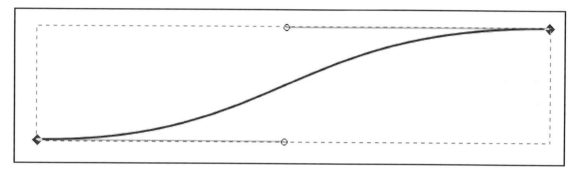

Bezier curve

Of course, if you are familiar with the SVG path commands, then you can generate the d formula without using the `d3.path` generator. In this case, we are essentially using M and C commands. However, the `d3.path` generator function is more readable and works well with both SVG and Canvas, hence, it yields more maintainable code in general. For more information on SVG path command, refer to https://www.w3.org/TR/SVG/paths.html#PathDataCubicBezierCommands .

At this point, we now have the entire tree graph visualized. As you can see with the help of the `d3.tree` layout, drawing this kind of complex visualization is relatively straightforward if not easy.

See also

- The `d3.tree` offers several functions that allow customization. For more details, check out its API documentation at https://github.com/d3/d3-hierarchy/blob/master/README.md#tree.

- The `d3.path` generator is capable of generating any arbitrary line on canvas and SVG; for more information, refer to its API document at `https://github.com/d3/d3-path/blob/master/README.md#path`.
- Refer to the *Animating multiple elements* recipe in `Chapter 6`, *Transition with Style*, for explanations on object constancy.
- This recipe is inspired by Mike Bostock's Tidy Tree example, which you can find at `http://bl.ocks.org/mbostock/4339184`.

Building an enclosure diagram

An enclosure diagram is an interesting visualization of hierarchical data structures that use the recursive circle packing algorithm. It uses containment (nesting) to represent hierarchy. Circles are created for each leaf node in a data tree, while its size is proportional to a particular quantitative dimension of each data element. In this recipe, you will learn how to implement this kind of visualization using the D3 pack layout.

Getting ready

Open your local copy of the following file in your web browser:

`https://github.com/NickQiZhu/d3-cookbook-v2/blob/master/src/chapter9/pack.html`

How to do it...

In this recipe, let's see how we can implement an enclosure diagram using `d3.pack`:

```
function pack() {
    var _chart = {};

    var _width = 1280, _height = 800,
            _svg,
            _valueAccessor,
            _nodes,
            _bodyG;

    _chart.render = function () {
        if (!_svg) {
            _svg = d3.select("body").append("svg")
                    .attr("height", _height)
                    .attr("width", _width);
```

```
            }

            renderBody(_svg);
        };

        function renderBody(svg) {
          if (!_bodyG) {
              _bodyG = svg.append("g")
                      .attr("class", "body");
          }

          var pack = d3.pack() // <-A
                  .size([_width, _height]);

          var root = d3.hierarchy(_nodes) // <-B
                          .sum(_valueAccessor)
                          .sort(function(a, b) {
                            return b.value - a.value;
                          });

          pack(root); // <-C

          renderCircles(root.descendants());

          renderLabels(root.descendants());
        }

    function renderCircles(nodes) {
      // will be explained in the 'how it works...' section
      ...
    }

    function renderLabels(nodes) {
      // omitted
      ...
    }

    // accessors omitted
    ...

    return _chart;
}
```

This recipe generates the following visualization:

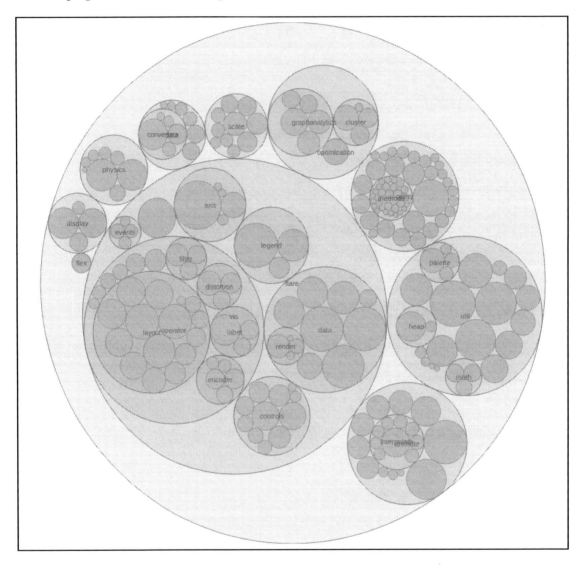

Enclosure diagram

How it works...

In this recipe, we continue to use hierarchical JSON data source that describes Flare project package relationship. For more information on the data source, refer to the *Build a treemap* recipe in this chapter. The JSON data structure looks like the following:

```
{
  "name": "flare",
  "children": [
    {
      "name": "analytics",
      "children": [
        {
          "name": "cluster",
          "children": [
            {"name": "AgglomerativeCluster", "size": 3938},
            {"name": "CommunityStructure", "size": 3812},
            {"name": "HierarchicalCluster", "size": 6714},
            {"name": "MergeEdge", "size": 743}
          ]
        },
        ...
      ]
    }
  ]
}
```

This data is loaded into the chart object in the `flare` function:

```
function flare() {
    d3.json("../../data/flare.json", function (nodes) {
        chart.nodes(nodes).valueAccessor(size).render();
    });
}
```

In this visualization, the first thing we need to take care of is to define our layout; in this case, we need to use the `d3.pack` layout:

```
var pack = d3.pack() // <-A
            .size([_width, _height]);
```

We set the size of our visualization on layout so it can calculate accordingly. After that, before we can pass our JSON data to the `d3.pack` layout once again, we need to first process it using the `d3.hierachy` function (refer to line B), which is a prerequisite for any D3 hierarchical visualization:

```
var root = d3.hierarchy(_nodes) // <-B
            .sum(_valueAccessor)
```

```
                    .sort(function(a, b) { return b.value - a.value; });
    pack(root); // <-C
```

In this case, we told `d3.hierarchy` function to sum up all values using the
`_valueAccessor` function, which takes `d.size` as the value by default. Additionally, we
also asked the `d3.hierachy` function to sort the nodes based on the values. Finally, we
then pass the processed data to the `pack` function on line C. The layout data after this
process now look like this:

```
▼ Node {data: Object, height: 4, depth: 0, parent: null, children: Array[10]…} ▨
  ▶ children: Array[10]
  ▼ data: Object
    ▶ children: Array[10]
      name: "flare"
    ▶ __proto__: Object
    depth: 0
    height: 4
    parent: null
    r: 400
    value: 956129
    x: 640
    y: 400
  ▶ __proto__: Object
```

Pack layout data

Circle rendering is done in the `renderCircle` function:

```
function renderCircles(nodes) { // <-C
    var circles = _bodyG.selectAll("circle")
            .data(nodes);
    circles.enter().append("circle")
            .merge(circles)
            .transition()
        .attr("class", function (d) {
            return d.children ? "parent" : "child";
        })
        .attr("cx", function (d) {return d.x;}) // <-D
        .attr("cy", function (d) {return d.y;})
        .attr("r", function (d) {return d.r;});
    circles.exit().transition()
            .attr("r", 0)
            .remove();
}
```

Then, we simply bind the layout data and create the `svg:circle` elements for each node. For update, we set `cx`, `cy`, and `radius` to the value that the pack layout has calculated for us for each circle (refer to line D). Finally, when removing the circle, we reduce the size of the circle down to zero first, before removing them to generate a more smooth transition. Label rendering in this recipe is pretty straightforward with some help from the auto-hiding technique we introduced in this chapter, so we will not cover the function in detail here.

See also

- The `d3.pack` function offers several functions that allow customization. For more details, please check out its API documentation at
  `https://github.com/d3/d3-hierarchy/blob/master/README.md#pack`.
- The *Building a treemap* recipe for auto label hiding technique.
- This recipe is inspired by Mike Bostock's pack layout example, which you can find at `http://bl.ocks.org/mbostock/ca5b03a33affa4160321`.

10
Interacting with Your Visualization

In this chapter, we will cover:

- Interacting with the mouse
- Interacting with a multi-touch device
- Implementing the zoom and pan behavior
- Implementing the drag behavior

Introduction

The ultimate goal of visualization design is to optimize applications so that they help us perform cognitive work more efficiently.

Ware C. (2012)

The goal of data visualization is to help the audience gain information from a large quantity of raw data quickly and efficiently through metaphor, mental model alignment, and cognitive magnification. So far, in this book, we have introduced various techniques to leverage D3 library by implementing many types of visualization. However, we haven't touched a crucial aspect of visualization: human interaction. Various research have concluded the unique value of human interaction in information visualization.

> *Visualization combined with computational steering allows faster analyses of more sophisticated scenarios...This case study adequately demonstrate that the interaction of a complex model with steering and interactive visualization can extend the applicability of the modelling beyond research*

Barrass I. & Leng J (2011)

In this chapter, we will focus on D3 human visualization interaction support; or, as mentioned earlier, you will learn how to add computational steering capability to your visualization.

Interacting with mouse events

The mouse is the most common and popular human-computer interaction control found on most desktop and laptop computers. Even today, with multi-touch devices rising to dominance, touch events are still commonly emulated with mouse events. In this recipe, we will learn how to handle standard mouse events in D3.

Getting ready

Open your local copy of the following file in your web browser:

```
https://github.com/NickQiZhu/d3-cookbook-v2/blob/master/src/chapter10/mouse.htm
l
```

How to do it...

In the following code example, we will explore techniques of registering and handling mouse events in D3. Although in this particular example we are handling only `click` and `mousemove`, the techniques utilized here can be applied easily to all other standard mouse events supported by modern browsers:

```
<script type="text/javascript">
    var r = 400;

    var svg = d3.select("body")
            .append("svg");

    var positionLabel = svg.append("text")
            .attr("x", 10)
            .attr("y", 30);

    svg.on("mousemove", function () { //<-A
        printPosition();
    });
    function printPosition() { //<-B
        var position = d3.mouse(svg.node()); //<-C
        positionLabel.text(position);
    }

    svg.on("click", function () { //<-D
        for (var i = 1; i < 5; ++i) {
            var position = d3.mouse(svg.node());

            var circle = svg.append("circle")
                    .attr("cx", position[0])
                    .attr("cy", position[1])
                    .attr("r", 0)
                    .style("stroke-width", 5 / (i))
                    .transition()
                        .delay(Math.pow(i, 2.5) * 50)
                        .duration(2000)
                        .ease(d3.easeQuadIn)
                    .attr("r", r)
                    .style("stroke-opacity", 0)
                    .on("end", function () {
                        d3.select(this).remove();
                    });
        }
    });
</script>
```

This recipe generates the following interactive visualization when you click on the SVG image:

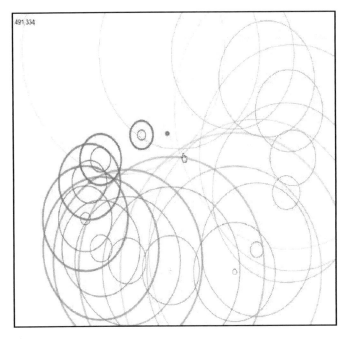

Mouse interaction

How it works...

In D3, to register an event listener, we need to invoke the on function on a particular selection. The given event listener will be attached to all the selected elements for the specified event (refer to line A). The following code in this recipe attaches a mousemove event listener, which displays the current mouse position (refer to line B):

```
svg.on("mousemove", function () { //<-A
    printPosition();
});
function printPosition() { //<-B
    var position = d3.mouse(svg.node()); //<-C
    positionLabel.text(position);
}
```

On line C, we used d3.mouse function to obtain the current mouse position relative to the given container element. This function returns a two-element array [x, y]. After this, we also registered an event listener for a mouse click event on line D using the same on function:

```
svg.on("click", function () { //<-D
        for (var i = 1; i < 5; ++i) {
            var position = d3.mouse(svg.node());

        var circle = svg.append("circle")
                .attr("cx", position[0])
                .attr("cy", position[1])
                .attr("r", 0)
                .style("stroke-width", 5 / (i)) // <-E
                .transition()
                    .delay(Math.pow(i, 2.5) * 50) // <-F
                    .duration(2000)
                    .ease('quad-in')
                .attr("r", r)
                .style("stroke-opacity", 0)
                .each("end", function () {
                    d3.select(this).remove(); // <-G
                });
        }
});
```

Once again, we retrieved the current mouse position using the d3.mouse function and then generated five concentric expanding circles to simulate the ripple effect. The ripple effect was simulated using geometrically increasing delay (refer to line F) with decreasing stroke-width (refer to line E). Finally, when the transition effect is over, the circles were removed using a transition end listener (refer to line G). If you are not familiar with this type of transition control, refer to Chapter 6, *Transition with Style*, for more details.

There's more...

Although we have only demonstrated how to listen on the click and mousemove events in this recipe, you can listen on any event that your browser supports through the on function. The following is a list of mouse events that are useful to know when building your interactive visualization:

- click: Dispatched when a user clicks on a mouse button
- dbclick: Dispatched when a mouse button is clicked twice

- `mousedown`: Dispatched when the mouse button is pressed
- `mouseenter`: Dispatched when the mouse button is moved onto the limits of an element or one of its descendent elements
- `mouseleave`: Dispatched when the mouse button is moved off the limits of an element and all of its descendent elements
- `mousemove`: Dispatched when the mouse button is moved over an element
- `mouseout`: Dispatched when the mouse button is moved off of the boundaries of an element
- `mouseover`: Dispatched when the mouse button is moved onto the limits of an element
- `mouseup`: Dispatched when a mouse button is released over an element

See also

- Refer to `Chapter 6`, *Transition with Style*, for more details on the ripple effect technique used in this recipe.
- Refer to W3C DOM Level 3 Events specification for a complete list of event types at `https://www.w3.org/TR/DOM-Level-3-Events/`.
- Refer to the `d3.mouse` API document for more details on mouse detection at `https://github.com/d3/d3-selection/blob/master/README.md#mouse`.

Interacting with a multi-touch device

Today, with the proliferation of multi-touch devices, any visualization that targets mass consumption needs to worry about its interact-ability not only through the traditional pointing device but also through multi-touches and gestures. In this recipe, we will explore touch support offered by D3 to see how it can be leveraged to generate some pretty interesting interaction with multi-touch-capable devices.

Getting ready

Open your local copy of the following file in your web browser:

```
https://github.com/NickQiZhu/d3-cookbook-v2/blob/master/src/chapter10/touch.html
.
```

How to do it...

In this recipe, we will generate a progress-circle around the user's touches, and once the progress is completed, a subsequent ripple effect will be triggered around the circle. However, if the user prematurely ends their touch, we shall stop the progress-circle without generating the ripples:

```javascript
<script type="text/javascript">
    var initR = 100,
        r = 400,
        thickness = 20;

    var svg = d3.select("body")
            .append("svg");

    d3.select("body") // <-A
            .on("touchstart", touch)
            .on("touchend", touch);

    function touch() {
        d3.event.preventDefault(); // <-B

        var arc = d3.arc()
                .outerRadius(initR)
                .innerRadius(initR - thickness);

        var g = svg.selectAll("g.touch") // <-C
                .data(d3.touches(svg.node()), function (d, i) {
                    return i;
                });

        g.enter()
            .append("g")
            .attr("class", "touch")
            .attr("transform", function (d) {
                return "translate(" + d[0] + "," + d[1] + ")";
            })
            .append("path")
                .attr("class", "arc")
```

```
                        .transition().duration(2000).ease(d3.easeLinear)
                        .attrTween("d", function (d) { // <-D
                            var interpolate = d3.interpolate(
                                    {startAngle: 0, endAngle: 0},
                                    {startAngle: 0, endAngle: 2 * Math.PI}
                                );
                            return function (t) {
                                return arc(interpolate(t));
                            };
                        })
                        .on("end", function (d) {
                            if (complete(d)) // <-E
                                ripples(d);
                            g.remove();
                        });

            g.exit().remove().each(function (d) {
                console.log("Animation stopped");
                d[2] = "stopped"; // <-F
            });
        }

    function complete(d) {
        console.log("Animation completed? " + (d.length < 3));
        return d.length < 3;
    }

    function ripples(position) {
        console.log("Producing ripple effect...");

        for (var i = 1; i < 5; ++i) {
            var circle = svg.append("circle")
                    .attr("cx", position[0])
                    .attr("cy", position[1])
                    .attr("r", initR - (thickness / 2))
                    .style("stroke-width", thickness / (i))
                .transition()
                    .delay(Math.pow(i, 2.5) * 50)
                    .duration(2000).ease(d3.easeQuadIn)
                    .attr("r", r)
                    .style("stroke-opacity", 0)
                    .on("end", function () {
                        d3.select(this).remove();
                    });
        }
    }
    }
</script>
```

This recipe generates the following interactive visualization on a touch-enabled device:

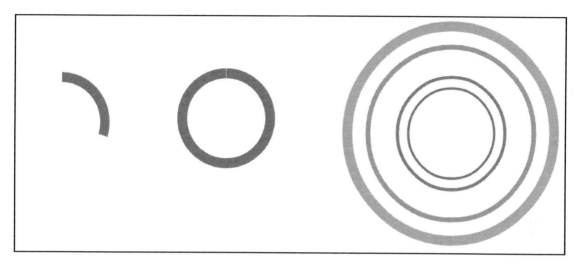

Touch Interaction

How it works...

Event listener for touch events are registered through D3 selection's on function similar to what we have done with mouse events in the previous recipe (refer to line A):

```
d3.select("body") // <-A
        .on("touchstart", touch)
        .on("touchend", touch);
```

One crucial difference here is that we have registered our touch event listener on the body element instead of the svg element since there are default touch behaviors defined with many OS and browsers and we would like to override it with our custom implementation. This is done through the following function call (refer to line B):

```
d3.event.preventDefault(); // <-B
```

Once the touch event is triggered, we will retrieve multiple touch point data using the d3.touches function, as illustrated by the following code snippet:

```
var g = svg.selectAll("g.touch") // <-C
            .data(d3.touches(svg.node()), function (d, i) {
                return i;
            });
```

Instead of returning a two-element array as the d3.mouse function does, d3.touches returns an array of two-element arrays since there could be multiple touch points for each touch event. Each touch position array has data structure that looks like the following:

```
▼ [Array[2]] ▥
    ▼ 0: Array[2]
        0: 216
        1: 142
        length: 2
      ▶ __proto__ : Array[0]
      length: 1
    ▶ __proto__ : Array[0]
```

Touch position array

Here, we also used array index in this recipe to establish object constancy. Once the touch data is bound to the selection, the progress circle was generated for each touch around the user's touch point:

```
g.enter()
    .append("g")
    .attr("class", "touch")
    .attr("transform", function (d) {
        return "translate(" + d[0] + "," + d[1] + ")";
    })
    .append("path")
        .attr("class", "arc")
        .transition().duration(2000).ease(d3.easeLinear)
        .attrTween("d", function (d) { // <-D
            var interpolate = d3.interpolate(
                    {startAngle: 0, endAngle: 0},
                    {startAngle: 0, endAngle: 2 * Math.PI}
                );
            return function (t) {
                return arc(interpolate(t));
            };
        })
        .on("end", function (d) {
            if (complete(d))
                ripples(d); // <-E
            g.remove();
        });
```

This is done through a standard arc transition with arc attribute tweening (refer to line D) as explained in `Chapter 7`, *Getting into Shape*. If the progress-circle has not yet been canceled by the user even though the transition is over, then a ripple effect similar to what we have done in the previous recipe is generated on line E. Since we have registered the same event listener `touch` function on both the `touchstart` and `touchend` events, we can use the following lines to remove progress-circle and also set a flag to indicate that this progress circle has stopped prematurely:

```
g.exit().remove().each(function (d) {
    console.log("Animation stopped");
    d[2] = "stopped"; // <-F
});
...
function complete(d) {
    console.log("Animation completed? " + (d.length < 3));
    return d.length < 3;
}
```

We need to set this stateful flag on d, which is the touch data array, since there is no way to cancel a transition once it starts; hence, even after you remove the progress-circle element from the DOM tree, the transition will still complete and trigger line E.

There's more...

We have demonstrated touch interaction through the `touchstart` and `touchend` events; however, you can use the same pattern to handle any other touch events supported by your browser. The following list contains the proposed touch event types recommended by W3C:

- `touchstart`: It is dispatched when the user places a touch point on the touch surface.
- `touchend`: It is dispatched when the user removes a touch point from the touch surface.
- `touchmove`: It is dispatched when the user moves a touch point along the touch surface.
- `touchcancel`: It is dispatched when a touch point is disrupted in an implementation-specific manner.

See also

- Refer to `Chapter 6`, *Transition with Style*, for more details on object constancy and the ripple effect technique used in this recipe.
- Refer to `Chapter 7`, *Getting into Shape*, for more details on the progress-circle attribute tween transition technique used in this recipe
- Refer to the W3C Touch Events proposed recommendation for a complete list of touch event types at `https://www.w3.org/TR/touch-events`
- Refer to the `d3.touch` API document for more details on multi-touch detection at `https://github.com/d3/d3-selection/blob/master/README.md#touches`

Implementing zoom and pan behavior

Zooming and panning are common and useful techniques in data visualization, which work particularly well with SVG-based visualization, since vector graphic does not suffer from pixilation as its bitmap counterpart would. Zooming is especially useful when you are dealing with large dataset when it is impractical or impossible to visualize the entire dataset, thus a zoom and drill-down approach needs to be employed. In this recipe, we will explore D3's built-in support for both zooming and panning.

Getting ready

Open your local copy of the following file in your web browser:

`https://github.com/NickQiZhu/d3-cookbook-v2/blob/master/src/chapter10/zoom.html`

How to do it...

In this recipe, we will implement geometric zooming and panning using D3 zoom support. Let's see how this is done in the following code:

```
<script type="text/javascript">
    var width = 600, height = 350, r = 50;

    var data = [
        [width / 2 - r, height / 2 - r],
        [width / 2 - r, height / 2 + r],
        [width / 2 + r, height / 2 - r],
        [width / 2 + r, height / 2 + r]
    ];

    var svg = d3.select("body").append("svg")
            .attr("style", "1px solid black")
            .attr("width", width)
            .attr("height", height)
            .call( // <-A
                    d3.zoom() // <-B
                    .scaleExtent([1, 10]) // <-C
                    .on("zoom", zoomHandler) // <-D
            )
            .append("g");

    svg.selectAll("circle")
            .data(data)
            .enter().append("circle")
            .attr("r", r)
            .attr("transform", function (d) {
                return "translate(" + d + ")";
            });

    function zoomHandler() {
        var transform = d3.event.transform;

        svg.attr("transform", "translate("
            + transform.x + "," + transform.y
            + ")scale(" + transform.k + ")");
    }
</script>
```

This recipe generates the following zooming and panning effect:

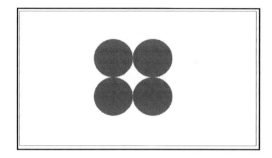

Original

The previous image show the original state of the visualization while the following one shows what happen when user zooms in either through scrolling the mouse wheel on a desktop or using multi-gesture on touch screen devices.

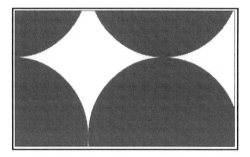

Zoom

The following screenshot shows what happen when user drags (pan) the image either with their mouse or finger.

Pan

How it works...

At this point, you might be surprised to see how little code is necessary to implement this fully functional zoom and pan effect with D3. If you have this recipe open in your browser, you will also notice zooming and panning reacts perfectly well to both mouse wheel and multi-touch gesture. Most of the heavy lifting is done by D3 library. What we have to do here is simply define what a zoom behavior is. Let's see how this is done in the code; firstly, we need to define zoom behavior on a SVG container:

```
var svg = d3.select("body").append("svg")
            .attr("style", "1px solid black")
            .attr("width", width)
            .attr("height", height)
            .call( // <-A
                d3.behavior.zoom() // <-B
                    .scaleExtent([1, 10]) // <-C
                    .on("zoom", zoomHandler) // <-D
            )
            .append("g");
```

As we can see on line A, a d3.zoom function was created (refer to line B) and invoked on the svg container. The d3.zoom will automatically create event listeners to handle the low-level zooming and panning gesture on the associated SVG container (in our case, the svg element itself). The low-level zoom gesture will then be translated to a high-level D3 zoom event. The default event listeners support both mouse and touch events. On line C, we define scaleExtent with a two-element array [1, 10] (a range). The scale extent defines how much zoom should be allowed (in our case, we allow 10X zoom). Finally, on line D, we register a custom zoom event handler to handle D3 zoom events. Now, let's take a look at what task this zoom event handler performs:

```
function zoomHandler() {
    var transform = d3.event.transform;

    svg.attr("transform", "translate("
        + transform.x + "," + transform.y
        + ")scale(" + transform.k + ")");
}
```

In the zoom function, we simply delegate the actual zooming and panning to SVG transformation. To further simplify this task, the D3 zoom event has also calculated the necessary translate and scale. So, all we need to do is embed them into a SVG transform attribute. Here are the properties contained in a zoom event:

- transform.x and transform.y: Current translation vector

- `transform.k`: A number representing the current scale

At this point, you might be asking what the point of having this `zoomHandler` function is. Why can't D3 take care of this step for us? The reason is that D3 zoom behavior is not designed specifically for SVG, but rather designed as a general zoom behavior support mechanism. Therefore, this zoom function implements the translation of general zoom and pan events into SVG-specific transformation.

There's more...

The zoom function is also capable of performing additional tasks other than the simple coordinate system transformation. For example, a common technique is to load additional data when the user issues a zoom gesture, hence implementing the drill-down capability in zoom function. A well-known example is a digital map; as you increase zoom level on a map, more data and details then can be loaded and illustrated.

See also

- Refer to `Chapter 2`, *Be Selective*, for more details on `d3.selection.call` function and selection manipulation
- Refer to W3C SVG coordinate system transformations specification for more information on how zoom and pan effect was achieved in SVG at `https://www.w3.org/TR/SVG/coords.html#EstablishingANewUserSpace`
- Refer to the `d3.zoom` API document for more details on D3 zoom support at `https://github.com/d3/d3-zoom/blob/master/README.md#zoom`

Implementing drag behavior

Another common behavior in interactive visualization that we will cover in this chapter is **dragging**. Drag is useful to provide capabilities in visualization that allow graphical rearrangement or even user input through force; we will discuss this in the next chapter. In this recipe, we will explore how the drag behavior is supported in D3.

Getting ready

Open your local copy of the following file in your web browser:

`https://github.com/NickQiZhu/d3-cookbook-v2/blob/master/src/chapter10/drag.html`

How to do it...

Here, we will produce four circles that can be dragged using D3 drag behavior support and additionally with SVG boundary detection while being dragging. Now, let's see how to implement this in code:

```
<script type="text/javascript">
    var width = 960, height = 500, r = 50;

    var data = [
        [width / 2 - r, height / 2 - r],
        [width / 2 - r, height / 2 + r],
        [width / 2 + r, height / 2 - r],
        [width / 2 + r, height / 2 + r]
    ];

    var svg = d3.select("body").append("svg")
            .attr("width", width)
            .attr("height", height)
            .append("g");

    var drag = d3.drag() // <-A
            .on("drag", move);

    svg.selectAll("circle")
            .data(data)
            .enter().append("circle")
            .attr("r", r)
            .attr("transform", function (d) {
                return "translate(" + d + ")";
            })
            .call(drag); // <-A

    function move(d) {
        var x = d3.event.x, // <-C
            y = d3.event.y;

        if(inBoundaries(x, y))
            d3.select(this)
                .attr("transform", function (d) { // <-D
```

```
                        return "translate(" + x + ", " + y + ")";
                });
        }
        function inBoundaries(x, y){
            return (x >= (0 + r) && x <= (width - r))
                && (y >= (0 + r) && y <= (height - r));
        }
    </script>
```

This recipe generates the drag behavior on the following four circles:

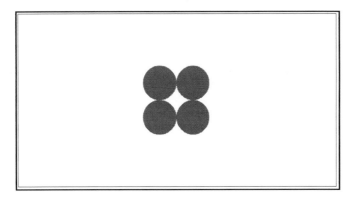

Original

The preceding image shows what this recipe renders in its original state while the following image show what happens when user drags each circle away from the center.

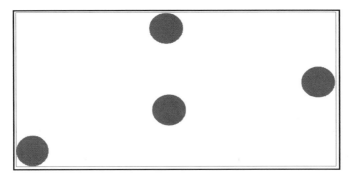

Dragged

How it works...

As we can see, drag support follows a pattern similar to the D3 zoom support. The main drag capability is provided by the d3.drag function (refer to line A). D3 drag behavior automatically creates appropriate low-level event listeners to handle drag gestures on the given element and then translates low-level events to high-level D3 drag events. Both mouse and touch events are supported, as follows:

```
var drag = d3.behavior.drag() // <-A
        .on("drag", move);
```

In this recipe, we are interested in the drag event, and it is handled by our move function. Similar to the zoom behavior, the D3 drag behavior support is event driven, therefore, it allows maximum flexibility in implementation, supporting not only SVG but also the HTML canvas. Once defined, the behavior can be attached to any element by calling it on a given selection:

```
svg.selectAll("circle")
        .data(data)
        .enter().append("circle")
        .attr("r", r)
        .attr("transform", function (d) {
            return "translate(" + d + ")";
        })
        .call(drag); // <-B
```

Next, in the move function, we simply use SVG transformation to move the dragged element to a proper location (refer to line D) based on the information conveyed by the drag event (refer to line C):

```
function move(d) {
    var x = d3.event.x, // <-C
        y = d3.event.y;

    if(inBoundaries(x, y))
        d3.select(this)
            .attr("transform", function (d) { // <-D
                return "translate(" + x + ", " + y + ")";
            });
}
```

One additional condition we check here is to calculate the SVG boundaries constraint so the user cannot drag an element outside of the SVG. This is achieved by the following check:

```
function inBoundaries(x, y){
    return (x >= (0 + r) && x <= (width - r))
```

```
                  && (y >= (0 + r) && y <= (height - r));
  }
```

There's more...

Other than the drag event, the D3 drag behavior also supports two other event types. The following list shows all supported drag event types and their attributes:

- `dragstart`: It is triggered when a drag gesture starts.
- `drag`: It is fired when the element is dragged. The `d3.event` object will contain *x* and *y* properties that represent the current absolute drag coordinates of the element. It will also contain the *dx* and *dy* properties representing the element's coordinates relative to its position at the beginning of the gesture.
- `dragend`: It is triggered when a drag gesture has finished.

See also

- Refer to `Chapter 2`, *Be Selective*, for more details on `d3.selection.call` function and selection manipulation.
- Refer to the `d3.behavior.drag` API document for more details on D3 drag support at `https://github.com/d3/d3-drag/blob/master/README.md#drag`.

11
Using Force

In this chapter, we will cover:

- Using gravity and charge
- Customizing velocity
- Setting the link constraint
- Using force to assist visualization
- Manipulating force
- Building a force-directed graph

Introduction

Use the force, Luke!

A master's words of wisdom to his apprentice

In this chapter, we will cover one of the most fascinating aspects of D3: force. Force simulation is one of the most awe-inspiring techniques that you can add to your visualization. Through a number of highly interactive and fully functional examples, we will help you explore not only the typical application of D3 force (for example, the force-directed graph), but also other essential aspects of force manipulation.

D3 force simulation support was created not as a separate capability, but rather as a kind of additional D3 layout. As we mentioned in `Chapter 9`, *Lay Them Out*, D3 layouts are nonvisual data-oriented layout management programs designed to be used with different visualization. Force simulation was originally created for the purpose of implementing a specific type of visualization called **force-directed graph**. Its implementation uses standard **velocity verlet integration** simulating physical forces on particles.

In other words, D3 implements a numeric method that is capable of loosely simulating the motion of particles using its velocity with stepped temporal functions. This kind of simulation, of course, was ideal in implementing particular visualization, such as a force-directed graph; however, you will also discover through recipes in this chapter that force simulation is capable of generating many other interesting visualization effects, thanks to its flexibility in custom force manipulation. The application of such techniques introduced in this chapter goes even beyond the data visualization realm and has practical applications in many other domains, for example, user interface design. Of course, in this chapter, we will also cover the classical application of force: the force-directed graph.

Using gravity and charge

In this recipe, we will introduce you to the first two fundamental forces: gravity and charge. As we have mentioned before, one objective of force layout's design is to loosely simulate the motion of particles, and one major feature of this simulation is the force of charge. Additionally, force simulation also implements pseudo gravity, or more accurately, a weak geometric constraint typically centered on the canvas that can be leveraged to keep your visualization from escaping the canvas. In the following example, you will learn how these two fundamental, sometimes opposing, forces can be leveraged to generate various effects with a particle system.

Getting ready

Open your local copy of the following file in your web browser:

```
https://github.com/NickQiZhu/d3-cookbook-v2/blob/master/src/chapter11/gravity-a
nd-charge.html.
```

How to do it...

In the following example, we will experiment with the force simulating gravity and charge settings so you can better understand different opposing forces involved and their interaction:

```javascript
<script type="text/javascript">
    var w = 1280, h = 800, r = 4.5,
        nodes = [],
        force = d3.forceSimulation()
                .velocityDecay(0.8)
                .alphaDecay(0)
                .force("collision",
                    d3.forceCollide(r + 0.5).strength(1));

    var svg = d3.select("body")
        .append("svg")
            .attr("width", w)
            .attr("height", h);

    force.on("tick", function () {
        svg.selectAll("circle")
            .attr("cx", function (d) {return d.x;})
            .attr("cy", function (d) {return d.y;});
    });

    svg.on("mousemove", function () {
        var point = d3.mouse(this),
            node = {x: point[0], y: point[1]}; // <-A

        svg.append("circle")
                .data([node])
            .attr("class", "node")
            .attr("cx", function (d) {return d.x;})
            .attr("cy", function (d) {return d.y;})
            .attr("r", 1e-6)
        .transition()
            .attr("r", r)
        .transition()
            .delay(7000)
            .attr("r", 1e-6)
            .on("end", function () {
                nodes.shift(); // <-B
                force.nodes(nodes);
            })
            .remove();
```

```
            nodes.push(node); // <-C
            force.nodes(nodes);
    });

    function noForce(){
        force.force("charge", null);
        force.force("x", null);
        force.force("y", null);
        force.restart();
    }

    function repulsion(){
        force.force("charge", d3.forceManyBody().strength(-10));
        force.force("x", null);
        force.force("y", null);
        force.restart();
    }

    function gravity(){
        force.force("charge", d3.forceManyBody().strength(1));
        force.force("x", null);
        force.force("y", null);
        force.restart();
    }

    function positioningWithGravity(){
        force.force("charge", d3.forceManyBody().strength(0.5));
        force.force("x", d3.forceX(w / 2));
        force.force("y", d3.forceY(h / 2));
        force.restart();
    }

    function positioningWithRepulsion(){
        force.force("charge", d3.forceManyBody().strength(-20));
        force.force("x", d3.forceX(w / 2));
        force.force("y", d3.forceY(h / 2));
        force.restart();
    }

</script>

<div class="control-group">
    <button onclick="noForce()">
        No Force
    </button>
    <button onclick="repulsion()">
        Repulsion
    </button>
```

```
        <button onclick="gravity()">
            Gravity
        </button>
        <button onclick="positioningWithGravity()">
            Positioning with Gravity
        </button>
        <button onclick="positioningWithRepulsion()">
            Positioning with Repulsion
        </button>
    </div>
```

This recipe generates a force-enabled particle system that is capable of operating in the modes shown in the following diagram:

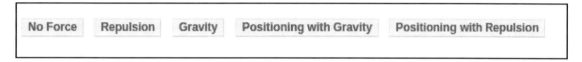

Force simulation modes

How it works...

Before we get our hands dirty with the preceding code example, let's first dig a little bit deeper into the fundamental concepts of alpha decay, velocity decay, charge, positioning, and collision so we can have an easier time understanding all the magic number settings we will use in this recipe.

Alpha decay

Alpha determines how hot a simulation is. A simulation starts with alpha of 1 and decay toward 0 by default over 300 iterations. Therefore, if you set the alpha decay to 0 meaning there is no decay therefore simulation will never stop. This is the setting we will use in this chapter in order to better demonstrate the effects. In real-life visualization, you will typically use some level of decay so that the simulation will cool down after a while, similar to how particles work in the real world.

Velocity decay

At each tick of the simulation particle, velocity is scaled down by a specified decay. Thus, a value of 1 corresponds to a frictionless environment, whereas a value of 0 freezes all particles in place since they lose their velocity immediately.

Charge

Charge is specified to simulate mutual n-body forces among the particles. A negative value will result in mutual node repulsion, whereas a positive value will result in a mutual node attraction.

Positioning

If X or Y positioning forces are specified, the simulation will push particles toward a desired position along a given dimension with configured strength. This is typically used as a global force that applies to all particles in the simulation.

Collision

The collision force treats particles as circles with a certain radius instead of size-less points. This will prevent particles from overlapping in a simulation.

Alright, now with the dry definition behind us, let's take a look at how these forces can be leveraged to generate interesting visual effects.

Setting up zero force layout

To set up zero force layout, we simply set up force layout with neither gravity nor charge. The force layout can be created using the `d3.forceSimulation` function:

```
var w = 1280, h = 800, r = 4.5,
        nodes = [],
        force = d3.forceSimulation()
                .velocityDecay(0.8)
                .alphaDecay(0)
                .force("collision",
                    d3.forceCollide(r + 0.5).strength(1));
```

First of all, we disable `alphaDecay` so that simulation will continue to run without cooling down while setting the `velocityDecay` to `0.8` to simulate the effect of friction. Next, we set the `collision` to slightly larger than the radius of the `svg:circle` element we will create later. With this setting in place, we then create additional nodes represented as `svg:circle` on SVG whenever the user moves the mouse:

```
svg.on("mousemove", function () {
        var point = d3.mouse(this),
            node = {x: point[0], y: point[1]}; // <-A
```

```
svg.append("circle")
        .data([node])
    .attr("class", "node")
    .attr("cx", function (d) {return d.x;})
    .attr("cy", function (d) {return d.y;})
    .attr("r", 1e-6)
.transition()
    .attr("r", r)
.transition()
    .delay(7000)
    .attr("r", 1e-6)
    .on("end", function () {
        nodes.shift(); // <-B
        force.nodes(nodes);
    })
    .remove();

nodes.push(node); // <-C
force.nodes(nodes);
});
```

Node object was created initially on line A with its coordinates set to the current mouse location. Like all other D3 layouts, force simulation is not aware and has no visual elements. Therefore, every node we create needs to be added to the layout's nodes array on line C and removed when the visual representation of these nodes was removed on line B. By default, force simulation starts automatically as soon as the simulation was created. With zero gravity and charge, this setting essentially lets us place a string of nodes with our mouse movement, as shown in the following screenshot:

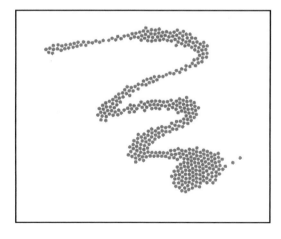

No Gravity or Charge

Setting up mutual repulsion

In the next mode, we will set the charge to a negative value without any global positioning force in order to generate a mutual repulsive force field:

```
function repulsion(){
    force.force("charge", d3.forceManyBody().strength(-10));
    force.force("x", null);
    force.force("y", null);
    force.restart();
}
```

These lines tell force layout to apply -10 charge on each node and update the node's {x, y} coordinate accordingly, based on the simulation result on each tick. However, only doing this is still not enough to move the particles on SVG since the layout has no knowledge of the visual elements. Next, we need to write some code to connect the data that is being manipulated by force layout to our graphical elements. Following is the code to do that:

```
force.on("tick", function () {
    svg.selectAll("circle")
        .attr("cx", function (d) {return d.x;})
        .attr("cy", function (d) {return d.y;});
});
```

Here, we register a `tick` event listener function that updates all circle elements to its new position based on the force layout's calculation. Tick listener is triggered on each tick of the simulation. At each tick, we set the `cx` and `cy` attributes to be the x and y values on d. This is because we have already bound the node object as datum to these circle elements. Therefore, they already contain the new coordinates calculated by force layout. This effectively establishes force layout's control over all the particles.

 Force simulation also sets values other than x and y on the node object, which we will cover and leverage in later recipes to implement force drag and custom forces. In this recipe, let's just focus on the simple force-based positioning first.

Other than `tick`, force layout also supports some other events:

- `tick`: Triggered on each tick of the simulation
- `end`: Triggered when a simulation ends

This force setting generates the following visual effect:

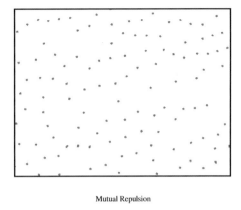

Mutual Repulsion

Setting up gravity

When we change the charge to a positive value, it generates mutual attraction or gravity among the particles:

```
function gravity(){
    force.force("charge", d3.forceManyBody().strength(1));
    force.force("x", null);
    force.force("y", null);
    force.restart();
}
```

This generates the following visual effect:

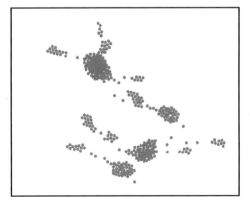

Gravity

Setting up positioning with gravity

When we turn on gravity with central positioning force, then it generates a somewhat similar effect as the mutual attraction; however, you can notice the strong gravitational pull as the mouse cursor moves away from the center:

```
function positioningWithGravity(){
    force.force("charge", d3.forceManyBody().strength(0.5));
    force.force("x", d3.forceX(w / 2));
    force.force("y", d3.forceY(h / 2));
    force.restart();
}
```

This recipe generates the following effect:

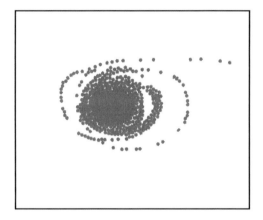

Positioning with gravity

Setting up positioning with repulsion

Finally, we can turn on both positioning and mutual repulsion. The result is an equilibrium of forces that keeps all particles somewhat stable, neither escaping nor colliding with each other:

```
function positioningWithRepulsion(){
    force.force("charge", d3.forceManyBody().strength(-20));
    force.force("x", d3.forceX(w / 2));
    force.force("y", d3.forceY(h / 2));
    force.restart();
}
```

Here is what this force equilibrium looks like:

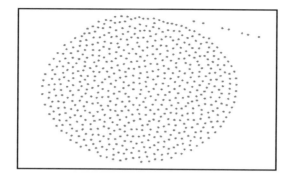

Positioning with repulsion

See also

- Refer to Velocity Verlet integration at
  `https://en.wikipedia.org/wiki/Verlet_integration`
- Refer to scalable, versatile, and simple constrained graph layout at
  `http://www.csse.monash.edu.au/~tdwyer/Dwyer2009FastConstraints.pdf`
- Refer to physical simulation at
  `http://www.gamasutra.com/resource_guide/20030121/jacobson_pfv.htm`
- The content of this chapter is inspired by Mike Bostock's brilliant talk on D3 Force that can be found at `http://mbostock.github.io/d3/talk/20110921/`
- Refer to `Chapter 10`, *Interacting with Your Visualization*, for more details on how to interact with the mouse in D3
- Refer to D3 Force Simulation API document for more details on force at
  `https://github.com/d3/d3-force`

Customizing velocity

In our previous recipe, we touched upon force simulation node object and its {x, y} attributes, which determine the location of a node on the layout. In this recipe, we will discuss another interesting aspect of physical motion simulation: velocity. The D3 force layout has a built-in support for velocity simulation, which relies on the {vx, vy} attributes on the node object. Let's see how this can be done in the example described in this recipe.

Getting ready

Open your local copy of the following file in your web browser:

`https://github.com/NickQiZhu/d3-cookbook-v2/blob/master/src/chapter11/velocity.html`.

How to do it...

In this recipe, we will modify the previous recipe by first disabling both positioning and charge and then giving newly added node some initial velocity. As a result, now, the faster you move the mouse higher the initial velocity and momentum will be for each node. Here is the code to do that:

```
<script type="text/javascript">
    var r = 4.5, nodes = [];

    var force = d3.forceSimulation()
                    .velocityDecay(0.1)
                    .alphaDecay(0)
                    .force("collision",
                        d3.forceCollide(r + 0.5).strength(1));

    var svg = d3.select("body").append("svg:svg");

    force.on("tick", function () {
        svg.selectAll("circle")
                .attr("cx", function (d) {return d.x;})
                .attr("cy", function (d) {return d.y;});
    });

    var previousPoint;

    svg.on("mousemove", function () {
        var point = d3.mouse(this),
            node = {
                x: point[0],
                y: point[1],
                vx: previousPoint?
                    point[0]-previousPoint[0]:point[0],
                vy: previousPoint?
                    point[1]-previousPoint[1]:point[1]
            };

        previousPoint = point;
```

```
svg.append("svg:circle")
            .data([node])
        .attr("class", "node")
        .attr("cx", function (d) {return d.x;})
        .attr("cy", function (d) {return d.y;})
        .attr("r", 1e-6)
    .transition()
        .attr("r", r)
    .transition()
    .delay(5000)
        .attr("r", 1e-6)
        .on("end", function () {
            nodes.shift();
            force.nodes(nodes);
        })
        .remove();

    nodes.push(node);
    force.nodes(nodes);
});
</script>
```

This recipe generates a particle system with initial directional velocity proportional to the user's mouse movement, as shown in the following screenshot:

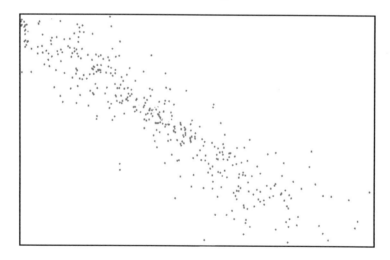

Velocity

How it works...

The overall structure of this recipe is pretty similar to the previous one. It also generates particles as the user moves the mouse around. Moreover, once the force simulation starts, the particle position is fully controlled by the force layout in its `tick` event listener function. However, in this recipe, we have turned off both positioning and charge so that we can focus more clearly on momentum alone. We left some friction so that the velocity decay, making simulation look more realistic. Here is our force layout configuration:

```
var force = d3.forceSimulation()
                    .velocityDecay(0.1)
                    .alphaDecay(0)
                    .force("collision",
                        d3.forceCollide(r + 0.5).strength(1));
```

The major difference in this recipe is that we keep track of not only the current mouse position, but also the previous mouse position. Additionally, whenever the user moves the mouse, we generate a node object containing the current location (`point[0]`, `point[1]`) and the previous location (`previousPoint.x`, `previousPoint.y`):

```
var previousPoint;

svg.on("mousemove", function () {
    var point = d3.mouse(this),
        node = {
            x: point[0],
            y: point[1],
            vx: previousPoint?
                point[0]-previousPoint[0]:point[0],
            vy: previousPoint?
                point[1]-previousPoint[1]:point[1]
        };

    previousPoint = point;
    ...
}
```

Since user's mouse location is sampled on fixed interval, the faster the user moves the mouse the further apart these two positions will be. This property and the directional information gained from these two positions are nicely translated automatically by force simulation into initial velocity for each particle we create as we have demonstrated in this recipe.

Besides the {x, y, vx, vy} attributes we have discussed so far, the force layout node object also supports some other useful attributes that we will list here for your reference:

- index: Zero-based index of the node within the node's array
- x: The x-coordinate of the current node position
- y: The y-coordinate of the current node position
- vx: The node's current x-velocity
- vy: The node's current y-velocity
- fx: The node's fixed x-position
- fy: The node's fixed y-position

 We will cover fx and fy and their usage in later recipe that involves dragging, which is one of the most common way to leverage fixed positioning of a node.

See also

- Refer to the *Interacting with mouse events* recipe in Chapter 10, *Interacting with Your Visualization*, for more details on how to interact with the mouse in D3.
- Refer to the D3 Force Simulation Nodes API for more details on node attributes at https://github.com/d3/d3-force#simulation_nodes.

Setting the link constraint

So far, we have covered some important aspects of the force layout, such as gravity, charge, friction, and velocity. In this recipe, we will discuss another critical functionality: links. As we have mentioned in the introduction section, D3 force simulation supports a scalable simple graph constraint, and in this recipe, we will demonstrate how link constraint can be leveraged in conjunction with other forces.

Getting ready

Open your local copy of the following file in your web browser:

`https://github.com/NickQiZhu/d3-cookbook-v2/blob/master/src/chapter11/link-cons`
`traint.html`.

How to do it...

In this recipe, whenever the user clicks on the mouse, we will generate a force-directed ring of particles constrained by links between nodes. Here is how it is implemented:

```
<script type="text/javascript">
    var w = 1280, h = 800,
            r = 4.5, nodes = [], links = [];

    var force = d3.forceSimulation()
                    .velocityDecay(0.8)
                    .alphaDecay(0)
                    .force("charge",
                        d3.forceManyBody()
                            .strength(-50).distanceMax(h / 4))
                    .force("collision",
                        d3.forceCollide(r + 0.5).strength(1));

    var duration = 10000;

    var svg = d3.select("body")
            .append("svg")
                .attr("width", w)
                .attr("height", h);

    force.on("tick", function () {
        svg.selectAll("circle")
            .attr("cx", function (d) {return boundX(d.x);})
            .attr("cy", function (d) {return boundY(d.y);});

        svg.selectAll("line")
            .attr("x1", function (d) {return boundX(d.source.x);})
            .attr("y1", function (d) {return boundY(d.source.y);})
            .attr("x2", function (d) {return boundX(d.target.x);})
            .attr("y2", function (d) {return boundY(d.target.y);}
        );
    });

    function boundX(x) {
```

```
        return x > (w - r) ? (w - r): (x > r ? x : r);
}

function boundY(y){
        return y > (h - r) ? (h - r) : (y > r ? y : r);
}

function offset() {
        return Math.random() * 100;
}

function createNodes(point) {
        var numberOfNodes = Math.round(Math.random() * 10);
        var newNodes = [];

        for (var i = 0; i < numberOfNodes; ++i) {
            newNodes.push({
                x: point[0] + offset(),
                y: point[1] + offset()
            });
        }

        newNodes.forEach(function(e){nodes.push(e)});

        return newNodes;
}

function createLinks(nodes) {
        var newLinks = [];
        for (var i = 0; i < nodes.length; ++i) { // <-A
            if(i == nodes.length - 1)
                newLinks.push(
                    {source: nodes[i], target: nodes[0]}
                );
            else
                newLinks.push(
                    {source: nodes[i], target: nodes[i + 1]}
                );
        }

        newLinks.forEach(function(e){links.push(e)});

        return newLinks;
}

svg.on("click", function () {
        var point = d3.mouse(this),
                newNodes = createNodes(point),
```

```
              newLinks = createLinks(newNodes);

    newNodes.forEach(function (node) {
        svg.append("circle")
                .data([node])
            .attr("class", "node")
            .attr("cx", function (d) {return d.x;})
            .attr("cy", function (d) {return d.y;})
            .attr("r", 1e-6)
                .call(d3.drag() // <-D
                        .on("start", dragStarted)
                        .on("drag", dragged)
                        .on("end", dragEnded))
                .transition()
            .attr("r", 7)
                .transition()
                .delay(duration)
            .attr("r", 1e-6)
            .on("end", function () {nodes.shift();})
            .remove();
    });

    newLinks.forEach(function (link) {
        svg.append("line") // <-B
                .data([link])
            .attr("class", "line")
            .attr("x1", function (d) {return d.source.x;})
            .attr("y1", function (d) {return d.source.y;})
            .attr("x2", function (d) {return d.target.x;})
            .attr("y2", function (d) {return d.target.y;})
                .transition()
                .delay(duration)
            .style("stroke-opacity", 1e-6)
            .on("end", function () {links.shift();})
            .remove();
    });

    force.nodes(nodes);
    force.force("link",
                    d3.forceLink(links)
                        .strength(1).distance(20)); // <-C
    force.restart();
});

function dragStarted(d) {
    d.fx = d.x; // <-E
    d.fy = d.y;
}
```

```
function dragged(d) {
    d.fx = d3.event.x; // <-F
    d.fy = d3.event.y;
}

function dragEnded(d) {
    d.fx = null; // <-G
    d.fy = null;
}
</script>
```

This recipe generates force-directed particle rings on a mouse click, as shown in the following screenshot:

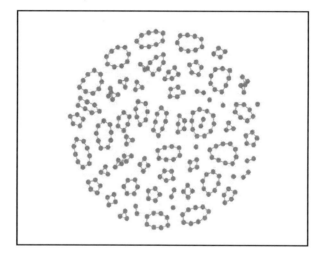

Force-directed particle rings

How it works...

Link constraint adds another useful dimension to force-assisted visualization. In this recipe, we set up our force layout with the following parameters:

```
var force = d3.forceSimulation()
                    .velocityDecay(0.8)
                    .alphaDecay(0)
                    .force("charge", d3.forceManyBody()
                            .strength(-50).distanceMax(h / 4))
                    .force("collision",
                            d3.forceCollide(r + 0.5).strength(1));
```

Besides collision, charge, and friction, this time we also bound charge-force interaction to 25% of the maximum height to simulate a more localized force interaction. When the user clicks on their mouse, a random number of nodes are being created and put under force simulation's control similar to what we have done in the previous recipes. The major addition in this recipe is the link creation, and its control logic is shown in the following code snippet:

```
function createLinks(nodes) {
    var newLinks = [];
    for (var i = 0; i < nodes.length; ++i) { // <-A
        if(i == nodes.length - 1)
            newLinks.push(
                {source: nodes[i], target: nodes[0]}
            );
        else
            newLinks.push(
                {source: nodes[i], target: nodes[i + 1]}
            );
    }

    newLinks.forEach(function(e){links.push(e)});

    return newLinks;
}
svg.on("click", function () {
    var point = d3.mouse(this),
            newNodes = createNodes(point),
            newLinks = createLinks(newNodes);

    newNodes.forEach(function (node) {
        svg.append("circle")
                .data([node])
            .attr("class", "node")
            .attr("cx", function (d) {return d.x;})
            .attr("cy", function (d) {return d.y;})
            .attr("r", 1e-6)
                .call(d3.drag() // <-D
                        .on("start", dragStarted)
                        .on("drag", dragged)
                        .on("end", dragEnded))
                .transition()
            .attr("r", 7)
                .transition()
                .delay(duration)
            .attr("r", 1e-6)
            .on("end", function () {nodes.shift();})
            .remove();
```

```
    });

    newLinks.forEach(function (link) {
        svg.append("line") // <-B
                .data([link])
            .attr("class", "line")
            .attr("x1", function (d) {return d.source.x;})
            .attr("y1", function (d) {return d.source.y;})
            .attr("x2", function (d) {return d.target.x;})
            .attr("y2", function (d) {return d.target.y;})
                .transition()
                .delay(duration)
            .style("stroke-opacity", 1e-6)
            .on("end", function () {links.shift();})
            .remove();
    });

    force.nodes(nodes);
    force.force("link",
                    d3.forceLink(links)
                        .strength(1).distance(20)); // <-C
    force.restart();
});
```

In the `createLinks` function, the n-1 link objects were created connecting a set of nodes into a ring (for loop on line A). Each link object must have two attributes specified as `source` and `target`, telling force layout which pair of nodes are connected by this link object. Once this is created, we decided to visualize the links in this recipe using a `svg:line` element (refer to line B). However, we will see in the next recipe that this does not have to always be the case. As a matter of fact, you can use pretty much anything; you can imagine to visualize (including hiding them, but retain the links for layout computation) the links as long as it makes sense for the audience of your visualization. After that, we also need to add link objects to force layout's links array (on line C) so that they can be put under force layout's control. The `d3.forceLink` function has two important parameters: link distance and link strength; both parameters are exclusively link related:

- `linkDistance`: This could be a constant or a function, which defaults to 20 pixels. Link distances are evaluated when the simulation is initialized, and it is implemented as weak geometric constraints. For each tick of the layout, the distance between each pair of linked nodes is computed and compared to the target distance. The links are then moved toward each other or away from each other.

- linkStength: This could be a constant or a function, which defaults to 1. Link strength sets the strength (rigidity) of links with a value in the range of [0, 1]. Link strength is also evaluated on initialization or reset.

Finally, we will need to translate the positioning data generated by force layout to SVG implementation in the tick function for each link similar to what we did for the nodes:

```
force.on("tick", function () {
    svg.selectAll("circle")
        .attr("cx", function (d) {return boundX(d.x);})
        .attr("cy", function (d) {return boundY(d.y);});

    svg.selectAll("line")
        .attr("x1", function (d) {return boundX(d.source.x);})
        .attr("y1", function (d) {return boundY(d.source.y);})
        .attr("x2", function (d) {return boundX(d.target.x);})
        .attr("y2", function (d) {return boundY(d.target.y);});
});
function boundX(x) {
    return x > (w - r) ? (w - r): (x > r ? x : r);
}

function boundY(y){
    return y > (h - r) ? (h - r) : (y > r ? y : r);
}
```

As we can see here, the D3 force simulation has again done most of the heavy lifting, therefore, all we need to do is simply set {x1, y1} and {x2, y2} on the svg:line elements in the tick function. Additionally, we have also used two bounded X and Y function to make sure that the particles and rings will not escape our SVG canvas area. For reference, the following screenshot is what a link object looks like after it is manipulated by force layout:

```
▼ Object {source: Object, target: Object} 
    index: 0
  ▼ source: Object
      index: 0
      vx: 0.053197899638804266
      vy: 0.15091190262538895
      x: 766.0524727424921
      y: 244.44706999976313
    ▶ __proto__: Object
  ▼ target: Object
      index: 1
      vx: -0.15306578127921316
      vy: 0.07160339431685558
      x: 752.5331134429422
      y: 281.48223643116603
    ▶ __proto__: Object
  ▶ __proto__: Object
```

Link object

One last additional technique worth mentioning in this recipe is the force-enabled dragging. All nodes generated by this recipe are "drag gable," and force simulation automatically re-computes all forces and constraints, as the user drags the rings around, as shown in the following screenshot:

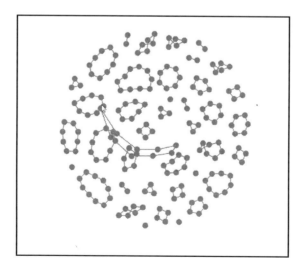

Dragging, with force simulation

This is accomplished by registering the d3.drag event handler as shown on line D in the following code snippet:

```
newNodes.forEach(function (node) {
    svg.append("circle")
            .data([node])
        .attr("class", "node")
        .attr("cx", function (d) {return d.x;})
        .attr("cy", function (d) {return d.y;})
        .attr("r", 1e-6)
            .call(d3.drag() // <-D
                    .on("start", dragStarted)
                    .on("drag", dragged)
                    .on("end", dragEnded))
            .transition()
        .attr("r", 7)
            .transition()
            .delay(duration)
        .attr("r", 1e-6)
        .on("end", function () {nodes.shift();})
        .remove();
});
```

The implementation of each of the drag event handler is pretty straightforward:

```
function dragStarted(d) {
    d.fx = d.x; // <-E
    d.fy = d.y;
}

function dragged(d) {
    d.fx = d3.event.x; // <-F
    d.fy = d3.event.y;
}

function dragEnded(d) {
    d.fx = null; // <-G
    d.fy = null;
}
```

When dragging happens on a particular node, we use fx and fy to fix that particular node to its initial position as shown on line E. While the dragging is happening, we continue to update the node's position with the user's mouse position, thus, moving the node while being dragged (refer to line F). Finally, when drag ends, we unfix the node position, thus, allowing force simulation to take control once again, as shown on line G. This is a very general drag support pattern you will see quite often with force-assisted visualization, including some later recipes in this chapter.

See also

- Scalable, versatile, and simple constrained graph layout:
  `http://www.csse.monash.edu.au/~tdwyer/Dwyer2009FastConstraints.pdf`
- For more information about force.links() function please refer to:
  `https://github.com/d3/d3-force#links`

Using force to assist visualization

So far, we learned to use force simulation visualizing particles and links similar to how you would use force in its classic application, the forced-directed graph. This kind of visualization is what force simulation was designed for in the first place. However, this is by no means the only way to utilize force in your visualization. In this recipe, we will explore techniques that I call force-assisted visualization. With this technique, you can add some randomness and arbitrariness into your visualization by leveraging force.

Getting ready

Open your local copy of the following file in your web browser:

`https://github.com/NickQiZhu/d3-cookbook-v2/blob/master/src/chapter11/arbitrary-visualization.html`.

How to do it...

In this recipe, we will generate bubbles on the user's mouse click. The bubbles are made of `svg:path` elements filled with gradient color. The `svg:path` elements are not strictly controlled by force layout though they are influenced by force, therefore, giving them the randomness required to simulate a bubble in real life:

```
<svg>
    <defs>
        <radialGradient id="gradient" cx="50%" cy="50%"
                                r="100%" fx="50%" fy="50%">
            <stop offset="0%"
              style="stop-color:blue;stop-opacity:0"/>
            <stop offset="100%"
              style="stop-color:rgb(255,255,255);stop-opacity:1"/>
        </radialGradient>
    </defs>
```

```
    </svg>

    <script type="text/javascript">
        var w = 1280, h = 800,
                    r = 4.5, nodes = [], links = [];

        var force = d3.forceSimulation()
                        .velocityDecay(0.8)
                        .alphaDecay(0)
                        .force("charge", d3.forceManyBody()
                                .strength(-50).distanceMax(h / 4))
                        .force("collision",
                                d3.forceCollide(r + 0.5).strength(1))
                        .force("position", d3.forceY(h / 2));

        var duration = 60000;

        var svg = d3.select("svg")
                    .attr("width", w)
                    .attr("height", h);


        var line = d3.line() // <-A
                .curve(d3.curveBasisClosed)
                .x(function(d){return d.x;})
                .y(function(d){return d.y;});

        force.on("tick", function () {
            svg.selectAll("path")
                .attr("d", line);
        });

        function offset() {
            return Math.random() * 100;
        }

        function createNodes(point) {
            var numberOfNodes = Math.round(Math.random() * 10);
            var newNodes = [];

            for (var i = 0; i < numberOfNodes; ++i) {
                newNodes.push({
                    x: point[0] + offset(),
                    y: point[1] + offset()
                });
            }

            newNodes.forEach(function(e){nodes.push(e)});
```

```
                return newNodes;
        }

    function createLinks(nodes) {
            var newLinks = [];
            for (var i = 0; i < nodes.length; ++i) {
                if(i == nodes.length - 1)
                    newLinks.push(
                        {source: nodes[i], target: nodes[0]}
                    );
                else
                    newLinks.push(
                        {source: nodes[i], target: nodes[i + 1]}
                    );
            }

            newLinks.forEach(function(e){links.push(e)});

            return newLinks;
        }

    svg.on("click", function () {
            var point = d3.mouse(this),
                    newNodes = createNodes(point),
                    newLinks = createLinks(newNodes);

            console.log(point);

            svg.append("path")
                    .data([newNodes])
                .attr("class", "bubble")
                .attr("fill", "url(#gradient)") // <-B
                .attr("d", function(d){return line(d);})
                    .transition().delay(duration) // <-C
                .attr("fill-opacity", 0)
                .attr("stroke-opacity", 0)
                .on("end", function(){d3.select(this).remove();});

            force.nodes(nodes);
            force.force("link",
                    d3.forceLink(links).strength(1).distance(20));
            force.restart();
        });
</script>
```

This recipe generates force-assisted bubbles on the user's mouse click as shown in the following screenshot:

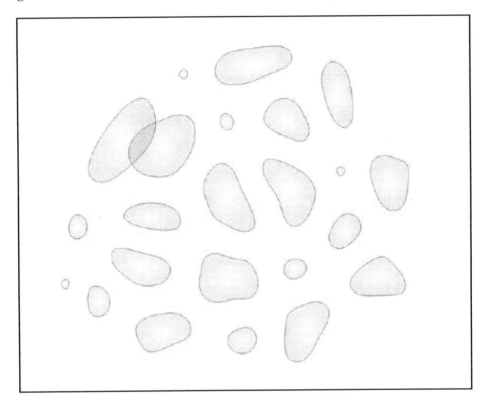

Force assisted bubbles

How it works...

This recipe is built on top of what we have done in the previous recipe, therefore, its overall approach is quite similar to the last recipe in which we created force-controlled particle rings on the user's mouse click. The major difference between this recipe and the last one is in this one we decided to use the d3.line generator to create the svg:path element that outlines our bubbles instead of using svg:circle and svg:line:

```
var line = d3.line() // <-A
            .curve(d3.curveBasisClosed)
            .x(function(d){return d.x;})
            .y(function(d){return d.y;});
    ...
```

```
svg.on("click", function () {
        var point = d3.mouse(this),
                newNodes = createNodes(point),
                newLinks = createLinks(newNodes);

        console.log(point);

        svg.append("path")
                .data([newNodes])
            .attr("class", "bubble")
            .attr("fill", "url(#gradient)") // <-B
            .attr("d", function(d){return line(d);}) // <-C
                .transition().delay(duration)
            .attr("fill-opacity", 0)
            .attr("stroke-opacity", 0)
            .on("end", function(){d3.select(this).remove();});

        force.nodes(nodes);
        force.force("link",
                d3.forceLink(links).strength(1).distance(20));
        force.restart();
    });
```

On line A, we created a line generator with a d3.curveBasisClosed curve mode since this gives us the smoothest outline for our bubble. Whenever a user clicks on the mouse, a svg:path element was created connecting all nodes (line C). Additionally, we also fill the bubble with our predefined gradient to give it a nice glow (line B). Finally, we also need to implement the force-based positioning in the tick function:

```
force.on("tick", function () {
    svg.selectAll("path")
        .attr("d", line);
});
```

In the tick function, we simply re-invoke the line generator function to update the d attribute for each path, thus, animating the bubbles using force layout computation.

See also

- Refer to SVG Gradients and Patterns at
  https://www.w3.org/TR/SVG/pservers.html.
- Refer to the *Using line generator* recipe in Chapter 7, *Getting into Shape*, for more information on D3 line generator.

Manipulating force

So far, we have explored many interesting aspects and applications of D3 force; however, in all of these prior recipes, we simply applied force layout's computation (gravity, charge, friction, collision, and velocity) directly to our visualization. In this recipe, we will go one step further to implement custom force manipulation, hence creating our own type of force.

In this recipe, we will first generate five sets of colored particles then assign corresponding colors and categorical force pull to user's touch, hence pulling only the particles that match the color. Since this recipe is a bit complex, I will give an example here: if I touch the visualization with my first finger, it will generate a blue circle and pull all blue particles to that circle, whereas my second touch will generate an orange circle and will only pull the orange particles. This type of force manipulation is commonly referred to as categorical multi-foci.

Getting ready

Open your local copy of the following file in your web browser:

```
https://github.com/NickQiZhu/d3-cookbook-v2/blob/master/src/chapter11/multi-foc
i.html.
```

How to do it...

Here is how you can achieve this in code:

```
<script type="text/javascript">
    var svg = d3.select("body").append("svg"),
            colors = d3.scaleOrdinal(d3.schemeCategory20c),
            r = 4.5,
            w = 1290,
            h = 800;

    svg.attr("width", w).attr("height", h);

    var force = d3.forceSimulation()
                    .velocityDecay(0.8)
                    .alphaDecay(0)
                    .force("charge",
                        d3.forceManyBody().strength(-30))
                    .force("x", d3.forceX(w / 2))
                    .force("y", d3.forceY(h / 2))
                    .force("collision",
```

```
                    d3.forceCollide(r + 0.5).strength(1));

var nodes = [], centers = [];

for (var i = 0; i < 5; ++i) {
    for (var j = 0; j < 50; ++j) {
        nodes.push({
            x: w / 2 + offset(),
            y: h / 2 + offset(),
            color: colors(i), // <-A
            type: i // <-B
        });
    }
}

force.nodes(nodes);

function offset() {
    return Math.random() * 100;
}

function boundX(x) {
    return x > (w - r) ? (w - r): (x > r ? x : r);
}

function boundY(y){
    return y > (h - r) ? (h - r) : (y > r ? y : r);
}

svg.selectAll("circle")
        .data(nodes).enter()
    .append("circle")
    .attr("class", "node")
    .attr("cx", function (d) {return d.x;})
    .attr("cy", function (d) {return d.y;})
    .attr("fill", function(d){return d.color;})
    .attr("r", 1e-6)
        .transition()
    .attr("r", r);

force.on("tick", function() {
    var k = 0.1;
    nodes.forEach(function(node) {
        var center = centers[node.type];
        if(center){
            node.x += (center[0] - node.x) * k;
            node.y += (center[1] - node.y) * k;
        }
```

```
        });

    svg.selectAll("circle")
        .attr("cx", function (d) {return boundX(d.x);})
        .attr("cy", function (d) {return boundY(d.y);});
});

d3.select("body")
    .on("touchstart", touch)
    .on("touchend", touch);

function touch() {
    d3.event.preventDefault();

    centers = d3.touches(svg.node());

    console.log(centers);

    var g = svg.selectAll("g.touch")
            .data(centers, function (d) {
                return d.identifier;
            });

    g.enter()
        .append("g")
        .attr("class", "touch")
        .attr("transform", function (d) {
            return "translate(" + d[0] + "," + d[1] + ")";
        })
        .append("circle")
            .attr("class", "touch")
            .attr("fill",
                    function(d){return colors(d.identifier);})
                .transition()
            .attr("r", 50);

    g.exit().remove();
    }
</script>
```

This recipe generates multi-categorical foci on touch, as shown in the following screenshot:

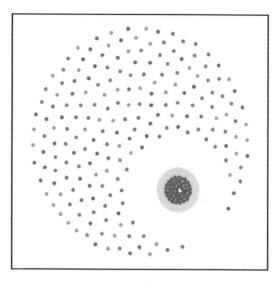

Multi-categorical foci on touch

How it works...

The first step of this recipe is to create colored particles and standard force equilibrium between positioning and repulsion. All node objects contain separate color and type ID attributes (line A and B), so they can be easily identified later. On line C, we let force simulation manage all the positioning of these particles as we have done in previous recipes:

```
var force = d3.forceSimulation()
                .velocityDecay(0.8)
                .alphaDecay(0)
                .force("charge",
                    d3.forceManyBody().strength(-30))
                .force("x", d3.forceX(w / 2))
                .force("y", d3.forceY(h / 2))
                .force("collision",
                    d3.forceCollide(r + 0.5).strength(1));

    var nodes = [], centers = [];

    for (var i = 0; i < 5; ++i) {
        for (var j = 0; j < 50; ++j) {
            nodes.push({
                x: w / 2 + offset(),
                y: h / 2 + offset(),
```

```
                    color: colors(i), // <-A
                    type: i // <-B
            });
        }
    }

    force.nodes(nodes); // <-C
```

Next, we will need to create a large `svg:circle` element on user touch to represent the touch point:

```
function touch() {
        d3.event.preventDefault();

        centers = d3.touches(svg.node());

        var g = svg.selectAll("g.touch")
                .data(centers, function (d) {
                    return d.identifier;
                });

        g.enter()
            .append("g")
            .attr("class", "touch")
            .attr("transform", function (d) {
                return "translate(" + d[0] + "," + d[1] + ")";
            })
            .append("circle")
                .attr("class", "touch")
                .attr("fill",
                    function(d){return colors(d.identifier);})
                    .transition()
                .attr("r", 50);

        g.exit().remove();
    }
```

This is the pretty standard multi-touch drawing that we saw in *Interacting with a multi-touch device* recipe in `Chapter 10`, *Interacting with Your Visualization*. Once the touch point is identified, all the custom force magic are implemented in the `tick` function. Now, let's take a look at the `tick` function:

```
force.on("tick", function() {
    var k = 0.1;
    nodes.forEach(function(node) {
        var center = centers[node.type]; // <-C
        if(center){
            node.x += (center[0] - node.x) * k; // <-D
            node.y += (center[1] - node.y) * k; // <-E
        }
    });

    svg.selectAll("circle") // <-F
        .attr("cx", function (d) {return boundX(d.x);})
        .attr("cy", function (d) {return boundY(d.y);});
});
```

In this tick function, we have the familiar part, on line F, where we let force simulation to control the position of all particles on the canvas; however, we have also introduced a custom force. On line C, we looped through all nodes to identify the nodes associated with a given center that represents user's touch. Once we detect the touch center, we started to move the particle closer to the center one tick at a time (line D and E) using the k coefficient. The larger the k the faster the particles will converge around a touch point.

See also

- Refer to the *Interacting with a multi-touch device* recipe in `Chapter 10`, *Interacting with your Visualization*, for more information on D3 multi-touch support.

Building a force-directed graph

Finally, we will show how to implement a force-directed graph, the classic application of D3 force. However, we believe with all the techniques and knowledge you have gained so far from this chapter, implementing force-directed graph should feel quite straightforward.

Getting ready

Open your local copy of the following file in your web browser:

https://github.com/NickQiZhu/d3-cookbook-v2/blob/master/src/chapter11/force-dir
ected-graph.html.

How to do it...

In this recipe, we will visualize the flare dataset as a force-directed tree (tree is a special type of graph):

```
<script type="text/javascript">
    var w = 1280,
            h = 800,
            r = 4.5,
            colors = d3.scaleOrdinal(d3.schemeCategory20c);

    var force = d3.forceSimulation()
            .velocityDecay(0.8)
            .alphaDecay(0)
            .force("charge", d3.forceManyBody())
            .force("x", d3.forceX(w / 2))
            .force("y", d3.forceY(h / 2));

    var svg = d3.select("body").append("svg")
            .attr("width", w)
            .attr("height", h);

    d3.json("../../data/flare.json", function (data) {
        var root = d3.hierarchy(data);
        var nodes = root.descendants();
        var links = root.links();

        force.nodes(nodes);
        force.force("link",
            d3.forceLink(links).strength(1).distance(20));

        var link = svg.selectAll("line")
            .data(links)
            .enter().insert("line")
                .style("stroke", "#999")
                .style("stroke-width", "1px");

        var nodeElements = svg.selectAll("circle.node")
            .data(nodes)
```

```
        .enter().append("circle")
          .attr("r", r)
          .style("fill", function(d) {
                return colors(d.parent && d.parent.data.name);
          })
          .style("stroke", "#000")
          .call(d3.drag()
                  .on("start", dragStarted)
                  .on("drag", dragged)
                  .on("end", dragEnded));

      force.on("tick", function(e) {
        link.attr("x1", function(d) { return d.source.x; })
            .attr("y1", function(d) { return d.source.y; })
            .attr("x2", function(d) { return d.target.x; })
            .attr("y2", function(d) { return d.target.y; });

        nodeElements.attr("cx", function(d) { return d.x; })
            .attr("cy", function(d) { return d.y; });
      });
    });

    function dragStarted(d) {
        d.fx = d.x;
        d.fy = d.y;
    }

    function dragged(d) {
        d.fx = d3.event.x;
        d.fy = d3.event.y;
    }

    function dragEnded(d) {
        d.fx = null;
        d.fy = null;
    }
</script>
```

This recipe visualizes the hierarchical flare dataset as a force-directed tree:

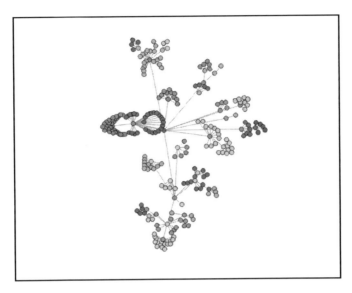

Force-directed graph (tree)

How it works...

As we can already see, this recipe is pretty short, and a quarter of the code was actually devoted to drag support. This is due to the fact that force-directed graph is what force simulation was designed for in the first place. Thus, there is really not much to do other than simply applying the force with correct data structure. First, we process the hierarchical dataset using the standard d3.hierarchy (line A) since this is how we can retrieve the nodes and links data structure d3.force expects:

```
d3.json("../../data/flare.json", function (data) {
        var root = d3.hierarchy(data); // <-A
        var nodes = root.descendants(); // <-B
        var links = root.links(); // <-C
        force.nodes(nodes); // <-D
        force.force("link", // <-E
                d3.forceLink(links).strength(1).distance(20));
        ...
}
```

On line B, we leverage the d3.hierarchy.descendants function to retrieve all nodes contained in the tree and the links among nodes on line C using the d3.hierachy.links function. These are the data structure d3.force expects; once we have them, they can be directly passed to simulation on line D and E. The rest of the recipe is very similar to the *Setting the link constraint* recipe in this chapter. We created the svg:link element to represent links and svg:circle elements to represent the nodes in the graph:

```
var link = svg.selectAll("line")
    .data(links)
  .enter().insert("line")
    .style("stroke", "#999")
    .style("stroke-width", "1px");

var nodeElements = svg.selectAll("circle.node")
    .data(nodes)
  .enter().append("circle")
    .attr("r", r)
    .style("fill", function(d) { // <-F
        return colors(d.parent && d.parent.data.name);
    })
    .style("stroke", "#000")
    .call(d3.drag() // <-G
            .on("start", dragStarted)
            .on("drag", dragged)
            .on("end", dragEnded));
```

The only parts worth mentioning here is that we colored the node using its parent's name on line F, so all siblings will be colored consistently, and on line G, we used the common drag support pattern mentioned in the *Setting the link constraint* recipe to allow dragging with this graph. Finally, we let force simulation to control both nodes and links positioning completely in the tick function:

```
force.on("tick", function(e) {
  link.attr("x1", function(d) { return d.source.x; })
      .attr("y1", function(d) { return d.source.y; })
      .attr("x2", function(d) { return d.target.x; })
      .attr("y2", function(d) { return d.target.y; });

  nodeElements.attr("cx", function(d) { return d.x; })
      .attr("cy", function(d) { return d.y; });
});
```

See also

- Refer to the *Building a tree* recipe in `Chapter 9`, *Lay Them Out*, for more information on D3 tree layout.
- For more information on force-directed graphs, visit `https://en.wikipedia.org/wiki/Force-directed_graph_drawing`.

12
Knowing Your Map

In this chapter we will cover:

- Projecting the US map
- Projecting the world map
- Building a choropleth map

Introduction

The ability to project and correlate data points to geographic regions is crucial in many types of visualizations. Geographic visualization is a complex topic with many competing standards emerging and maturing for today's web technology. D3 provides a few different ways to visualize geographic and cartographic data. In this chapter, we will introduce basic D3 cartographic visualization techniques and how to implement a fully-functional choropleth map (a special purpose colored map) in D3.

Projecting the US map

In this recipe we are going to start with projecting the US map using D3 GEO API, while also getting familiar with a few different JSON data formats for describing geographic data. Let's first take a look at how geographic data are typically presented and consumed in JavaScript.

GeoJSON

The first standard JavaScript geographic data format we are going to touch upon is called **GeoJSON**. GeoJSON format was originally written and maintained by an Internet working group of developers. Later it was standardized by the **Internet Engineering Task Force (IETF)** with RFC 7946 and published in August 2016.

> *GeoJSON is a format for encoding a variety of geographic data structures. GeoJSON supports the following geometry types: Point, LineString, Polygon, MultiPoint, MultiLineString, and MultiPolygon. Geometric objects with additional properties are Feature objects. Sets of features are contained by FeatureCollection objects.*

> *Source:* http://www.geojson.org/

GeoJSON format is a very popular standard for encoding GIS information and is supported by numerous open source as well as commercial software. GeoJSON format uses latitude and longitude points as its coordinates; therefore, it requires any software, including D3, to find the proper projection, scale and translation method in order to visualize its data. The following GeoJSON data describes the state of Alabama in feature coordinates:

```
{
  "type":"FeatureCollection",
  "features":[{
    "type":"Feature",
    "id":"01",
    "properties":{"name":"AL"},
    "geometry":{
      "type":"Polygon",
      "coordinates":[[
        [-87.359296,35.00118],
        [-85.606675,34.984749],
        [-85.431413,34.124869],
        [-85.184951,32.859696],

        ...
        [-88.202745,34.995703],
        [-87.359296,35.00118]
      ]]
    }
  }]
}
```

GeoJSON is currently the de facto GIS information standard for JavaScript project and is well supported by D3; however, before we jump right into D3 geographic visualization using this data format, we want to also introduce you to another emerging technology closely related to GeoJSON.

TopoJSON

TopoJSON is an extension of GeoJSON that encodes topology. Rather than representing geometries discretely, geometries in TopoJSON files are stitched together from shared line segments called arcs. This technique is similar to Matt Bloch's MapShaper and the Arc/Info Export format, .e00.

TopoJSON Wiki `https://github.com/topojson/topojson`

TopoJSON was created by D3's author *Mike Bostock* originally and designed to overcome some of the drawbacks in GeoJSON while providing a similar feature set when describing geographic information. In most cases concerning cartographic visualization TopoJSON can be a drop-in replacement for GeoJSON with much smaller footprint and better performance. Therefore, in this chapter, we will use TopoJSON instead of GeoJSON. Nevertheless, all techniques discussed in this chapter will work perfectly fine with GeoJSON as well. We will not list TopoJSON example here since its arcs-based format is not very human readable. However, you can easily convert your **shapefiles** (popular open source geographic vector format file) into TopoJSON using ogr2ogr command line tool provided by GDAL (`http://www.gdal.org/ogr2ogr.html`).

Now equipped with this background information let's see how we can make a map in D3.

Getting ready

Open your local copy of the following file in your web browser hosted on your local HTTP server:

`https://github.com/NickQiZhu/d3-cookbook-v2/blob/master/src/chapter12/usa.html`

How to do it...

In this recipe we will load US TopoJSON data and render them using D3 Geo API. Here is the code sample:

```
<script type="text/javascript">
    var width = 960,
            height = 500;

    var projection = d3.geoAlbersUsa();

    var path = d3.geoPath()
```

```
                    .projection(projection);

        var svg = d3.select("body").append("svg")
                .attr("width", width)
                .attr("height", height);

        var g = svg.append('g')
                .call(d3.zoom()
                        .scaleExtent([1, 10])
                        .on("zoom", zoomHandler));


        d3.json("../../data/us.json", function (error, us) { // <- A
            g.insert("path")
                    .datum(topojson.feature(us, us.objects.land))
                    .attr("class", "land")
                    .attr("d", path);

            g.selectAll("path.state")
                    .data(topojson.feature(us,
                            us.objects.states).features)
                    .enter()
                        .append("path")
                        .attr("class", "state")
                        .attr("d", path);
        });

        function zoomHandler() {
            var transform = d3.event.transform;

            g.attr("transform", "translate("
                    + transform.x + "," + transform.y
                    + ")scale(" + transform.k + ")");
        }
    </script>
```

This recipe projects US map with Albers USA mode:

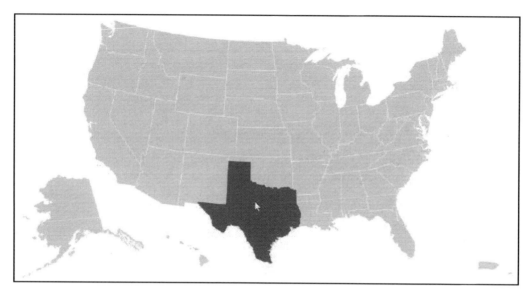

US map projected with Albers USA mode

How it works...

As you can see, the code required to project a US map using TopoJSON and D3 is quite short, especially the part concerning map projection. This is because both D3 geographic API and TopoJSON library are built explicitly to make this kind of job as easy as possible for developers. To make a map, first you need to load the TopoJSON data file (line A). The following screenshot shows what the topology data looks like once loaded:

```
▼ Object {type: "Topology", transform: Object, objects: Object, arcs: Array[10890]}
  ▶ arcs: Array[10890]
  ▼ objects: Object
    ▶ counties: Object
    ▶ land: Object
    ▼ states: Object
      ▶ geometries: Array[53]
        type: "GeometryCollection"
      ▶ __proto__: Object
    ▶ __proto__: Object
  ▶ transform: Object
    type: "Topology"
  ▶ __proto__: Object
```

Topology data from TopoJSON

Once the topology data is loaded, all we have to do is to use the TopoJSON library `topojson.feature` function to convert topology arcs into coordinates similar to what GeoJSON format provides as shown in the following screenshot:

```
▼ Object {type: "FeatureCollection", features: Array[53]}
  ▶ features: Array[53]
    type: "FeatureCollection"
  ▶ __proto__: Object
```

Feature collection converted using topojson.feature function

Then `d3.geo.path` will automatically recognize and use the coordinates to generate `svg:path` highlighted in the following code snippet:

```
var path = d3.geoPath()  // <- A
             .projection(d3.geoAlbersUsa());
...
g.insert("path")  // <-B
             .datum(topojson.feature(us, us.objects.land))
             .attr("class", "land")
             .attr("d", path);

    g.selectAll("path.state")
             .data(topojson.feature(us,
                us.objects.states).features)  // <-C
             .enter()
                .append("path")
                .attr("class", "state")
                .attr("d", path);
```

On line A, we first create a D3 GEO path object configured with Albers USA projection mode. Then we insert a `svg:path` that describe the outline of US, since this can be achieved by a single `svg:path` element (on line B). For the outline of each states we use the feature collection generated on line C to create one `svg:path` for each state that allow us to highlight the state on hover. With separate SVG element representing the states will also allow you to respond user interaction like click and touch.

That's it! This is all you need to do to project a map in D3 using TopoJSON. Additionally, we have also attached a zoom handler to the parent `svg:g` element:

```
var g = svg.append('g')
            .call(d3.zoom()
                    .scaleExtent([1, 10])
                    .on("zoom", zoomHandler));
```

This allows the user to perform simple geometric zoom on our map.

See also

- GeoJSON v1.0 specification: `http://geojson.org/geojson-spec.html`
- TopoJSON Wiki: `https://github.com/topojson/topojson/wiki`
- `Chapter 3`, *Dealing with Data,* for more information on asynchronous data loading
- `Chapter 10`, *Interacting with Your Visualization,* for more information on how to implement zooming
- Mike Bostock's post on Albers USA projection on which this recipe is based `http://bl.ocks.org/mbostock/4090848`

Projecting the world map

What if our visualization project is not just about US, but rather concerns the whole world? No worries, D3 comes with various built-in projection modes that work well with the world map that we will explore in this recipe.

Getting ready

Open your local copy of the following file in your web browser hosted on your local HTTP server:

`https://github.com/NickQiZhu/d3-cookbook-v2/blob/master/src/chapter12/world.html`

How to do it...

In this recipe we will project the world map using various different D3 built-in projection modes. Here is the code sample:

```
<script type="text/javascript">
    var width = 300,
        height = 300,
        translate = [width / 2, height / 2];

    var projections = [ // <-A
        {name: 'geoAzimuthalEqualArea', fn: d3.geoAzimuthalEqualArea()
                .scale(50)
                .translate(translate)},
        {name: 'geoConicEquidistant', fn: d3.geoConicEquidistant()
                .scale(35)
                .translate(translate)},
        {name: 'geoEquirectangular', fn: d3.geoEquirectangular()
                .scale(50)
                .translate(translate)},
        {name: 'geoMercator', fn: d3.geoMercator()
                .scale(50)
                .translate(translate)},
        {name: 'geoOrthographic', fn: d3.geoOrthographic()
                    .scale(90)
                    .translate(translate)},
        {name: 'geoStereographic', fn: d3.geoStereographic()
                        .scale(35)
                        .translate(translate)}
    ];

    d3.json("../../data/world-50m.json",
            function (error, world) { // <-B
        projections.forEach(function (projection) {
            var path = d3.geoPath() // <-C
                    .projection(projection.fn);

            var div = d3.select("body")
                    .append("div")
                    .attr("class", "map");

            var svg = div
                    .append("svg")
                    .attr("width", width)
                    .attr("height", height);

            svg.append("path") // <-D
                    .datum(topojson.feature(world,
```

```
                        world.objects.land))
                .attr("class", "land")
                .attr("d", path);

        svg.append("path") // <-E
                .datum(topojson.mesh(world,
                        world.objects.countries))
                .attr("class", "boundary")
                .attr("d", path);

        div.append("h3").text(projection.name);
        });
    });
</script>
```

This recipe generates world maps with different projection modes as shown in the following screenshot:

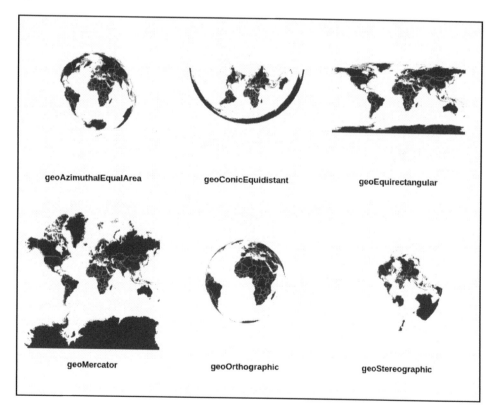

World map projection

How it works...

In this recipe, we first define an array containing six different D3 projection modes on line A. A world topology data was loaded on line B. Similar to the previous recipe we have a `d3.geoPath` generator defined on line C. We also customized the projection mode for geo path generator calling its `projection` function. The rest of the recipe is almost identical to what we have done in the previous recipe. The `topojson.feature` function was used to convert topology data into geographic coordinates so `d3.geoPath` can generate `svg:path` required for map rendering (line D). On line E, one new function `mesh` from TopoJSON was used worth mentioning here. `topojson.mesh` function returns the GeoJSON `MultiLineString` geometry object representing complicated topology. This is a very compact way to render complex geometric shapes since all shared arcs are only included once. In our case since we don't really need to visualize country outline on each continent separately and they are share their borders therefore this is the most efficient option in rendering.

See also

- D3 wiki Geo Projection page (`https://github.com/d3/d3-geo/blob/master/README.md#projections`) for more information on different projection modes as well as on how raw custom projection can be implemented

Building a choropleth map

Choropleth map is a thematic map, in other words, a specially designed map not a general purpose one, which is designed to show measurement of statistical variable on the map using different color shades or patterns; or sometimes referred as geographic heat-map in simpler terms. We have already seen in the previous two recipes that geographic projection in D3 consists of a group of `svg:path` elements, therefore, they can be manipulated as any other `svg` elements including coloring. We will explore this feature in geo-projection and implement a Choropleth map in this recipe.

Getting ready

Open your local copy of the following file in your web browser hosted on your local HTTP server:

```
https://github.com/NickQiZhu/d3-cookbook-v2/blob/master/src/chapter12/choropl
eth.html.
```

How to do it...

In a choropleth map different geographic regions are colored according to their corresponding variables, in this case based on 2008 unemployment rate in US by county. Now, let's see how to do it in code:

```
<script type="text/javascript">
    var width = 960,
            height = 500;

    var color = d3.scaleThreshold()
            .domain([.02, .04, .06, .08, .10]) // <-A
            .range(["#f2f0f7", "#dadaeb", "#bcbddc",
                    "#9e9ac8", "#756bb1", "#54278f"]);

    var projection = d3.geoAlbersUsa();

    var path = d3.geoPath()
            .projection(projection);

    var svg = d3.select("body").append("svg")
            .attr("width", width)
            .attr("height", height);

    var g = svg.append("g")
            .call(d3.zoom()
            .scaleExtent([1, 10])
            .on("zoom", zoomHandler));

    d3.json("../../data/us.json", function (error, us) { // <-B
        d3.tsv("../../data/unemployment.tsv",
                function (error, unemployment) {
            var rateById = {};

            unemployment.forEach(function (d) { // <-C
                rateById[d.id] = +d.rate;
            });
```

```
        g.append("g")
                .attr("class", "counties")
                .selectAll("path")
                .data(topojson.feature(us,
                        us.objects.counties).features)
                .enter().append("path")
                .attr("d", path)
                .style("fill", function (d) {
                    return color(rateById[d.id]); // <-D
                });

        g.append("path")
                .datum(topojson.mesh(us, // <-E
                        us.objects.states,
                        function(a, b) {
                                return a !== b;
                }))
                .attr("class", "states")
                .attr("d", path);
    });
});

function zoomHandler() {
    var transform = d3.event.transform;

    g.attr("transform", "translate("
            + transform.x + "," + transform.y
            + ")scale(" + transform.k + ")");
    }
</script>
```

This recipe generates the following choropleth map:

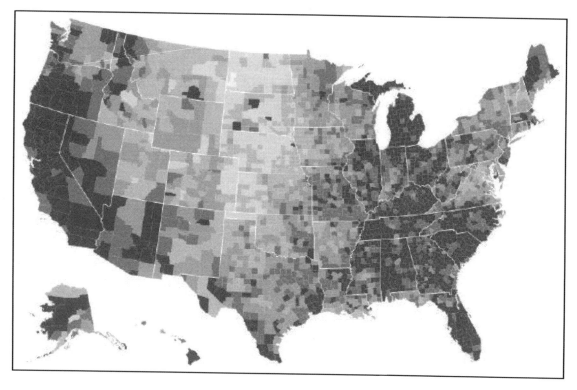

Choropleth Map of 2008 Unemployment Rate

How it works...

In this recipe we loaded two different data sets: one for the US topology and the other containing unemployment rate by county in 2008 (line B). This technique is generally considered as layering and is not necessarily limited to only two layers. The unemployment data are stitched to counties by their ID (line B and C). Region coloring is achieved by using a threshold scale defined on line A.

See also

- TopoJSON Wiki for more information on mesh function:
  `https://github.com/topojson/topojson-client#mesh`
- D3 Wiki for more information on threshold scale:
  `https://github.com/d3/d3-scale/blob/master/README.md#scaleThreshold`
- Mike Bostock's post on choropleth map which this recipe is based on:
  `http://bl.ocks.org/mbostock/4090848`

13
Test Drive Your Visualization

In this chapter we will cover:

- Getting Jasmine and setting up the test environment
- Test driving your visualization – chart creation
- Test driving your visualization – SVG rendering
- Test driving your visualization – pixel-perfect bar rendering

Introduction

Whenever we program as a professional programmer it is always important to test the program we write in order to make sure it functions as designed and produces the expected outcome. D3 data visualization mainly consists of JavaScript programs hence just like any other program we write, data visualization needs to be tested to make sure it represents the underlying data accurately. Obviously, we can perform our validation through visual examination and manual testing, which is always a critical part of the process of building data visualization since visual observation gives us a chance to verify not only the correctness, but also the aesthetics, usability, and many other useful aspects. However, manual visual inspection can be quite subjective, therefore, in this chapter we will focus our effort on automated unit testing. Visualization well covered by unit tests can free the creator from the manual labor of verifying correctness by hand, additionally allowing the creator to focus more on the aesthetics, usability, and other important aspects where it is hard to automate with machine.

Introduction to unit testing

Unit testing is a method in which a smallest unit of the program is tested and verified by another program called the test case. The logic behind unit testing is that at unit level the program is typically simpler and more testable. If we can verify that every unit in the program is correct then putting these correct units together will give us a higher confidence in which the integrated program is also correct. Furthermore, since unit tests are typically cheap and fast to execute, a group of unit test cases can be quickly and frequently executed to provide feedback whether our program is performing correctly or not.

Software testing is a complex topic and so far we have only scratched the surface; however, due to limited scope in this chapter, we will have to stop our introduction now and dive into developing unit tests.

For more information on some of the important concepts in software testing please check out the following links:

Unit test: `https://en.wikipedia.org/wiki/Unit_testing`

Test driven development: `https://en.wikipedia.org/wiki/Test-driven_development`

Code coverage: `https://en.wikipedia.org/wiki/Code_coverage`

Getting Jasmine and setting up the test environment

Before we start writing our unit test cases we need to set up an environment where our test cases can be executed to verify our implementation. In this recipe, we will show how this environment and necessary libraries can be set up for a visualization project.

Getting ready

Jasmine (`https://jasmine.github.io/`) is a **Behavior-Driven Development (BDD)** framework for testing JavaScript code.

BDD is a software development technique that combines **Test Driven Development (TDD)** with domain driven design.

We chose Jasmine as our testing framework because of its popularity in JavaScript community as well as its nice BDD syntax. You can download the Jasmine library from, `https://github.com/jasmine/jasmine/releases`.

Once downloaded you need to unzip it into the `lib` folder. Besides the `lib` folder we also need to create the `src` and `spec` folders for storing source files as well as test cases (in BDD terminology, test cases are called specification). See the following screenshot for the folder structure:

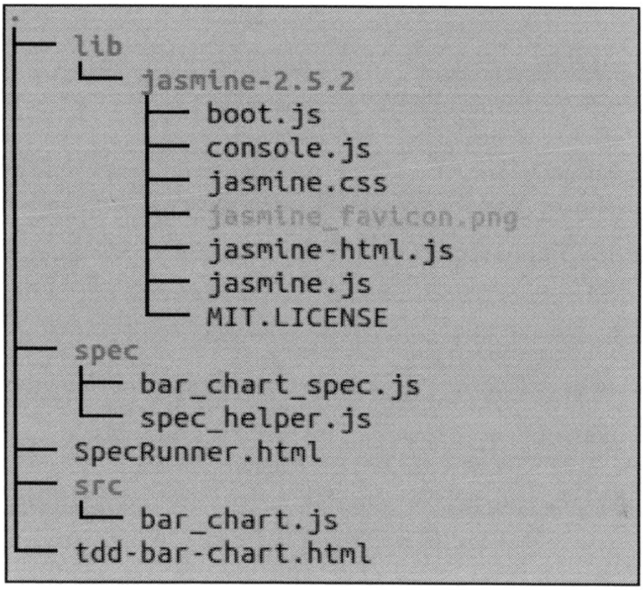

```
├── lib
│   └── jasmine-2.5.2
│       ├── boot.js
│       ├── console.js
│       ├── jasmine.css
│       ├── jasmine_favicon.png
│       ├── jasmine-html.js
│       ├── jasmine.js
│       └── MIT.LICENSE
├── spec
│   ├── bar_chart_spec.js
│   └── spec_helper.js
├── SpecRunner.html
├── src
│   └── bar_chart.js
└── tdd-bar-chart.html
```

Testing directory structure

How to do it...

Now, we have Jasmine in our environment, next thing to do is to set up an HTML page that will include Jasmine library as well as our source code plus test cases so they can be executed to verify our program. This file is called `SpecRunner.html` in our setup which includes the following code:

```
<!DOCTYPE html>
<html>
<head>
  <meta charset="utf-8">
  <title>Jasmine Spec Runner v2.5.2</title>
```

```
<link rel="shortcut icon" type="image/png"
        href="lib/jasmine-2.5.2/jasmine_favicon.png">
<link rel="stylesheet" href="lib/jasmine-2.5.2/jasmine.css">

<script src="lib/jasmine-2.5.2/jasmine.js"></script>
<script src="lib/jasmine-2.5.2/jasmine-html.js"></script>
<script src="lib/jasmine-2.5.2/boot.js"></script>

<!-- include source files here... -->
<script src="src/bar_chart.js"></script>

<!-- include spec files here... -->
<script src="spec/spec_helper.js"></script>
<script src="spec/bar_chart_spec.js"></script>

</head>

<body>
</body>
</html>
```

How it works...

This code follows standard Jasmine spec runner structure and generates execution report directly into our HTML page. Now, you have a fully functional test environment set up for your visualization development. If you open the `SpecRunner.html` file with your browser you will see a blank page at this point; however, if you check out our code sample you will see the following report:

Jasmine report

See also

- **Jasmine:** https://jasmine.github.io/
- **Jasmine 2.5 Reference Document:**
  https://jasmine.github.io/2.5/introduction
- **Behavior**
  Driven Development: https://en.wikipedia.org/wiki/Behavior-driven_deve
  lopment

Test driving your visualization – chart creation

With test environment ready, we can move on and develop a simple bar chart very similar to what we have done in the *Creating a bar chart* recipe in `Chapter 8`, *Chart Them Up*, though this time in a test-driven fashion. You can see how the bar chart looks if you open the `tdd-bar-chart.html` page:

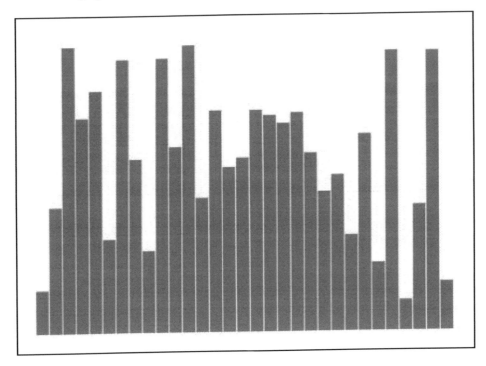

Test driven bar chart

By now we all know very well how to implement a bar chart using D3; however, building a bar chart is not the focus of this recipe. Instead, we want to show how we can build test cases every step of the way and verify automatically that our bar chart implementation is doing what it is supposed to do. The source code of this recipe was built using test driven development method; however, we will not show you every step in the TDD process due to limited scope in this book. Instead, we have grouped multiple steps into three larger sections with different focuses in this chapter and this recipe is the first step we take.

Getting ready

Open your local copy of the following file in your text editor:

- https://github.com/NickQiZhu/d3-cookbook-v2/blob/master/src/chapter13/src/bar_chart.js
- https://github.com/NickQiZhu/d3-cookbook-v2/blob/master/src/chapter13/spec/bar_chart_spec.js

How to do it...

First step we need to take is to make sure our bar chart implementation exists and can receive the data. The starting point of our development could be arbitrary and we decide to drive from this simplest function to set up the skeleton for our object. Here is what the test case looks like:

```
describe('BarChart', function () {
    var div,
        chart,
        data = [
            {x: 0, y: 0},
            {x: 1, y: 3},
            {x: 2, y: 6}
        ];

    beforeEach(function () {
        div = d3.select('body').append('div');
        chart = BarChart(div);
    });

    afterEach(function () {
        div.remove();
    });

    describe('.data', function () {
        it('should allow setting and retrieve chart data',
        function () {
            expect(chart.data(data).data()).toBe(data);
        });
    });
});
```

How it works...

In this first test case we used a few Jasmine constructs:

- `describe`: This function defines a suite of test cases; within `describe` a sub-suite can be nested and test cases can be defined
- `it`: This function defines a test case
- `beforeEach`: This function defines a pre-execution hook which will execute the given function before the execution of each test case
- `afterEach`: This function defines a post-execution hook which will execute the given function after the execution of each test case
- `expect`: This function defines an expectation in your test case which can then be chained with matchers (for example, `toBe` and `toBeEmpty`) to perform assertion in your test case

In our example we use the `beforeEach` hook to set up a `div` container for each test case and then remove `div` after execution in `afterEach` hook to improve the isolation between different test cases. The test case itself is almost trivial; it checks if the bar chart can take data and also return data attribute correctly. At this point if we run our `SpecRunner`, it will display a red message complaining there is no `BarChart` object, so let's create our object and function:

```
function BarChart(p) {
    var that = {};
    var _parent = p, _data;
    that.data = function (d) {
        if (!arguments.length) return _data;
        _data = d;
        return that;
    };

    return that;
}
```

Now, if you run `SpecRunner.html` again it will give you a happy green message showing our only test case is passing.

Test driving your visualization – SVG rendering

Now we have the basic skeleton of our bar chart object created, and we feel that we are ready to try to render something, so in this second iteration we will try to generate the `svg:svg` element.

Getting ready

Open your local copy of the following file in your text editor:

- `https://github.com/NickQiZhu/d3-cookbook-v2/blob/master/src/chapter13/src/bar_chart.js`
- `https://github.com/NickQiZhu/d3-cookbook-v2/blob/master/src/chapter13/spec/bar_chart_spec.js`

How to do it...

Rendering the `svg:svg` element should not only simply add the `svg:svg` element to the HTML body, but also translate the width and height setting on our chart object to proper SVG attributes. Here is how we express our expectation in our test cases:

```
describe('.render', function () {
    describe('svg', function () {
        it('should generate svg', function () {
            chart.render();
            expect(svg()).not.toBeEmpty();
        });

        it('should set default svg height and width',
          function () {
            chart.render();
            expect(svg().attr('width')).toBe('500');
            expect(svg().attr('height')).toBe('350');
        });

        it('should allow changing svg height and width',
          function () {
            chart.width(200).height(150).render();
            expect(svg().attr('width')).toBe('200');
            expect(svg().attr('height')).toBe('150');
```

```
            });
        });
    });

    function svg() {
        return div.select('svg');
    }
```

How it works...

At this point, all of these tests will fail since we don't even have the render function; however, it clearly articulates that we expect the render function to generate the svg:svg element and setting the width and height attributes correctly. The second test case also makes sure that if the user does not provide the height and width attributes we will supply a set of default values. Here is how we will implement the render method to satisfy these expectations:

```
. . .
var _parent = p, _width = 500, _height = 350
        _data;

    that.render = function () {
        var svg = _parent
            .append("svg")
            .attr("height", _height)
            .attr("width", _width);
    };

    that.width = function (w) {
        if (!arguments.length) return _width;
        _width = w;
        return that;
    };

    that.height = function (h) {
        if (!arguments.length) return _height;
        _height = h;
        return that;
    };
};
. . .
```

At this point our SpecRunner.html is once again all green and happy. However, it's still not doing much since all it does is generate an empty svg:svg element on the page and not even use the data at all.

Test driving your visualization – pixel-perfect bar rendering

In this iteration we will finally generate the bars using the data we have. Through our test cases we will make sure all bars are not only rendered but rendered with pixel-perfect precision.

Getting ready

Open your local copy of the following file in your text editor:

- https://github.com/NickQiZhu/d3-cookbook-v2/blob/master/src/chapter13/ src/bar_chart.js
- https://github.com/NickQiZhu/d3-cookbook-v2/blob/master/src/chapter13/ spec/bar_chart_spec.js

How to do it...

Let's see how we test it:

```
describe('chart body', function () {
    it('should create body g', function () {
        chart.render();
        expect(chartBody()).not.toBeEmpty();
    });

    it('should translate to (left, top)', function () {
        chart.render();
         expect(chartBody().attr('transform')).
         toBe('translate(30,10)')
    });
});

describe('bars', function () {
    beforeEach(function () {
        chart.data(data).width(100).height(100)
            .x(d3.scaleLinear().domain([0, 3]))
            .y(d3.scaleLinear().domain([0, 6]))
            .render();
    });
```

```
        it('should create 3 svg:rect elements', function () {
            expect(bars().size()).toBe(3);
        });

        it('should calculate bar width automatically',
          function () {
            bars().each(function () {
              expect(d3.select(this).attr('width')).
              toBe('18');
            });
        });

        it('should map bar x using x-scale', function () {
            expect(bar(0).attr('x')).toBe('0');
            expect(bar(1).attr('x')).toBe('20');
            expect(bar(2).attr('x')).toBe('40');
          });

          it('should map bar y using y-scale', function () {
              expect(bar(0).attr('y')).toBe('60');
              expect(bar(1).attr('y')).toBe('30');
              expect(bar(2).attr('y')).toBe('0');
            });

            it('should calculate bar height based on y', function () {
                expect(bar(0).attr('height')).toBe('10');
                expect(bar(1).attr('height')).toBe('40');
                expect(bar(2).attr('height')).toBe('70');
              });
          });
      });

  function svg() {
      return div.select('svg');
  }

  function chartBody() {
      return svg().select('g.body');
  }

  function bars() {
      return chartBody().selectAll('rect.bar');
  }

  function bar(index) {
      return d3.select(bars().nodes()[index]);
  }
});
```

How it works...

In the preceding test suite we describe our expectations of having the chart body svg:g element correctly transform and correct number of bars with appropriate attributes (width, x, y, height) set. The implementation is actually going to be shorter than our test case which is quite common in well tested implementation:

```
...
var _parent = p, _width = 500, _height = 350,
        _margins = {top: 10, left: 30, right: 10, bottom: 30},
        _data,
        _x = d3.scaleLinear(),
        _y = d3.scaleLinear();

that.render = function () {
        var svg = _parent
            .append("svg")
            .attr("height", _height)
            .attr("width", _width);

        var body = svg.append("g")
            .attr("class", 'body')
            .attr("transform", "translate(" + _margins.left + ","
            + _margins.top + ")")

        if (_data) {
            _x.range([0, quadrantWidth()]);
            _y.range([quadrantHeight(), 0]);

            body.selectAll('rect.bar')
                .data(_data).enter()
                .append('rect')
                .attr("class", 'bar')
                .attr("width", function () {
                    return quadrantWidth() / _data.length -
                    BAR_PADDING;
                })
                .attr("x", function (d) {return _x(d.x); })
                .attr("y", function (d) {return _y(d.y); })
                .attr("height", function (d) {
                    return _height - _margins.bottom - _y(d.y);
                });
        }
};
...
```

I think you are getting the picture and now you can repeat this cycle over and over to drive your implementation. D3 visualization is built on HTML with SVG and both are simple mark-up languages that can be verified easily. Well thought-out test suite can make sure your visualization is pixel-perfect even sub-pixel perfect.

See also

- **Test driven development**:
  https://en.wikipedia.org/wiki/Test-driven_development

Building Interactive Analytics in Minutes

In this appendix we will cover:

- Learning Crossfilter.js library
- Charting with dimensions using dc.js

Introduction

Congratulations! You have finished an entire book on data visualization with D3. Together we have explored various topics and techniques. At this point you will probably agree that building interactive, accurate, and aesthetically appealing data visualization is not a trivial matter even with the help of a powerful library like D3. It typically takes days or even weeks to finish a professional data visualization project even without counting the effort usually required on the backend. What if you need to build an interactive visualization quickly, or a proof-of-concept before a full-fledged visualization project can be commenced, and you need to do just that not in weeks or days, but minutes. In this appendix we will introduce you to two interesting JavaScript libraries that allow you to do just that: building quick in-browser interactive multidimensional data visualization in minutes.

The crossfilter.js library

Crossfilter is also a library created by D3's author *Mike Bostock,* initially used to power analytics for Square Register.

> *Crossfilter is a JavaScript library for exploring large multivariate datasets in browser. Crossfilter supports extremely fast (<30ms) interaction with coordinated views, even with datasets containing a million or more records.*

> *-Crossfilter Wiki (August 2013)*

In other words, Crossfilter is a library that you can use to generate data dimensions on large and typically flat multivariate datasets. So what is a data dimension? A data dimension can be considered as a type of data grouping or categorization while each dimensional data element is a categorical variable. Since this is still a pretty abstract concept, let's take a look at the following JSON dataset and see how it can be transformed into dimensional dataset using Crossfilter. Assume that we have the following flat dataset in JSON describing payment transactions in a bar:

```
[
  {"date": "2011-11-14T01:17:54Z", "quantity": 2, "total": 190,   "tip":
100, "type": "tab"},
  {"date": "2011-11-14T02:20:19Z", "quantity": 2, "total": 190,   "tip":
100, "type": "tab"},
  {"date": "2011-11-14T02:28:54Z", "quantity": 1, "total": 300,   "tip":
200, "type": "visa"},
  ..
]
```

 Sample dataset borrowed from Crossfilter Wiki:
https://github.com/square/crossfilter/wiki/API-Reference.

How many dimensions do we see here in this sample dataset? The answer is: it has as many dimensions as the number of different ways that you can categorize the data. For example, since this data is about customer payment, which is observation on time series, obviously the date is a dimension. Secondly, the payment type is naturally a way to categorize data; therefore, type is also a dimension.

The next dimension is bit tricky since technically we can model any of the field in the dataset as dimension or its derivatives; however, we don't want to make something as a dimension if it does not help us slice the data more efficiently or provide more insight into what the data is trying to say. The total and tip fields have very high cardinality, which usually is an indicator for poor dimension unless we group them into different buckets (though tip/total, that is, tip in percentage could be an interesting dimension); however, the `quantity` field is likely to have a relatively small cardinality assuming people don't buy thousands of drinks in this bar, therefore, we choose to use quantity as our third dimension. Now, here is what the dimensional logical model looks like:

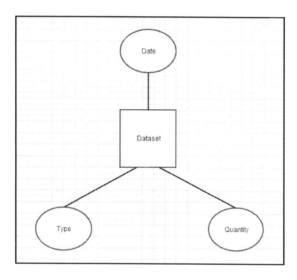

Dimensional Dataset

These dimensions allow us to look at the data from a different angle, and if combined will allow us to ask some pretty interesting questions, for example:

- Are customers who pay by tab more likely to buy in larger quantity?
- Are customers more likely to buy larger quantity on Friday night?
- Are customers more likely to tip when using tab versus cash?

Now, you can see why dimensional dataset is such a powerful idea. Essentially, each dimension gives you a different lens to view your data, and when combined, they can quickly turn raw data into knowledge. A good analyst can quickly use this kind of tool to formulate a hypothesis, hence gaining knowledge from data.

How to do it...

Now, we understand why we would want to establish dimensions with our dataset; let's see how this can be done using Crossfilter:

```
var timeFormat = d3.time.format.iso;
var data = crossfilter(json); // <-A

var hours = data.dimension(function(d){
    return d3.time.hour(timeFormat.parse(d.date)); // <-B
});
var totalByHour = hours.group().reduceSum(function(d){
    return d.total;
});

var types = data.dimension(function(d){return d.type;});
var transactionByType = types.group().reduceCount();
var quantities = data.dimension(function(d){return d.quantity;});
var salesByQuantity = quantities.group().reduceCount();
```

How it works...

As shown in the preceding section, creating dimensions and groups are quite straight-forward in Crossfilter. First step before we can create anything is to feed our JSON dataset, loaded using D3, through Crossfilter by calling the `crossfilter` function (line A). Once that's done, you can create your dimension by calling the `dimension` function and pass in an accessor function that will retrieve the data element that can be used to define the dimension. In the case for `type` we will simply pass in `function(d){return d.type;}`. You can also perform data formatting or other task in dimension function (for example, date formatting on line B). After creating the dimensions, we can perform the categorization or grouping by using the dimension, so `totalByHour` is a grouping that sums up total amount of the sale for each hour, while `salesByQuantity` is a grouping of counting the number of transactions by quantity. To better understand how `group` works, we will take a look at what the group object looks like. If you invoke the `all` function on the `transactionsByType` group you will get the following objects back:

```
[▼ Object 🛈          , ▼ Object 🛈          , ▼ Object 🛈                ]
    key: "cash"            key: "tab"             key: "visa"
    value: 4               value: 16              value: 5
    ▶ __proto__: Object    ▶ __proto__: Object    ▶ __proto__: Object
```

Crossfilter group objects

We can clearly see that `transactionByType` group is essentially a grouping of the data element by its type while counting the total number of data elements within each group since we had called `reduceCount` function when creating the group.

The following are the description for functions we used in this example:

- `crossfilter`: Creates a new crossfilter with given records if specified. Records can be any array of objects or primitives.
- `dimension`: Creates a new dimension using the given value accessor function. The function must return naturally-ordered values, that is, values that behave correctly with respect to JavaScript's <, <=, >=, and > operators. This typically means primitives: Booleans, numbers, or strings.
- `dimension.group`: Creates a new grouping for the given dimension, based on the given `groupValue` function, which takes a dimension value as input and returns the corresponding rounded value.
- `group.all`: Returns all groups, in ascending natural order by key.
- `group.reduceCount`: A shortcut function to count the records; returns this group.
- `group.reduceSum`: A shortcut function to sum records using the specified value accessor function.

There's more...

We have only touched a very limited number of Crossfilter functions. Crossfilter provides a lot more capability when it comes to how dimension and group can be created; for more information please check out its API reference:
`https://github.com/square/crossfilter/wiki/API-Reference`.

See also

- Data Dimension: `http://en.wikipedia.org/wiki/Dimension_(data_warehouse)`
- Cardinality: `http://en.wikipedia.org/wiki/Cardinality`

At this point we have everything we want to analyze. Now, let's see how this can be done in minutes instead of hours or days.

Dimensional charting – dc.js

Visualizing Crossfilter dimensions and groups is precisely the reason why dc.js was created. This handy JavaScript library was created by your humble author and is designed to allow you to visualize Crossfilter dimensional dataset easily and quickly. This library was originally created by your humble author now maintained by a group of community contributor led by Gordon Woodhull.

 dc.js version 2.0 beta that we used in this chapter has not yet been upgrade to D3 v4.x therefore you will notice usage and references to old D3 v3 API which is somewhat different from what we have witnessed so far in this book.

Getting ready

Open your local copy of the following file as reference:

```
https://github.com/NickQiZhu/d3-cookbook-v2/blob/master/src/appendix-a/dc.html
```

How to do it...

In this example we will create three charts:

- A line chart for visualizing total amount of transaction on time series
- A pie chart to visualize number of transactions by payment type
- A bar chart showing number of sales by purchase quantity

Here is what the code looks like:

```
<div id="area-chart"></div>
<div id="donut-chart"></div>
<div id="bar-chart"></div>
...
dc.lineChart("#area-chart")
            .width(500)
            .height(250)
            .dimension(hours)
            .group(totalByHour)
            .x(d3.time.scale().domain([
            timeFormat.parse("2011-11-14T01:17:54Z"),
              timeFormat.parse("2011-11-14T18:09:52Z")
]))
```

```
            .elasticY(true)
            .xUnits(d3.time.hours)
            .renderArea(true)
            .xAxis().ticks(5);

dc.pieChart("#donut-chart")
        .width(250)
        .height(250)
        .radius(125)
        .innerRadius(50)
        .dimension(types)
        .group(transactionByType);
dc.barChart("#bar-chart")
        .width(500)
        .height(250)
        .dimension(quantities)
        .group(salesByQuantity)
        .x(d3.scale.linear().domain([0, 7]))
        .y(d3.scale.linear().domain([0, 12]))
        .centerBar(true);

dc.renderAll();
```

This generates a group of coordinated interactive charts:

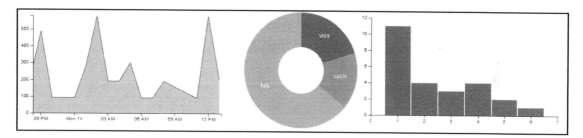

Interactive dc.js charts

When you click or drag your mouse across these charts you will see the underlying Crossfilter dimensions being filtered accordingly on all charts:

Filtered dc.js charts

How it works...

As we have seen through this example, dc.js is designed to generate standard chart-based visualization on top of Crossfilter. Each dc.js chart is designed to be interactive so user can apply dimensional filter by simply interacting with the chart. dc.js is built entirely on D3, therefore, its API is very D3-like and I am sure with the knowledge you have gained from this book you will feel quite at home when using dc.js. Charts are usually created in the following steps.

1. First step creates a chart object by calling one of the chart creation functions while passing in a D3 selection for its anchor element, which in our example is the div element to host the chart:

```
<div id="area-chart"></div>
...
dc.lineChart("#area-chart")
```

2. Then we set the width, height, dimension, and group for each chart:

```
chart.width(500)
     .height(250)
     .dimension(hours)
     .group(totalByHour)
```

For coordinate charts rendered on a Cartesian plane you also need to set the x and y scale:

```
chart.x(d3.time.scale().domain([
   timeFormat.parse("2011-11-14T01:17:54Z"),
   timeFormat.parse("2011-11-14T18:09:52Z")
])).elasticY(true)
```

In this first case, we explicitly set the x axis scale while letting the chart automatically calculate the y-scale for us. While in the next case we set both x and y scale explicitly.

```
chart.x(d3.scale.linear().domain([0, 7]))
     .y(d3.scale.linear().domain([0, 12]))
```

There's more...

Different charts have different functions for customizing their look-and-feel and you can see the complete API reference at
`https://github.com/dc-js/dc.js/blob/master/web/docs/api-latest.md`.

Leveraging `crossfilter.js` and `dc.js` allows you to build sophisticated data analytics dashboard fairly quickly. The following is a demo dashboard for analyzing the NASDAQ 100 Index for the last 20 years `https://dc-js.github.io/dc.js/`:

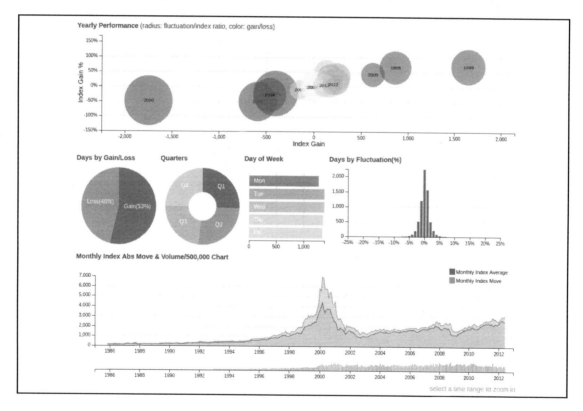

dc.js NASDAQ demo

At the time of writing this book, `dc.js` supports the following chart types:

- Bar chart (stackable)
- Line chart (stackable)
- Area chart (stackable)
- Pie chart
- Bubble chart
- Composite chart
- Choropleth map
- Boxplot
- Heatmap
- Sparkline
- Bubble overlay chart

And many more, see this page for a complete list of supported chart types `http://dc-js.github.io/dc.js/examples/`. For more information on the `dc.js` 'library please check out our Wiki page at `https://github.com/dc-js/dc.js`.

See also

The following are some other useful D3 based reusable charting libraries. Although, unlike `dc.js` they are not designed to work with Crossfilter natively nevertheless they tend to be richer and more flexible when tackling general visualization challenges:

- NVD3: `http://nvd3.org/`
- Rickshaw: `http://code.shutterstock.com/rickshaw/`

Index

82612786R00213

Made in the USA
San Bernardino, CA
17 July 2018